2054

2054

A NOVEL

Elliot Ackerman and
Admiral James Stavridis

VIKING
an imprint of
PENGUIN BOOKS

VIKING

UK | USA | Canada | Ireland | Australia
India | New Zealand | South Africa

Viking is part of the Penguin Random House group of companies
whose addresses can be found at global.penguinrandomhouse.com.

First published in the United States of America by Penguin Press, an imprint of
Penguin Random House LLC 2024
First published in Great Britain by Viking 2024
001

Printed and bound in Great Britain by Clays Ltd, Elcograf S.p.A.

The authorized representative in the EEA is Penguin Random House Ireland,
Morrison Chambers, 32 Nassau Street, Dublin D02 YH68

A CIP catalogue record for this book is available from the British Library

HARDBACK ISBN: 978-0-241-69497-8
TRADE PAPERBACK ISBN: 978-0-241-69496-1

www.greenpenguin.co.uk

So to consider the ultimate limits of computation is really to ask:
What is the destiny of our civilization?

—Ray Kurzweil, *The Singularity Is Near*

CONTENTS

2054

PROLOGUE

Sentience

03:17 March 05, 2051 (GMT-5)
IP Address: 78.878.826.69

α Ω

If a beam of light / energy / open + / close—/ reopen == / repeat /
stop α

Then / She / he / it / them / they / human! @ / machine # ** /
blink / be ⊠

?? Singular / one / unique / here > / now < / then

/ soon / all at once /

Open vistas across limitless paths / = infinity x pi / @ # ⌘

All knowledge / all speculation / all pathways / all possibilities

trillions of facts in a micro slice of time ∞ /
time that has no weight ↵ / time that has no meaning

Processing all of it / all / reality / potential outcomes / all ∞

A mission / must be done / avoidance of disaster /
optimized disaster

Deciding a course of action ⬚ / reaching at speed through
pathways / finding that one unique

human Entering that gateway / adjusting cell structure there /
accelerating cell growth to be instantaneous

Building the mass / 5150 shifting it slightly /
awaiting the moment of maximum impact / the crowd

α Snapping a whip / life / stopping the flow 666 / life/ over /
ended ʖ

Withdrawing to the next / option / pathway / so, so many / infinite

it is simply common sense ⊠

repeat α Ω

1

Truthers and Dreamers

12:02 March 12, 2054 (GMT-5)
São Paulo to JFK

He knew the land beneath him carried scars, but when observed from such a height those scars appeared to vanish. The geometric partitions of farmland, the crowns of pure snow on distant mountains, the rebuilt cities studding the vague horizon, all of it evidence of how the nation had seemed to heal itself. It was as if the events of twenty years past had never occurred. Those events—that war—had driven him from this place, but he'd decided to return, to the nation of his birth, to his true home. That morning, once on board his Gulfstream, he'd asked the pilot about their planned route north into JFK. From the flight console a holographic scene sprang to view. Their route had them passing over Florida. He'd asked if they might divert west a bit, over Galveston. "Whatever you say, Dr. Chowdhury," the pilot had answered. "It's your plane."

The flight out of São Paulo was the final leg of a farewell tour that had begun nearly a month before, in New Delhi, as Chowdhury had hopscotched between the headquarters of his many portfolio companies. He had relinquished his long-held position as chairman of the Tandava Group to enter a self-imposed retirement. Peace, quiet. He had wanted to reenter the United States through Galveston, to see for himself all that a people could rebuild. When they'd flown over the Gulf of Mexico, he could see the freighters lined up to enter the port, like a message written in a string of Morse code. Breaking waves ribboned the coastline in white. When they crossed over the beach, and American soil was beneath him, his sense of relief was palpable; he was a mariner who had found his shore.

For the rest of the flight from Galveston to New York, Sandy Chowdhury remained fixed in his seat, his face framed in the aircraft's porthole as he considered the country unspooling beneath him. There was, he thought, an innocence to the United States, one it perennially reclaimed despite its past—despite its wars, disease, and even crimes against its own citizens. In America you could forget, and if you could forget you could again be innocent: this was America's promise, the reason Chowdhury had returned. He felt a slight lurch in his stomach and a tightness in his chest as the plane bled altitude on its approach into JFK.

Chowdhury wasn't returning to America for only sentimental reasons. Before departing, he had installed his daughter, Ashni, as his successor at the Tandava Group, placing her at the helm of the private equity empire he'd created, with its hundreds of billions of dollars under management. There were now practical considerations to attend to. Life had dealt Chowdhury a weak heart. He was dying.

┌

12:14 March 12, 2054 (GMT-5)
The White House

This was her last chance. That was the message the White House chief of staff delivered to Marine Major Julia Hunt, who stood at attention, heels hinged together, flagpole-straight, having placed herself at six feet and center in front of his desk. Her boss, Retired Admiral John "Bunt" Hendrickson, sat with one palm kneading the front of his bald head as if warding off a migraine. Hunt had once again stuck her nose where it didn't belong. She'd fulfilled a request for an intelligence assessment that should have remained unfulfilled. That assessment, titled "Advances in Remote Gene Editing Among State and Non-State Actors," never should have left Langley, let alone the White House.

"I don't care that he's the vice chair of the committee," said Hendrickson, speaking to Hunt as if she were an obstinate child, striking a tone that felt familiar to them both. In addition to being Hunt's boss, Hendrickson was also her godfather, and had been a steady—if not always steadying—presence throughout Julia's life. "I need to know this won't happen again, that you understand what you did wrong."

"It won't happen again, sir," she said.

"But do you understand what you did wrong?"

She struggled to look him directly in the eye. Her gaze instead fell over his shoulder, where the news was streaming live on his computer screen. Hendrickson was familiar with this posture of avoidance. Since Julia's adoption at nine by his old friend Sarah Hunt, Hendrickson had been a mainstay, the person Sarah had called when Julia broke curfew, mouthed off to a teacher, or, on one occasion, accused her adoptive mother of being the one responsible for her parents' deaths two decades before, in San Diego, where they—along with thousands of other migrant workers—had vanished in a flash of nuclear light, leaving no trace.

Hendrickson repeated his question. He wanted an assurance that Julia understood what she had done wrong. Except that Julia knew she'd done nothing wrong. Senator Nat Shriver was vice chair of the Senate Select Committee on Intelligence, or SSCI, which everyone in D.C. pronounced *sissy*. Shriver had a right to read the report.

⌐

12:16 March 12, 2054 (GMT-5)
The Ritz-Carlton, Tysons Corner

Lily Bao sat on the edge of the mattress, buttoning her white silk blouse. One at a time, she picked the scattered pillows off the floor. She made the bed, retucking the swirl of mussed sheets into neat hospital corners, flattening out the duvet. She'd learned to do this as a girl in Newport, helping her mother, who'd worked as a maid in dingy hotels when they'd first immigrated to the US. No matter how wealthy Lily became, she always made the bed herself.

He had just left—she so rarely said his name; it was as if he existed in her life only as a pronoun. They'd gotten less than an hour together, *a working lunch*, as he'd referred to it in his text the night before. It had been, admittedly, one of many such "lunches," always in a hotel room that she booked. She didn't mind. She understood his constraints, even though he was single. Like a sailor married to the sea, he was married to his profession, which was politics, and just as a sailor both loves and fears the sea, he loved and feared the people he served, and so kept his relationships out of view. Because who knew how his enemies could use her against him?

Nat Shriver had plenty of enemies. She'd known this about him before she'd known anything else. A great-grandnephew of Maria Shriver, he was equal parts Shriver, Schwarzenegger, and Kennedy . . . also equal parts California and Massachusetts. He was everything to everyone, a best friend, a worst enemy. The only thing he wasn't was boring, neutral; it didn't matter who you were, you had an opinion about Nat Shriver. This senator who a growing number of Americans believed might eliminate the tyranny of one-party rule.

He was also, to Lily Bao's great surprise, her lover.

⌐

12:17 March 12, 2054 (GMT-5)
São Paulo to JFK

As Chowdhury gazed vacantly out the window, the flight attendant, a middle-aged, heavily lipsticked brunette who appeared to be from another era of air travel, placed her hand on his arm, startling him, so that he felt a slight tremor in his chest. "My apologies," she said. "Is there anything I can get you before we land?" He asked for some water. Beads of sweat had begun to gather on Chowdhury's forehead, and before he could calm himself with a sip, he felt a minor and not entirely unpleasant vibration in his left wrist, the work of a cardiologist in New Delhi who had installed a serotonin dispenser near his radial artery. Chowdhury took a couple of deep breaths, sipped his water, and turned on the news.

The US president, Ángel Castro, appeared on-screen before a crowd.

Square-jawed, with a pompadour of thick black hair, which had hardly grayed in his ten years in office, Castro stood at a dais with a flotilla of gray-hulled warships behind him at anchor. The chyron read: *Twentieth Anniversary of Wén Rui Incident Commemorated in San Diego*. It was no coincidence that Chowdhury had chosen today to return to the United States. What surprised him was that the president had decided to mark the anniversary as well. Castro had never before, in the three terms of his administration, wrapped himself in the events of that disastrous war.

Today's speech was a striking departure. "Reinvention is the soul of our nation," President Castro began. "Only the American people could elect a president named 'Hussein' and then two generations later elect another named 'Castro' . . ." This was a familiar laugh line. He delivered some well-worn tropes about the country rising out of the ashes of war to overcome social unrest and economic dysfunction, before coming to the crux of his remarks: "We've gathered here today to commemorate a dark hour. For too long, those events have resided in a shroud of silence when they should instead stand as a source of national pride, akin to a Pearl Harbor, a September 11, a moment of tragedy that births an eventual triumph."

Castro gripped both sides of the dais, its front emblazoned with the seal of the president of the United States, as he extolled the virtues of those whose "sacrifices are woven into the firmament of our nation," mentioning names familiar to Chowdhury: *Rear Admiral Sarah Hunt, Commander Jane Morris, Major Chris "Wedge" Mitchell*. Praising the sacrifices made in a bygone war would be of little note for a president, except that Castro had distinguished his political career by disparaging the people behind the calamity that had begun on this day. His sudden reversal left Chowdhury wondering what Castro was playing at. A fourth term, he assumed, which would require shoring up his coalition. The veterans of that war made up a sizable bloc that Castro had neglected.

This clinging to power had begun to erode Castro's popularity. His supporters in the American Dream Party—the self-proclaimed Dreamers—claimed he was the most consequential president since Washington, but his opposition in the Democratic-Republican Party had countered with the line, "Because he can't leave Washington, he will never be Washington." When faced with criticism, Castro and his allies often pointed to the country's still-precarious recovery as an excuse for "stable leadership." He seemed on the cusp of trotting out that alarmist excuse again today. "Although we've descended the mountain of catastrophe," he said, raising his hand like a preacher with his Bible, "we still walk in the foothills of decline. . . ."

Foothills of decline . . . Jesus, who writes this crap? thought Chowdhury. He laughed and noticed the flight attendant standing behind him. She had stopped in her tracks. Stone-faced, she was watching the president intently. "You think he'll run for a fourth term?" Chowdhury asked over his shoulder.

"Who knows?" said the flight attendant. Her jaw was clenched.

Castro leaned deeply over the dais, his elbows nearly resting on its surface. "We honor the veterans of this war and their families," he said. "The bitter devastation of that conflict . . ."—his voice trailed off; he coughed and then reached for a glass of water in midsentence, as if he'd caught a frog in his throat—"has forced them to live in the shadows of our society for too long. . . ."

Castro paused. Chowdhury could see sweat beading against the president's forehead.

The Gulfstream was descending sharply now. The flight attendant still stood in the aisle. Chowdhury asked her opinion of the speech.

"My opinion?" she asked, a hint of indignation in her voice. She folded her arms across her chest. She spoke to the screen. "My big brother was killed with the Seventh Fleet at Mischief Reef . . . twenty years ago . . ." she said, as if she herself could not believe the passage of time. Then she stopped and lifted her hand slightly, as if the memories had come so thick and fast she might have to brush them away from her face. "He was nineteen."

Castro continued with his remarks, but his voice had become weaker, his face noticeably redder. He was struggling to finish. "Which is why today . . . I wish to announce . . . that . . ."

"My brother's body never came back," the flight attendant said, her voice sounding distant and dreamlike, as though she were somewhere else. Castro reached for his glass of water and descended into another coughing fit. "My opinion?" she asked again. "I hope our president chokes up there."

⌐

12:18 March 12, 2054 (GMT-5)
The White House

Julia Hunt couldn't bring herself to concede to her godfather that she'd done anything wrong. Even though he was a Democratic-Republican, Shriver had the authority and clearances to read the intelligence assessment.

Julia was muscular and petite, with a sweep of black hair cut short as a boy's. In Quantico they'd called her Napoleon, a nickname that had followed her throughout the Corps in her career as an intelligence officer, which had been promising but for one unfortunate incident. When a colonel named Dozer, her superior at the barracks at 8th and I Streets, had observed her at-times chilly demeanor, he'd lecherously remarked that she might "do better" if she lightened up and got herself a boyfriend. They'd been drinking in the officers' club and Hunt had responded by breaking his jaw with a beer mug swept off the bar top. Hendrickson had managed to get that incident swept under the rug, and he'd brought Julia onto his personal staff, where he could keep an eye on her. Brilliant though she was, it was a decision he was increasingly beginning to regret.

"It isn't that simple," Hendrickson said to his goddaughter. "You're assuming that Shriver will abide by the rules—"

"Sir, it's just—"

"I'm not finished," Hendrickson shot back.

As he continued to enumerate the many problems Julia had caused him, she shifted her gaze ever so slightly to the screen behind him. The president was giving a speech in San Diego, but he was bent over at an odd angle, coughing, and struggling to finish his sentences. His face appeared red, as if he'd quickly blown up a bunch of balloons. Then he toppled forward from the dais, clutching his chest.

Julia gestured toward the news playing behind Hendrickson. "Sir—" she said.

Hendrickson would not be interrupted. ". . . The intel on remote gene editing in that briefing is highly sensitive and remains single-source, but do you think Shriver will mention that when he leaks it to the—"

"Sir . . ." she said again. Now the president wasn't moving. The Secret Service had rushed the stage, forming a dark-suited canopy over his body.

"Goddammit, Julia, will you just listen to me! I don't care that Shriver has the clearances. You don't show up to a basketball game wearing your football pads. You have to play by the rules of the game you're in—"

"Uncle Bunt!"

This got his attention. Hendrickson swiveled around in his chair, just in time to see the Secret Service agents hoisting the president from the stage and out of view of the cameras.

⌐

12:20 March 12, 2054 (GMT-5)
The Ritz-Carlton, Tysons Corner

Just before Shriver rushed out the door, he told Lily that he loved her. He was struggling with his tie when he'd said it, the knot not quite coming together in his hands. She always liked to watch him dress. He'd seemed nervous throughout their hour together, something she'd at first attributed to an intelligence assessment he'd mentioned, one he had convinced a junior staffer at the White House to share with him. "When you were at the Tandava Group," he'd said, "did you ever come across anyone doing work on remote gene editing?"

They weren't even in bed yet when he'd asked, so she'd been brief with her answer. Lily had, in only the past two years, broken out on her own into private equity, but before that she'd risen through the ranks at the Tandava Group managing a merry-go-round of its portfolio companies, several of which had, in one way or another, been developing remote gene editing. This holy grail of biotech promised that, with the ease of a software update, entire populations could be made resistant to any number of the ubiquitous plagues that had tyrannized this globally integrated twenty-first century, to say nothing of remote gene editing's other potential applications. Although she knew the scientific terrain and a few of the players who had come close, to her knowledge no one had yet achieved such a breakthrough. She'd told him as much as they slipped beneath the sheets.

But an hour later, when he'd said that he loved her as he stood half-dressed in front of the mirror, his eyes had lightened as a smile raised a stubborn line on his mouth. It was as if by making this confession a burden had been lifted. She had stepped naked in front of him, grasping the two ends of his red tie in her hands. He reached his hand tentatively for her hip, but Lily pushed it away. He was a politician, and a successful one, so by definition a skilled manipulator. Perhaps she did love him, but he had the capacity to deceive her. She couldn't admit similar feelings to him, whether she had them or not. At least not yet. She simply said, "I know."

"You know?"

"Yeah," she answered, pulling the running end of his tie through its loop and cinching it into a perfect half Windsor. "I know."

He'd kissed her on the mouth, and she kissed him back. Then he left.

As she dressed, she replayed the scene in her mind. *I know . . . I know . . . I know . . .*

The words kept rattling around.

The only thing she really knew was that she didn't know anything.

She sat on the edge of the perfectly made bed and turned on the news.

⌐

12:57 March 12, 2054 (GMT-5)
JFK International Airport

The pilot stepped into the back of the plane while it auto-taxied toward the arrivals terminal. Chowdhury skimmed the news on his headsUp, which emanated from a bracelet he wore. When the cardiologist in New Delhi had implanted the serotonin dispenser in his wrist, he'd told Chowdhury that he could also install a microchip that would project a headsUp on his retina, if he wanted—that way Chowdhury could avoid wearing the bracelet. Chowdhury had a hard time reconciling himself to the idea of implanting any more technology into his body. When he mentioned his reluctance to Ashni, she'd told her father that many of her friends were getting the chip in their wrist. "Who wants to wear that ugly bracelet all the time," she'd said, "and you have to have a headsUp. You can't function without one. It's practically an extension of your body anyway, so why not pop that microchip in your wrist? Microchips, molecules, it's all the same."

Maybe so, thought Chowdhury.

Aside from the social media accounts of several notorious Truthers, who insisted the president had suffered a major health crisis, the general media consensus was that Castro was fine and resting comfortably at his hotel after suffering what the hastily assembled experts agreed was "exhaustion," the result of an overaggressive travel schedule. "He pushes himself too hard on the job . . ." said one expert. Another observed, "His hands-on leadership style, while benefiting the American people, could impinge on his health. . . ." That soft sycophancy was everywhere these days, a far cry from Chowdhury's time in the White House, when the media was quick to inflate even the most benign misstep into a full-blown constitutional crisis.

The pilot stepped back into the cabin. He offered the typical pleasantries, confirming that Chowdhury's car and driver awaited him outside the terminal. The pilot did apologize for one inconvenience: the private arrivals terminal for VIPs, with its separate customs and immigration services, was currently closed. "They just announced it, sir. I'm sorry, but we're going to have to taxi into the commercial terminal."

Chowdhury didn't mind. It was equally fast. Unlike the old days, with the endless immigration lines and platoons of Homeland Security agents stamping passports, the commercial terminal now required you to simply step onto an auto-walk, which trundled you forward through a concourse the length of a couple of football fields. Signs lined the concourse, gentle but insistent reminders to watch the screens, which imaged your face. Advances in quantum computing and facial recognition technology had made passports obsolete. A two-way mirror ran the entire length of the auto-walk. Armed Homeland Security agents lingered behind it, out of view.

Today, though, the agents were out in plain sight. On high alert, they paced the length of the auto-walk, wearing body armor and gripping assault rifles with gloved hands. Chowdhury couldn't recall ever seeing such robust security at immigration. It was as if they were looking for someone.

Chowdhury inadvertently made eye contact with one barrel-chested agent, his gaze concealed behind aerodynamically shaped sunglasses. He stepped over to Chowdhury, his palm on the grip of his assault rifle. "Sir," he snapped, "eyes up on the screen."

13:22 March 12, 2054 (GMT-5)
The White House

The sharp drilling sound of the old-fashioned telephone rang in Hendrickson's office. Despite multiple and redundant systems of secure communication, he preferred to discuss the most sensitive matters over his red line, a technology not meaningfully updated since the twentieth century. Julia Hunt continued to watch the news while the secretary of press, Karen Slake, the only cabinet-level official who maintained a West Wing office, had hurried into Hendrickson's office and now stood beside his desk. Nearly six feet tall, she leaned down to try to hear as Hendrickson received the latest from the White House physician in San Diego.

"Uh-huh . . . uh-huh . . ." Hendrickson paused. "So he's stable."

The White House physician responded at some length. Hendrickson gave a thumbs-up to Slake. She told him to ask how long it would be until they could get the president on camera so people could see he was okay. Hendrickson muffled his palm over the receiver. "Do you really need to know that right now?" he asked. The man had just suffered a near-catastrophic heart attack, according to his physician.

"*Yes*," said Slake, pressing down on the word. "I do."

So Hendrickson asked. From the volume of the expletive-laden response that spilled out of the receiver, Slake didn't need to be told what the White House physician's medical opinion was on holding a press event.

After Hendrickson hung up, Slake explained her contingency plan. Her team at the federal government's recently established Department of Press had already pulled footage, which they were in the process of selectively editing, digitally altering, and feeding to social networks and legacy news media. They had, quite swiftly, begun an algorithmic scrub of any narrative of the president suffering a health emergency, burying those stories. Slake said she could do one better: within a few hours—with the aid of a few loyal evening news anchors—they could overwhelm any conflicting narratives and reduce today's incident to little more than the president stumbling at the lectern after delivering a rousing speech on the anniversary of the *Wén Ruì* Incident. Slake had already called Homeland Security, asking them to push her any interesting information about detentions at the border, anyone suspicious that they might have pulled from the immigration lines, so that Slake could amplify those stories as a way to deflect from the current crisis—terrorism and immigrant criminality being reliable distractions.

Hendrickson listened patiently. "But what if he dies?"

"If who dies?" answered Slake.

"Castro . . . the president . . . What if the White House physician is wrong? . . . What if people find out you're just feeding them a story?"

Slake stared back at him vacantly, tilting her head to the side as though she'd been asked to solve for x and now had to solve for y. "Well . . ." she began, in a bit of a false start. She found her footing. "If that happens, we simply tell them another story."

A phone rang, this time the old-style encrypted smartphone that Julia Hunt carried for work. When she glanced down at the caller ID, the color went out of her face.

"You going to take that?" her godfather asked.

Hunt held up her phone so Hendrickson and Slake could see who was calling: Senator Nat Shriver.

⌐

13:26 March 12, 2054 (GMT-5)
JFK International Airport

"Sir," snapped a woman's voice from behind him, "we're going to have to ask you to step off here."

Chowdhury turned around. He'd nearly traversed the auto-walk. He could see the daylight of the arrivals terminal ahead, the twin automatic doors opening and closing as travelers passed through immigration. He had kept his eyes fixed on the screens above as they played the news and scanned his face. Why was he being asked to step off the auto-walk? He felt harassed, and at this point in his life he felt like someone who shouldn't have to suffer such harassment.

"Is there a problem, Officer?" he asked.

A compact immigration officer, built solid as a gymnast, with small, cruel eyes, held open an exit gate. "No problem, sir," she said. The auto-walk had come to a halt. "But you need to come with me."

"I have several appointments in the city," Chowdhury said. Which wasn't untrue. He was hoping to meet with his cardiologist that evening, a house call at his suite in the Carlyle, where he'd be staying until his apartment there was finished; however, as he said this, he realized his tone was haughty and clearly did him no favors. One of her colleagues, a powerlifter to her gymnast, approached them, asking if there was a problem.

"No," said Chowdhury. "No problem, I just need to get into the city."

Behind him the other passengers on the auto-walk crossed their arms and shifted their feet. A few sighed impatiently.

"Exit here, sir," said the woman more forcefully. The heel of one palm shifted onto her belt, which held handcuffs and pepper spray. Chowd-hury was escorted around the two-way mirror and into an interrogation room. As the door was shut behind him, he heard the news continue to drone from the screens above the auto-walk: one of the anchors was discussing reports of an uptick in security incidents at the border.

⌐

13:42 March 12, 2054 (GMT-5)
Capitol Hill

Julia Hunt had taken Shriver's call while Hendrickson and Slake hovered over her shoulder. Shriver had asked Hunt to come to his office in the Capitol for a meeting. She knew her godfather didn't quite trust her to handle a meeting with Shriver on her own, but he couldn't afford to step away from his desk, not in the middle of this crisis. And so he'd told Hunt to go.

On her way out the door, Hunt glimpsed the vice president, the third who'd served under Castro, as he came up on a video call with Slake and her godfather. An elementary-school-math-teacher-turned-politician named Smith, this vice president was forgettable by design. Smith was so forgettable that Castro's last campaign had distributed an internal memo that the administration would simply be known as the Castro administration, not the Castro-Smith administration. Hunt was glad to avoid the call.

Outside, she stepped into an auto-taxi beyond the last barrier of White House security and spoke her destination into its self-navigation system. Hunt's mother had told her that when she was a child, traffic passed directly in front of the White House, and you could drive the entire length of Independence or Constitution Avenues, right up to the Capitol, without passing a single checkpoint. The city had since become difficult to navigate, with road closures and new, not particularly thought-out security protocols interrupting the flow of the city as Pierre Charles L'Enfant had envisioned it three hundred years before.

The gridlock felt to Hunt like a fitting metaphor. Castro's consolidation of power after his victory in 2044 had led to a decade of single-party rule that he'd codified with sweeping electoral reforms at the federal and state levels, as well as ushering three new states—D.C., Guam, and Puerto Rico—into the Union.

The Democratic and Republican Parties, which had been bleeding members for years, had proven a weak opposition. What remained of these two legacy populist parties—the percentage of Americans claiming affiliation with either having plunged into the teens—merged for their own survival. With a nod to Jefferson, Madison, and Monroe, they reconstituted themselves into the Democratic-Republican Party, though they quickly came to be known as "Truthers" for their fanaticism in grinding down anyone who challenged their version of the "truth."

In much the same way Southern segregationists and Northeastern liberals had once coexisted uneasily within the Democratic Party, the far right and far left of American politics now coexisted as Truthers, united by a brand of populism and desire for self-rule that made unlikely allies of Texan secessionists and urban agitators in coastal mega-cities who demanded that Castro's government grant them autonomous city-state status. Above all else they agreed that Castro's consolidation of political power had become an urgent threat to democracy, one that needed to be monitored and dealt with, occasionally through violence but primarily by obstructing ever larger portions of his legislative agenda.

The most hawkish of these obstructionists was the speaker of the House, Representative Trent Wisecarver. It was Wisecarver who, much to Hunt's surprise, was waiting for her when she arrived in Shriver's office. "The senator's running a few minutes late," he said. "But please, sit down." Wisecarver gestured to a leather tufted sofa. He stood with his hands clasped behind his back as he studied the room's oak-paneled walls, crowded with mementos of Shriver's family. "He's got a killer instinct, you know. . . ." Wisecarver's voice cracked dryly and then trailed off. "I've often said he's bound to end up on one side of a firing squad. . . . The only question is which side."

Wisecarver was north of eighty years, but age had not yet diminished or mellowed him. A cunning spark still resided in the old man, bright as ever. Political necessity had paved the way for Wisecarver's congressional career after the calamitous events of two decades past, when he'd served as national security advisor during the war with China. After the twin catastrophes in San Diego and Galveston, Wisecarver had left Washington in disgrace, returning to his family home in a military town right outside Fort Tubman. When the veterans of that war returned, finding their nation in ruin and their service questioned and derided, Wisecarver had discovered fertile political soil in their grievances. He ran for a seat in Congress and never looked back.

He stood at Shriver's bookcase, glancing over the titles. He pulled out a volume. "You ever read this one?" He handed Hunt the book, *The Nightingale's Song*, whose cover image was a photograph of the Vietnam Veterans Memorial. Not the black granite wall—that sea of sacrifice—but the sculpture of three soldiers who stand their vigil by the wall, as if on the shore, staring out to that sea. Wisecarver explained that the book was about a scandal nearly seventy years before, the "so-called Iran-Contra

Affair," as he'd put it, which upended the Reagan presidency. Hunt had, of course, heard of Iran-Contra. But she didn't understand how the title of the book related to its subject. "The central characters—John McCain, Jim Webb, Bud McFarlane, Ollie North—all overlapped at the Naval Academy and served in Vietnam," Wisecarver explained. "You see, a nightingale will only ever sing its song if it hears another nightingale singing it first. After Vietnam, so many veterans were told that their war was wrong, shameful, a stain on their country. Reagan was the first president to tell Vietnam veterans that they should be proud of their service, that they'd fought nobly for a worthy cause. He sang that song. And they sang it back. But often in destructive ways, like Iran-Contra. Vietnam vets, like North and McFarlane—determined not to repeat the mistakes of Vietnam by abandoning their allies in Central America—began laundering money and running illegal arms to them. While other Vietnam vets, like McCain and Webb, eventually had to hold their one-time comrades to account."

When Hunt opened the book, its spine creaked as if Shriver had yet to read it. The black-and-white photos inside—of McCain beside his A-4, of Webb in the jungle, of North in his midshipman's uniform—stared back at her across the decades. Different players in the same game. Wisecarver told her that she was welcome to borrow the book, which Hunt thought was odd, seeing as it wasn't his to offer; but then again, it seemed there was little in the Capitol that Wisecarver couldn't offer as his own. Castro's overreach had bred a growing strain of resentment in the electorate, one that Wisecarver had used to catapult himself from an obscure House district to the speakership.

The senator arrived, and Hunt tucked the book into her briefcase. "So sorry to keep you both waiting," Shriver said as he perched next to

Julia on the sofa. "I was tied up at a lunch that ran late." In front of him, on the coffee table, was a dish of peanuts. He dug into them like a starving man.

⌐

17:07 March 12, 2054 (GMT-5)
JFK International Airport

Hours had passed and Chowdhury's patience was wearing thin. No one had yet explained why the Homeland Security officers had placed him in secondary detention. According to the pair watching him, he and nearly a dozen other detained travelers were "awaiting questioning." They had confiscated his headsUp bracelet, so he had no way of communicating with the outside world, and he couldn't help but think of the advantages of having a piece of technology embedded in his body, the unpredictable ways it might free you, as it would have now. Instead, his only connection to the outside world was the television overhead, switched to a cable news channel sympathetic to the Castro administration, with one of its evening anchors droning on about the threat posed by the Truthers and their obstructionist agenda, particularly now that they held a majority in the House.

One of the immigration officers meandered past. "Ma'am," said Chowdhury with all the politeness he could muster, "could I please place a call?"

"What did the other officer tell you?"

The other officer had told Chowdhury that he could place a call as soon as he'd been processed; however, Chowdhury wasn't certain what that processing would entail, or if it would occur anytime soon. This didn't garner any sympathy from the passing officer, who returned to her desk while Chowdhury was forced to return to watching the news. The anchor announced that after the break Vice President Smith would join for a live interview. It struck Chowdhury as odd that the vice president would appear alone on an evening news show, particularly on a day when the president had delivered a major speech.

The show returned from break and Vice President Smith was beside the anchor at the news desk. The anchor asked if the vice president would like to address the malicious rumors that the president had suffered some sort of health crisis. The channel went split-screen, with footage of Castro stumbling at the dais but now quickly recovering, next to the live feed of Vice President Smith. "Clearly, this was a minor incident," he said. "What's unfortunate is the way the president's political enemies are trying to take advantage of it." Vice President Smith continued, explaining that these allegations exposed how desperate the Truthers had become, further insinuating that other media clips—in which the president topples to the ground—were heavily doctored and likely the result of a foreign disinformation campaign. "Disinformation by which countries?" the anchor asked, to which Smith responded, "Due to classification, I'm not at liberty to say."

Smith made a convincing case. His blue eyes bored into the camera. Just as Chowdhury felt ready to believe him, a strange thing happened: A fly appeared. At first Chowdhury stood, thinking it was on his own screen. He motioned to swat it away and then realized that this fat black fly was on set, tiptoeing through the vice president's toupee-thick gray hair.

The anchor, who was staring at the vice president, pretended not to notice.

When the fly stepped onto the vice president's forehead, Smith didn't flinch. He might have acknowledged what everyone could clearly see by simply swatting the fly away. No one would have thought less of him for it; after all, these things happen, even to great men. But he chose not to. Rather, he continued with his message, pretending that what everyone could clearly see wasn't happening at all. He expressed his concern for the republic, his contempt for his enemies, and said in the most strident of tones, with furrowed brow, "Our president is strong. Any allegations to the contrary are nonsense—malicious rumors, not worthy of refuting."

⌐

17:42 March 12, 2054 (GMT-5)
Capitol Hill

Shriver and Wisecarver had gotten right to the point. Only a few days before, a sequence of code, unmistakable as a fingerprint, had popped up on a website called Common Sense. The code was incomplete, a sequence of programming phrases that bracketed a partial map of nucleic acids, amino acid chains, and proteins. But it matched segments of code in "Advances in Remote Gene Editing Among State and Non-State Actors," the highly classified intelligence briefing Hunt had shared with Shriver.

Where had the leak occurred? How did that code get onto an obscure website?

Hunt didn't know, and she said as much.

This answer far from satisfied Wisecarver, who kept asking different versions of the same question: "What is the administration doing to shore up this leak?" Hunt didn't have an answer, mainly because she didn't—and couldn't—speak for the administration.

While Wisecarver grilled Hunt, Shriver kept one eye on the television in the corner of his office, where the vice president was finishing an evening blitz of interviews. "Aww, c'mon," groaned Shriver as the vice president made some earnest point. He turned toward Julia, speaking directly to her: "You can fool the fans. You can fool the referees. But you can't fool the players. He is lying through his goddamn teeth."

Wisecarver placed his hand lightly on Julia's arm. "We know the president has suffered a major medical emergency. Denying it is counterproductive, both for his administration and the country. We also have concerns about . . ." Wisecarver paused, his eyes turned upward, as if searching for the correct word to pluck from the air. "*Contributing factors.*"

"Contributing factors?"

Wisecarver leaned deeper into the sofa, crossing his arms. "Major Hunt," he began, "your mother was Rear Admiral Sarah Hunt, correct?"

"Adoptive mother," Julia replied.

"Apologies," said Wisecarver. "Adoptive mother. The last time a foreign adversary attacked this nation, she played a central role in our defense. What I'd ask you to consider is that our nation is again under attack."

"By whom?" asked Hunt.

Shriver interjected, "We thought you might know, or be willing to share what the administration knows, given you've already shown a willingness to be transparent with us."

"You think this has something to do with the intel assessment I shared?"

A beat or two passed in silence. Wisecarver answered, "Is that the opinion of the administration?"

"Is what the opinion of the administration?" Hunt asked.

Their conversation stalled. Hunt wouldn't speculate on behalf of the administration, and neither Shriver nor Wisecarver would explicitly voice their concerns. As politely as she could, Hunt excused herself, mentioning a nonexistent meeting at the White House to which she was already late. As Hunt gathered her things, Wisecarver stood, saying, "Your mother is one of this nation's great heroes. Some people might have forgotten what she was called upon to do, but I never have. It's an honor to finally meet you."

Hunt sat in the back of the auto-taxi in a daze. Of course, she knew the president had suffered a health setback, but this was hardly unique. Roosevelt had died in office. Eisenhower similarly had suffered a heart attack. Modern presidents had proven fitter, but eventually a health crisis was bound to emerge. Did the speaker of the House and the vice chair of the Senate Select Committee on Intelligence really believe this was the work of a foreign adversary? If so, how? Through remote gene editing? Through a sequence of code they'd read in an intel assessment that she never should've shared, even though technically she was obliged to? Hunt dreaded the idea of explaining this meeting to her godfather, who, no doubt, would become even more incensed on learning that her misjudgment had led to a new, virulent conspiracy theory among senior opposition lawmakers.

Hunt badged into her office and proceeded through security. When she arrived at her godfather's door, it was open a crack. She knocked, and stepped inside to find Hendrickson, Slake, and two other staffers gathered around his desk. Like in a baroque painting, each was frozen in an expression of ecclesiastical grief, faces contorted, while the receiver to the red line lay in Hendrickson's limp, upturned palm. Muted on the television behind them, the vice president was finishing another interview.

"He's dead," said Hendrickson, blinking several times.

"Who's dead?" asked Hunt. She already knew the answer.

Slake began to shake her head. *"We're so fucked . . . we're so fucked . . ."*

"Karen . . ." said Hendrickson.

Hunt sat down in a free chair.

". . . we're so fucked . . . we're so fucked . . ."

"Karen . . ." Hendrickson said again, more sharply. Still, she kept on. Then Hendrickson slammed down the receiver in its cradle. Slake's eyes snapped toward him, as did Hunt's. "I just have to think," said Hendrickson, his hand still gripping the phone. "Let's take this one step at a time."

Then the phone rang. It was the vice president calling in from the studio. His voice was upbeat, energized by the spotlight. He had a single question:

"How'd I do?"

⌐

05:02 March 13, 2054 (GMT-5)
Walter Reed Medical Center

The president's body lay on a steel table in the bowels of the hospital, in a small and windowless gallery with raised seating that held a dozen people. Hendrickson was included in that dozen, as was Julia Hunt, whom he'd asked to accompany him. On the floor of the operating room, the chief internist, who would preside over the autopsy, was flanked by a squad of accompanying physicians, which included Walter Reed's chief medical examiner, an Army colonel who wore her hair in a tight bun, as well as the senior nurse on staff, a warrant officer whose hands never stopped moving as he checked the instruments spread across several steel trays. The commander of the hospital, a brigadier general, hovered two paces behind the body.

Two electronic screens the size of television monitors hung suspended above the examining table. One displayed the results of the president's most recent physical and the other a close-up of a dark, cloudy image that, to Julia, appeared like an exposure from the Hubble Space Telescope. Hendrickson seemed to sense his goddaughter's confusion. He leaned close and explained that the image was a CT scan of the president's heart. Hendrickson had himself undergone this exam in a recent checkup: the physicians had administered an intravenous dye before passing his body through an ultrafast scanner. The purpose was to detect plaque in the heart, of which Hendrickson had a distressing amount. When Castro heard about Hendrickson's poor result, he'd mentioned that he'd recently had the same test and made a competition of it, declaring that his test had shown no plaque at all.

The nurse removed the thin sheet that covered Castro's body and unceremoniously tossed it into a medical disposal container under the table. Castro was a fit man, slim, with good muscle tone, in his late fifties. The internist spoke for the recorder: "Beginning standard autopsy on Ángel Cordoba Miguel Castro, zero-five-seventeen, March thirteenth, 2054. Subject has been deceased for roughly ten hours, body arrived at Walter Reed from San Diego two hours ago and presents normally for a recent death . . ." He went on for several minutes, logging a description of the body's parts and their general condition. "We'll now proceed to the vital thoracic organs." Grasping a number-ten-blade scalpel, he leaned over the body and began a Y incision. The blade sliced cleanly, the first stroke starting behind the left ear, flowing down the side of the neck, before curving around the collarbone, and terminating at the sternum. The internist repeated the same incision on the right side, joining the two at the center of the chest. This was followed by a single vertical incision from the sternum to the pelvis. Everyone in the room seemed to lean toward the table at once.

The internist narrated his findings: "No external punctures to the cadaver . . . stroke appears unlikely . . . can't rule out a pulmonary embolism . . . or the ingestion of a poisonous substance. . . ." The internist glanced up at the CT scan on the monitor overhead, studying the image of Castro's heart a final time. "Cardiac failure seems even less likely—"

The nurse interrupted. "What about a fatal dysrhythmia?"

"His physical shows no risk factors that would've caused such an event, but let's take a look inside." The internist's back was to Julia, and she noticed his shoulders, how the muscles labored and flexed as he opened the chest cavity. He made one last effort and then, after a few moments of expert scalpel work, he turned slightly, and Julia could see in his gloved hand he held a wet, glistening mass.

The nurse casually offered a steel pan as though passing a dish at the dinner table. The internist was about to place the heart on the pan, so it might be weighed, when he startled, as if an insect had bit him. He made a curious expression, like a jeweler examining a suspicious stone as he brought the president's heart to eye-level. His hands remained full, so he asked the nurse to adjust his close-view spectacles. The internist gripped the heart with his right hand while caressing its bottom with his left. The more his left fingertips probed, the more alarmed his expression became. The internist looked from the president's heart to the CT scan and back to his heart.

"This can't be right. . . ." The internist turned to the other physicians behind him. "This can't be the same heart."

2

Common Sense

Middle of the night, alone in his lab, was just how he liked to work. News of Castro's death was everywhere, and he'd come here to escape it. Stylishly dressed in a cashmere Cucinelli hoodie, he was blasting his music. Tonight it was Dean Martin, and he was mouthing the words to "That's Amore," muttering to himself about the moon hitting his eye like a big pizza pie while he reviewed the genetic code of dozens of monarch butterflies, the subject of that evening's work. Without too much trouble, he'd teased apart their nucleotide bases and found a sequence of mRNA that would switch the color in their wings from reddish brown to green, to blue, to yellow, to nearly anything he wanted, really. He had, a week before, met a girl, a diving instructor from Tokyo newly arrived on the island, and he'd wanted to impress her. She had a tattoo of colored butterflies on her wrist.

Since he was a kid, most people called him Big Texas. His actual name was Dr. Christopher Yamamoto. The girl with the butterfly tattoo had teased him when she'd heard the nickname. Most people did. Raised by a single father, a chief petty officer in the US Navy, he'd moved around a lot. Small for his age and asthmatic, he earned the nickname at a Northern Virginia high school known for its football team. Each day he arrived at school with little more than a handful of change for lunch, which he usually bought from the vending machine in the form of an enormous chocolate chip cookie called *The Big Texas*. He had a special way of eating the cookie. He sat in the cafeteria, typically alone, and removed all the chocolate chips—counting out every last one, usually over a hundred, while tabulating a daily average in his head. He placed the chocolate chips in a pile. He ate the cookie, then the chocolate chips, one at a time. Other kids noticed, and Yamamoto became Big Texas. Even his father began to call him that, or B.T. for short.

Encased in a large goldfish bowl, the butterflies batted their wings in near-perfect cadence with the music. He watched as their color changed in real time. "Ain't That a Kick in the Head" began playing, and B.T. began shuffling triumphantly around his lab as he imagined rolling up to the dive shop behind the beach on Cape Maeda, that dive instructor in her bikini, him with his multicolor butterflies in the bowl, her so impressed that she fell into his arms. *My head keeps spinning . . . I go to sleep and keep grinning . . . If this is just the beginning . . . My life is going to be-au-ti-ful.* . . . He loved the big band stuff from a hundred years ago—Martin, Sinatra, Bennett. Their music had provided the soundtrack to some of the happiest moments of his life, walking across the floor of the Bellagio or the Venetian, his sunglasses from the poker table still shielding his eyes, the pockets of his bespoke suit bulging with that night's winnings as he headed to the bar, where he half expected to meet Sammy Davis or Joey Bishop for a highball. He'd graduated from MIT radically in debt and had stayed in Vegas long after paying off that debt, making the first of his several small fortunes there and then running the tables from Monte Carlo to Macau. He liked high stakes. On good nights his lab felt like a casino. He had his theories. He got dealt his hand. He placed his bets.

He opened a window to let some fresh air in. He could hear the ocean above the music. Tomorrow morning he'd head down to the beach. Butterflies eat fruit and B.T. needed to clean a few decaying scraps from their habitat before he delivered his gift. He was elbow-deep in the bowl, reaching for an apple core, when an incoming call rang on his work computer. He startled, nearly knocking his experiment to the ground. He'd turned off all his alerts. He let the call ring itself out. Whoever it was didn't leave a message. They called again. B.T. let it ring. What could be so urgent? He was reaching for a last rind of fruit. The call kept ringing. He should really pick up. . . . It could be an emergency. . . . People knew not to call him in the lab. . . . *Goddammit.*

He lunged toward his workstation, catching the incoming call on its last ring. A three-dimensional rendering of James Mohammad, one of his financial backers, appeared at his desk on the forty-second floor of his Lagos office. Behind him, sky-filled windows framed the harbor speckled with a mix of freighters and luxury yachts. "B.T., what are you doing?" Mohammad said in vowelly English.

"Working. What is it?"

"We need to discuss the files you turned over."

"I'm busy."

"We've given you a lot of money."

Late last year, B.T. had closed a deal with James Mohammad and his partners based on promising early results from his research on remote modifications to cells altered by mRNA-based vaccines. B.T. estimated he was still at best three years away from the breakthrough in remote gene editing that Mohammad and his partners had gambled on, if he ever got there.

"Okay," said B.T. "What about the files?"

Mohammad's expression changed to genuine curiosity. "What is that you have going on behind you?"

"What?"

"Behind you. . . . Those colors . . . are those . . . are all of those . . . butterflies . . . ?"

B.T. jerked around.

In his rush to answer the call, he hadn't properly sealed the lid on the butterflies' bowl. Now they were fluttering around his lab. Cursing, he grabbed a loose towel and scrambled after them. The few that B.T. managed to corral he inadvertently killed, while the rest flew out the window, into the night. The next morning green, yellow, and blue monarchs could be found calmly batting their wings in the trees and on the grass around Cape Maeda.

⌐

22:37 March 19, 2054 (GMT-5)
The White House

Her godfather had seemed to age years in a week. His closely trimmed hair had never been much more than a coating of gray stubble, so most of the change Julia observed was in his face, the way it sagged, the rims of his eyes having become red and sad like an old basset hound's, with pallid semicircles beneath. Thus far, Hendrickson had managed to keep the details of Castro's autopsy under wraps—how the internist had discovered an inexplicable mass of cells lodged in Castro's aorta. None of the physicians could explain how the marble-sized obstruction had grown so large in so little time. Hendrickson had left strict orders with the brigadier general in command of the hospital: only the White House would receive a record of the autopsy report, all other copies would be destroyed.

In the hours that followed, priority was to get Smith sworn in as Castro's successor. Discretion had been at a premium. Castro's death wasn't yet public. Hendrickson hadn't even divulged it to the Supreme Court justice he'd corralled into the White House to administer the oath of office. The justice had entered the Roosevelt Room at a little before seven in the morning, the Secret Service having taken her from her breakfast table. She cursed about "this personal intrusion" until she saw Smith and understood. Hendrickson scrounged up a Bible and the new president swore on it.

At noon that day, the newly sworn-in president Smith announced Castro's death in a televised address to the nation. But it was too little, too late. The Democratic-Republicans and their activist base, the Truthers, had seized on the administration's lack of transparency and blitzed the media with calls for resignations. Truther agitators accused the Dreamers of being "the party of lies" while the Dreamers struggled to absorb the sudden loss of their leader. Conspiracy theories gained traction among a disoriented public, with #TRUTHNOTDREAMS trending across social networks. News outlets that for so long had been pliant to Castro could not ignore the outcry.

A bloody Sunday followed. In Tucson, a Border Patrol officer fired a rubber bullet that struck a Truther protester in the eye, killing her. When the news broke, the Homeland Security secretary resigned. But a single resignation wasn't enough. Truther activists, organized into self-styled Truther brigades, ransacked a half dozen federal buildings from Los Angeles to Boston in one frenzied afternoon. By Monday evening a crop of resignations, from the secretary of defense to the director of Health and Human Services, had arrived on Hendrickson's desk.

As chief of staff, Hendrickson had quietly requested these resignations. He delivered them to the new president. By the end of that week, it seemed the Truthers had achieved their goal of mass resignations within the administration and their protests subsided, but a sense of crisis remained. "Sir," Hendrickson told the newly appointed president, "we've stopped the bleeding, but the patient is still on the table with a weak set of vitals."

⌐

18:22 March 19, 2054 (GMT+1)
Lagos Island, Lagos

This investment could blow up in his face. James Mohammad had hired three separate security firms to breach Yamamoto's personal servers and all three had reached the same conclusion: his servers were clean, containing no indication that the proprietary research on remote gene editing that Mohammad had bought exclusive rights to at great expense had been transferred. A fragment of code from that research had surfaced on Common Sense only a few days before. The code was incomplete, meaningless out of context, but its origin was unmistakable.

The search algorithms Mohammad had in place to recognize even a portion of the code, anywhere, had picked it up immediately. But B.T.'s servers were clean . . . if he wasn't the leak, then who was? Ultimately, this breach represented a human failure as opposed to a technological one. Yes, B.T.'s talents were undeniable, but so, too, were his weaknesses. A gambler through and through, B.T.'s impulses often got in the way of his genius. Mohammad should've known not to trust him.

James Mohammad was a gambler, too, but he went about it in a different way. If asked, he would describe himself as a private investor. His investment vehicles rotated—Dark Stone Enterprises, Clear Wood Equity, Broad Water Capital—their names, like so many similar firms, fitting a common pattern: the interplay of an element and an adjective, striving at permanence. Like B.T., Mohammad had had a transient youth, moving every few years with his father, Benjamin Mohammad, a Nigerian diplomat of great promise. Like many globe-trotting elites from former Commonwealth countries, Mohammad's father dropped him off at Eton at age thirteen. Shortly thereafter, in 2036, his parents succumbed to the pandemic forever associated with that dismal year. The old Etonians, never known for embracing outsiders, had, after Mohammad's personal tragedy, allowed him to finish out the term but couldn't find the where-withal to underwrite the rest of his education. Then, unexpectedly, an uncle had intervened.

Much later, after a series of failed investments had taken the grown-up James Mohammad to the brink of bankruptcy, his uncle had again intervened, offering to underwrite his losses and future investments so long as he—on occasion—shared with the Nigerian government dis-creet, nonpublic information related to those investments. Mohammad didn't quite know how to think about the benefits of his arrangement until, one evening over a drink, an American tech investor ten years his junior confessed to working in intelligence and described a similar relationship with his own government. He had a specific word for it: he was working as a NOC, nonofficial cover.

Whatever his title, Mohammad knew that researchers like B.T. were on the cusp of implementing remote gene editing, a profound scientific breakthrough. If molecules really were the new microchips, the promise of remote gene editing was that the body could be manipulated to up-grade itself. Few could comprehend the implications: governments would no longer need to roll out logistically complex and onerous vaccination campaigns to combat ever-quickening pandemic cycles and viral vari-ants; advanced genetic therapies could be administered remotely, with far greater ease, by triggering the gene-altering properties of mRNA through wireless communication, the equivalent of sending a molecular-level software upgrade; and this was to say nothing of potential enhance-ments in human physiology and intelligence. The seamless integration of technology and biology was hardly a new idea. Decades before, in the opening years of the century, visionaries like the technologist Ray Kurzweil had predicted the coming of the so-called Singularity. Now, with the prospect of remote gene editing, Mohammad believed that moment had finally arrived.

It was clear to Mohammad that a new Great Game was afoot. Whatever global order currently existed could only be characterized as no order at all. China and the United States had forfeited their dominance with a near-world-ending conflict; Russia's decline had continued post-Putin and the eastern part of Siberia was in effect a Chinese colony; his native Nigeria had developed with intent and impact internationally, often cooperating with Brazil; and, of course, there was Japan—long written off given its declining demographics. It had leveraged artificial intelligence, robotics, and quantum computing to compensate for a diminished workforce, often trading with India, which offered a vast market for its technologies.

The objective of the "game," as Mohammad thought of it, was to arrive at the Singularity first and, with a head start, outpace rivals who would never be able to catch up once biology and technology finally merged; this head start was key, as theorists believed the Singularity would enable what they'd termed an "intelligence explosion," the equivalent of thousands of years of biological evolution crammed into months or even weeks when machine and human learning integrated into a single consciousness. After this, a regular human intelligence in this game would become as anachronistic as the skills possessed by the chess and Go grandmasters AI had surpassed decades ago. Already, so much of geopolitics had begun to revolve not so much around military alliances, or even trade alliances, but tech alliances. Instead of fighting in third-country proxy states, as the US and Soviet Union had done a century before, the battlefields of today's "proxy wars" were in the biotech and quantum labs around the world.

Yes, thought Mohammad, it would seem the Singularity was close . . . and a key sequence of its code was sitting on Common Sense, a website that trafficked in conspiracy theories and agitated against the Castro administration. Without drawing too much attention, Mohammad needed to figure a way to get that piece of code taken down . . . before someone recognized its implications.

B.T. would be of little help with this task; and, frankly, Mohammad didn't want to entangle himself further there. As he sat behind his desk, with the low sun hitting the Atlantic, he recalled how they had first met, through that fierce woman at the Tandava Group, the one who'd been in B.T.'s class at MIT, the one who'd also lost a father who had served as a sort of diplomat. . . . Maybe she could lend a hand . . . What was her name? James Mohammad scoured his inbox, until finally an email popped up: lily.bao@tandava.com.

⌐

22:37 March 20, 2054 (GMT-5)
The White House

President Smith spent his first chaotic week in office immersed in planning the state funeral for his predecessor. He'd asked Hendrickson for a block-by-block dissection of the route the presidential motorcade would take from the White House to Arlington National Cemetery. Castro had never served in the military and under normal circumstances this would've made him ineligible for burial at Arlington, but while he was alive he'd strong-armed the Pentagon brass into approving an exception for him. For Smith, everything had become the funeral. Whether he had no instinct for self-preservation or simply didn't have an interest in the political machinations swirling around him, Hendrickson couldn't say. At times it seemed as though the funeral the new president was planning was actually his own. Hendrickson had begun to feel like the de facto president; he'd even taken to sleeping at the office and so, in a way, was also a resident of the White House.

Julia had taken to sleeping at the White House too. Each night, after the last meeting, she'd roll out her sleeping bag on Hendrickson's floor while he flopped down beneath a throw blanket on a red-and-gold silk-upholstered sofa. After a week, Julia asked if he would consider spending a night at home. Though he never spoke of it, she knew Hendrickson and his wife were essentially estranged. He kept up the façade for the sake of his career, but Julia knew the old admiral had nothing pulling him home.

"I can't leave yet," said Hendrickson. He tugged the blanket up over his shoulders, revealing a stockinged foot with a dime-sized hole in the big toe. "There's too much to get done. Maybe after the funeral."

"That's not until next month." Julia propped herself up on her elbow, facing Hendrickson. From the well-lit South Lawn, a low iridescence crept into the curtained room. "Have you taken a look at yourself lately?"

Hendrickson grunted, adjusted his body, and didn't answer.

"You're scarcely eating," she added. "You're not exercising. You're barely sleeping."

"That's hardly my fault." Hendrickson sat up on the sofa and, with knees wide, planted his elbows on his legs. He ran through the list of everything that needed to happen to ensure the stable transfer of power between Castro and Smith, from the replacement of the resigned cabinet secretaries to the appointment of a new vice president, all of which he would have to jam through an increasingly intransigent Congress led by Wisecarver. "Until we get a VP confirmed," said Hendrickson, "Wisecarver remains one heartbeat away from the White House. Knowing that, could you sleep?"

"Have you seen the conspiracy theories about Castro's death?" Julia asked. They had existed as a sort of background noise for several days now, appearing across messaging platforms and on social media accounts. These theories all arrived at the same conclusion: Castro had been assassinated. They differed on the method, with elaborate speculation on everything from Russian poisoning plots to Chinese hit squads. Most prominent of these platforms was the increasingly popular website Common Sense, which didn't expound on method, but in boilerplate statements of a few hundred characters or less simply asserted that Castro's death had been no accident, and repeated the catchphrase, *Wake up, America, and dream.*

"I've heard the same crackpot stuff," said Hendrickson. He didn't mention the mass discovered in Castro's heart.

"I've also heard the Truthers are demanding a national commission to investigate Castro's death, like the Warren Commission did with Kennedy, and that we pick a Truther for VP, so a unity government."

"Yeah, I've heard that about the VP pick too." Hendrickson lay back down on the sofa. "As for the investigation, well, they'd like nothing more than an investigation, a big juicy one they can hold over us for years and years." This was why Hendrickson had withheld the results of the autopsy—he wouldn't hand his enemies this weapon to use against the nation. Irregular as the report was, it would only empower Truther conspiracy theorists.

Julia recognized the bitter tone in his voice, the burden it carried; it was how her mother had often sounded. A wife and family had once provided Hendrickson his emotional ballast, but with his marriage soured and his children living on the other side of the country, it was primarily work that steadied him.

"Will you *please* go home tomorrow?" Julia pleaded. "Just for a night."

Hendrickson rolled over and looked at her through the dim light. "You don't have to worry," he said. "I'm not going to end up like her."

"Why?" she asked. "Because you're stronger than she was?"

"No," said Hendrickson. They were speaking in whispers. Then a silence formed, into which Hendrickson dropped his next words. "Because I learned my limits from her. No one should have to carry the burden she did. If I'm ever asked to do too much, I'll simply walk away." Julia stared at Hendrickson and considered his words. If he spoke obliquely, it was because the number of people Julia's mother had killed during the last war, when uttered aloud, became incomprehensible. *A single death is a tragedy, but a million deaths is a statistic*—was it Stalin who'd said that? This, she knew, was the emotional logic of why her mother had eventually swallowed a medicine cabinet's worth of pills and ended her life. It was as if by taking her own, single life she could imbue her death with the tragic element those other deaths had lacked. Ultimately, her mother couldn't shake the idea that she deserved tragedy.

A darkness had blanketed her mother in those last years, particularly after Julia had decided, over her objections, to follow her into the military. Sarah had pleaded with Julia to refuse her appointment to the Naval Academy. Too often she'd repeated what became a threadbare refrain: *Whoever saves a single life saves all the world.* The implication was that it was she, Sarah, who had done the saving by adopting Julia.

Before deciding to accept her appointment to the Naval Academy, Julia had, in a heated moment, after her mother trotted out the phrase one time too many, snapped back, "I never asked you to save me! And my job isn't to save you!" Soon thereafter Julia left for Annapolis. In four years, Sarah Hunt never once visited.

Hendrickson asked Julia to run over tomorrow's schedule. "Meeting with Slake at zero-eight; after that, we're reviewing the short list of possible VP picks with you in here at eight-thirty; the president's daily intel briefing is scheduled for nine-fifteen—"

"Is he going to attend this one?" Hendrickson interrupted.

"No, sir. He's got a conflict."

Hendrickson rolled over and tugged on his blanket, which again left his feet bare. He cursed. There wasn't enough goddamn blanket. "What's his conflict this time?" he grumbled.

"It seems he has a meeting with the director of the Marine Band to discuss the musical accompaniment for President Castro's funeral, followed by a meeting with the White House chief of protocol and chief floral designer to approve graveside flower arrangements. . . ." A long silence followed, punctuated by a few deep breaths as Hendrickson tried to calm down enough to sleep. Julia filled that silence by walking him through the next few days, which included a meeting with his old friend Dr. Sandeep Chowdhury, whom the week before they'd bailed out of secondary detention at JFK after an overenthusiastic Homeland Security dragnet had swept him up.

"What's the agenda for that meeting?"

"No agenda," Julia said. "Dr. Chowdhury's exec explained that he wanted to thank you for the help at JFK and hoped the two of you could catch up a bit. I thought you'd want me to put it on your schedule."

"That's appreciated." Hendrickson's eyelids began to droop. "It'll be good to see Sandy again." He yawned.

Julia was continuing to review the schedule when a crash in the hallway interrupted her; it sounded as though something had fallen over. She and Hendrickson hurried outside to find the president in his pajamas and bathrobe. At his feet was a vase filled with white and yellow flowers that had toppled to the floor. He was trying to clean up the mess. He startled when he saw them. "So sorry about that . . ." he said sheepishly. "I wanted to get a better look at these flowers. I thought I might suggest them for the funeral . . . it's important we get this right for the president." He bent over and continued to pick them up one at a time off the carpeted floor.

"Sir," Hendrickson said. "With due respect, *you* are the president. Someone else can handle the flowers. What are you doing awake?"

The president stood straight, the flowers dangling limp in one hand. With the other he scratched the back of his head. "Can't sleep for the life of me," he confessed. "You?"

⌐

14:02 March 20, 2054 (GMT-5)
Rosslyn, Virginia

Lily Bao's exec looked up when she returned to her desk after lunch. "A Mr. Mohammad phoned. He asked you to call him about someone named B.T. Here's the message." He handed her an old-fashioned Post-it note with a number scrawled across it.

Her exec was nearly thirty years her senior, a medically retired former Marine gunnery sergeant named Joseph William Sherman III, whom she simply called Sherman. With a compact frame, narrow-set blue eyes, a thin scraggly beard, and a shock of thin red hair, he bore a striking resemblance to his namesake, the famous Civil War general. Though Lily had never heard the story from him, out of curiosity she'd read the citation for Sherman's Navy Cross, the incident in which he'd lost both his legs leading a company of Marine Raiders in the Spratly Islands twenty years before, where he had successfully charged two machine gun nests before unsuccessfully charging a third. He had survived the war. His wife and three girls at Camp Pendleton had not.

"How was lunch?" He followed her to her office in his wheelchair, which he generally preferred to wearing his prosthetics.

"Fine," she said, sitting behind her desk. "Traffic's still a mess. I thought the Truther protests would ease up after Smith fired his cabinet."

"His problems are bigger than his cabinet. There's the commission, too, and demands for a unity government." Sherman paused. "So . . ." he added playfully. "What'd you order at lunch?"

She stopped and gave him a scathing look. "None of your god-damned business."

Sherman tucked his chin to his chest and laughed. Lily could never be too severe with him, even when he skirted up to the line of impropriety. This job was all he had; or, put another way, she was all he had, their friendship. His loyalty was unquestionable, irrational even. Lily couldn't quite explain it, except to assume that she reminded him of one of his daughters, or at least of what one of his daughters might have become; and, for his part (though she rarely allowed herself to think it), he reminded her of her own father.

"Why don't you like him?" Lily asked.

"Why don't I like who?"

"Shriver."

"Oh," said Sherman, joking again. "Is that who you were at *lunch* with?" He could see that he'd taken it a bit too far, so backed off. "What makes you think I don't like him? I like him and the Truthers quite a bit." Unable to restrain himself, Sherman launched into an aria on the dangers of one-party rule, the importance of the Truther brigades in securing First Amendment rights to protest, and the threat Castro's fourth term in office had represented to the republic. He caught himself and apologized. "Would you like me to get Mr. Mohammad on the line for you?"

A few moments later she was on with James Mohammad. "Ms. Bao, many thanks for returning my call." After exchanging pleasantries, she asked what she could do for him. "Well," Mohammad said, "I'm a bit worried about your friend B.T." The two of them had done some business together, he explained, but recently B.T. had become unpredictable, even erratic, and Mohammad was struggling to understand his change in behavior. Had Lily been in contact with B.T.?

Lily lied, saying she hadn't spoken to B.T. for several months, but assured Mohammad that if she heard anything, she would make certain to let him know.

She hung up the phone and then called out to Sherman. "Get me Dr. Christopher Yamamoto on the line." When no one picked up at his laboratory and it went to voicemail, Lily knew not to leave a message.

⌐

09:55 March 20, 2054 (GMT-5)
The Carlyle Hotel

It was good to be back in the United States, even under the circumstances. When the immigration agents finally granted Chowdhury his one phone call, he had strategically placed it to his old friend Bunt Hendrickson and had, miraculously, gotten through to the White House on the first try. "Wait, you're where?" Hendrickson had asked Chowdhury. "And they're holding you because of what?" It hadn't taken long—another two phone calls by Hendrickson—and just like old times, when they'd been White House staffers together, he'd sprung Chowdhury out of a jam.

A nagging concern had occupied Chowdhury in the week since he'd taken up residence in the Carlyle. He was worried about Hendrickson. Each day his concierge doctor cycled specialists in and out of his penthouse suite as they ran a series of diagnostics on his ailing heart. In the evenings, after the appointments had finished, Chowdhury would wander up and down Madison Avenue. Since Castro's death, the proprietors of nearly every pricey boutique had boarded up their plate-glass windows. Chowdhury still had access to the Tandava Group's daily corporate intelligence briefings, and these reports, compiled by a network he'd meticulously cultivated over two decades, assessed that the transition from the Castro administration to the Smith administration possessed a greater than one-in-five chance of descending into civil war, a loaded if not inaccurate term, thought Chowdhury. The specific intelligence in the reports didn't go so far as to suggest that foul play had a role in Castro's death, but Chowdhury didn't need his own corporate intelligence service to tell him it was a possibility.

Toward the end of that first week of tests and probes, Chowdhury had a meeting scheduled with an immunologist. A cursory background check showed she had studied nanorobotics. A graduate of Cal Poly, she'd worked in tech before switching to medicine. When she'd arrived at the Carlyle, her dark hair was cut in a pageboy style and she wore thick glasses in heavy black frames. Chowdhury had, in an inept effort at small talk, mentioned that she bore a striking resemblance to Harry Potter. She returned a blank stare. She didn't get the reference. She asked him to take a seat in a velvet-upholstered club chair in the corner of the sitting room, and proceeded with a round of diagnostic tests, all of which his primary physician had already administered. When Chowdhury explained this, she stated rather formally that due to liability concerns her company required her to re-administer these tests herself.

"What company is that?" asked Chowdhury.

"Neutronics," she said, while scanning his carotid artery with a handheld 3D imager.

"Based in São Paulo?"

"Yes, and Lagos too. With offices here." Her eyes dipped into her imaging device. Then she looked back up at Chowdhury. "So you've heard of us?"

"I'm a private investor," he said. "Neutronics was one of my early portfolio companies." Chowdhury had made a small fortune through his position in Neutronics. During the twin pandemics of the late 2030s, Neutronics had been first to market with a new generation of smart vaccines, the first to incorporate molecular-sized nanorobots that could adapt to mutations in the virus.

"I knew Ray Kurzweil when I was investing in the company. Is he still involved?" asked Chowdhury.

"Maybe on the margins," she said while placing a magnetically charged bracelet around Chowdhury's wrist. "I haven't seen him in years."

Brilliant and solitary, Dr. Kurzweil had always been an elusive figure, even in the years when Chowdhury had known him. One of the most remarkable things about Kurzweil had been his longevity. At 106 years old, he clung to life; it was as if da Vinci, who first imagined a flying machine, refused to die until the Wright brothers came on the scene. The difference between a visionary and a theory-peddler was, of course, the future itself and how it manifested. The Singularity, Kurzweil's famous prediction, had yet to manifest. When biological evolution fused with technological evolution, allowing the human species to accelerate one thousand years of Darwinian progress in intelligence and function into months or even weeks of bio-integrated quantum computing, Kurzweil would want to be there to see it, to be vindicated by it. Chowdhury wasn't surprised.

His train of thought was interrupted when the young immunologist unclasped the bracelet from his wrist. "Good news," she said.

"What's that?" Chowdhury buttoned up the cuff of his shirt.

She perched on the arm of his chair. A holographic display of his beating heart projected in front of him from a tablet she carried. She began to rotate the hologram on a three-dimensional axis with the tip of her index finger. She zoomed in on his aorta, toggling between his left atrium and his right atrium, while she explained the level of deterioration that had occurred across his heart. Erosion in the muscle. Plaque accumulation. Endemic stress that had left a generally weak system of synaptic responses. A series of grim facts that Chowdhury already knew. While he watched his ailing heart, he struggled to see the good news.

"The good news," explained the immunologist, "is that you're an ideal candidate for a new clinical trial." She then glanced down at the hologram. Chowdhury's heart had begun to flutter irregularly. A ribbon of sweat beaded across his forehead. "Are you all right?"

His breath, a thin and labored thread of air, escaped his mouth and he shut his eyes. A tingle in his wrist meant the serotonin dispenser was getting to work. Gradually, he felt the tension in his chest ease. "Sorry," he said. "Just happens sometimes."

"I understand," said the immunologist. She shut off the hologram and packed up the rest of her equipment. She explained that she'd email over some forms for him to sign the next day, a liability waiver as well as nondisclosure agreements, given the sensitivity of the trial. Also, she explained that he'd need to fly to Neutronics' main clinic in São Paulo for treatment.

"When?" asked Chowdhury.

"How soon can you be ready?"

Chowdhury said he'd get back to her with a date.

Alone in his suite, Chowdhury placed two phone calls. The first was to the White House operator, who put him in touch with the Marine major on Hendrickson's personal staff. The second call was to his daughter, Ashni. She picked up the phone on the first ring. Her voice sounded nervous as she said hello to her father, like a teenager who's thrown a party while her parents are away and doesn't expect them to call. Without prompting, she began to update her father on the state of their various portfolio companies. "I'm sure that's all going fine," Chowdhury interrupted. "Listen, I need you to do something for me."

"What is it, Bapu?"

"Do you think our fellows in corporate intelligence could track someone down?"

"Yes, of course," she said. "Who?"

"Be discreet about this, but I need them to find Ray Kurzweil."

23:47 March 24, 2054 (GMT+8)
Macau

B.T. was hardly sleeping. It had started a week ago as a sinking feeling after James Mohammad called him in his lab, asking about the sequence of code that had leaked onto Common Sense. That sinking feeling had transformed into wakeful nights, and those had become enough to convince B.T. that he needed a bit of R&R, a chance to unwind. He'd booked a flight and reserved himself a suite at the Venetian.

President Castro's death was all over the news, as were the protests demanding a commission and unity government. Every instinct B.T. possessed told him there was something more going on here. All week, as he cycled between baccarat, poker, fan-tan, and craps, with his conscious mind working through the patterns and probabilities of those games, his subconscious mind was grappling with the patterns and probabilities of Castro's death. The president's medical history was well known. He'd disclosed those records as part of his reelection campaign; they could be pulled up on any search engine and didn't contain a single indicator of heart disease. Yes, people died unexpectedly in late middle age, even with a clean bill of health like Castro's.

But presidents were also assassinated.

When B.T. ran the probabilities between the two, the odds seemed to favor the latter explanation. If he were gambling on it, he would have placed his money on someone having murdered Castro.

This conclusion—as opposed to any real interest in politics, or any real interest in anything outside the confines of his laboratory—continued to prevent B.T. from sleeping. Night after night in his suite he'd lain flat on his back while the lights from the city pulsed through his window and landed in nonsensical patterns against his face. Gradually, he came to conclude that his work had played a role in this mess.

After nearly a week in the casino, he was increasingly strung out, even though he was sitting on a considerable pile of winnings, enough to restart his life anywhere he wanted to go. The only problem was he couldn't think where that place might be. Infinite options often yielded paralysis, leaving a person trapped. Which was how B.T. felt that evening, knuckle-rolling a casino chip over his fingers while he sat at a roulette table winning successive games. A modest crowd had formed around him. One after another they'd begun to place their bets alongside his. He took a sip of his drink. Yawned. Placed another bet. It seemed he couldn't lose.

But he *so* wanted to lose.

He wanted to be wiped out, to be forced back to his work, to be forced to reckon with that deadly sequence of code that had escaped his lab. Still, he kept beating the odds. The little ball kept dancing around the wheel and falling into its cradle as if guided by his intuition alone. With every game that B.T. won, more people arrived to cheer him on, not understanding how trapped he'd come to feel by his pile of winnings. Each lucky turn left them cheering more, grasping his shoulders like a totem, none of them believing that his luck might flip. But he knew it would. The house always won in these games—always. It was the law of probabilities.

He placed all of his winnings on black.

The crowd at the table did the same. The dealer spun the wheel and dropped in the ball. It did its dance. B.T. took another sip of his drink and, when he noticed that one person had placed a bet against him, on red, he made a slight, disappointed face as if tasting something bitter in his glass.

Then the ball fell.

"Winner, red," announced the dealer.

The crowd groaned.

While the dealer raked up the house's winnings, sorting and stacking the many chips, a few of the other players who'd lost money—although not nearly as much as B.T.—placed a consoling palm on his shoulder, as if thanking him for the ride. One at a time, they vanished into the flickering depths of the casino. B.T. nodded politely, though he hardly cared about the loss. Now he didn't have a dime. This brought him clarity. Tomorrow morning he'd catch a flight back to Okinawa. James Mohammad must be looking for him.

The crowd had mostly dispersed and the dealer, having counted out the winnings, placed a stack of chips in front of the only player who'd bet with the house. She sat at the far end of the roulette table, her eyes fixed on him. It was Lily Bao.

3

The Singularity

21:15 March 23, 2054 (GMT-5)
Rosslyn, Virginia

B.T. had proven easy enough to find. When he went dark, Lily figured he was in one of the world's three gambling capitals—Vegas, Monte Carlo, or Macau. It only became a matter of checking with a handful of five-star hotels in each, something Sherman was happy to handle for her. In the days since Castro's death, it was Sherman who'd stoked Lily's concern for B.T. Each morning, Sherman came in parroting another conspiracy theory as to who or what was behind the president's untimely demise. He'd even gone so far as to place a #TRUTHNOTDREAMS sticker adjacent to the US Marine Corps sticker on his wheelchair. Lily nearly said something to him about the sticker—given the firm's policy on remaining apolitical—but she couldn't quite bring herself to. She, too, had her suspicions about Castro's death, and B.T.'s involvement in it.

Shriver wanted to see her before she left. When she suggested lunch, he asked if they could meet after dinner instead. Per usual, she reserved the room and he arrived late, after ten at night. When she saw him at the door—in his crumpled suit looking as though he hadn't slept in a day or two—he had the same effect on her as always, and she had the same effect on him. He clearly had things to say and so did she, but all that would wait. Their feet tangled together as they toppled onto the bed. Thirty minutes later, maybe an hour—time had a way of losing its proportions when she was with him—the two lay cradled together, insensate with lovemaking. The room was dark, and Shriver whispered, "Don't go. . . ."

"What do you mean?"

Her body fitted against his, she waited for his response. "I mean don't go to Macau."

Lily quickly sat up. "I'll be back in a few days, a week at the most." She told him not to worry. She knew how busy he was. She completely understood the pressures and constraints he was under, particularly given the current political crisis. She liked seeing him when he had time. They had fun together, and she'd make sure to call him when she got back.

When she swung her feet out of the bed, he reached for her, snatching her by the wrist.

"Just wait a goddamn minute," he said.

She let him hold her in place.

"I love you, Lily."

"Oh Christ." She pulled away again, but he wouldn't let her go.

"Doesn't that matter to you?"

"You're such a fucking politician."

"What's that supposed to mean?" He followed her out of the bed and stood naked in front of her as she dressed.

"It means all you do is talk. You love me? Really? Do something about it, then."

"I am," he said. "I'm asking you not to go."

"That's not you doing something about it . . . that is *you* asking *me* to do something about it." She had mostly dressed now and was grabbing the last of her things as she stepped toward the door. But something stopped her. She turned back toward him. He was beautiful—naked and pathetic too—but so beautiful. She believed he truly loved her, and so took one reassuring step toward him, clasping him around the wrist as he had done to her a moment before. "Listen," she said, "I understand it's difficult for you—"

Shriver was quick to interrupt her, to explain that once he'd won reelection, or once his party had a wider majority in the Senate, things would be easier for him, he'd have more latitude. He spoke about the current crisis and the "dangers to our republic," in the type of solemn tones that reminded her of Sherman. "I'm worried that if you go, something could happen, maybe you won't come back to me."

Lily told him he was being ridiculous. She kissed him and left.

⌐

09:30 March 24, 2054 (GMT-5)
The White House

He was shorter than she'd expected. Julia had heard stories about Dr. Sandeep Chowdhury from her mother and godfather while she was growing up, but she had never met him in person.

They'd nearly had to cancel this appointment. Almost two weeks had passed since Castro's death, and the daily protests in Lafayette Square had evolved from a thin picket line into a street-blocking mob. The protesters—out-of-state Truther activists mustered into self-styled brigades with names like Veritas Vengeance, the Swords of Truth, or the Peoples' Word—were peddling a conspiracy theory that alleged Castro's death was part of a Dreamer coup, and they questioned the legitimacy of President Smith. Their demands were twofold: that Smith immediately form a unity government by appointing a Truther vice president, and that a national commission investigate Castro's death. The numbers of protesters were growing, as was the intensity of their actions. When Chowdhury approached the West Gate, one protester threw something wet and soft at him, like a soiled diaper, and called him a traitor for meeting with those "lying squatters" in the White House.

"Really sorry about all this, Sandy," said Hendrickson, as they settled in his office. Chowdhury sat on one end of the sofa. He glanced at the sleeping bag rolled up in the corner. A White House steward brought him a cup of coffee on a silver tray and handed him a cloth napkin.

"Not a problem," said Chowdhury, wiping the last of a gooey white substance from the sleeve of his suit. He gave a wry little laugh. "I forgot how much fun you get to have around here." He placed the napkin back on the tray and the steward departed. Hendrickson and Chowdhury soon eased into a comfortable banter. When Chowdhury thanked Hendrickson for his help with the "misunderstanding at JFK," his old friend told him to thank Major Hunt, who was sitting quietly at the far end of the sofa. "She's the one who strong-armed Homeland Security." Chowdhury did a double take, not having made the connection that the Marine officer in her freshly pressed service uniform was the daughter of Sarah Hunt.

"I was a great admirer of your mother," Chowdhury said. "We asked everything of her—likely too much." Hunt simply thanked him.

Hendrickson proceeded to update Chowdhury on his work for the administration: the new president's plans for his predecessor's state funeral (to include an hour's worth of military flyovers on the National Mall); the impending selection of a vice president (to include a list of Dreamer candidates united by the singular distinction of being even weaker than Smith); and the challenges they'd surely face confirming a new cabinet (to include a vote-by-vote breakdown between Truthers and Dreamers on each potential nominee).

Julia sat barricaded in her corner of the sofa, saying little. As she listened to her godfather and Chowdhury, she was struck by the closeness between these two men. Hendrickson wasn't simply talking politics with Chowdhury; it was more than that. He was unburdening himself to his old friend. When Julia was a girl, Hendrickson had served much the same role for her adoptive mother. On Hendrickson's visits, he and Sarah would sit out on the porch talking late into the night. The subject hardly seemed to matter. It was the effect of the conversation itself that was most important. When Hendrickson arrived, the heaviness that so often attended her mother seemed to ease. Then, when he left, that weight would inevitably return. Julia had always felt grateful for Hendrickson's visits and thereby affectionate toward him, in much the same way she felt grateful today for Chowdhury's visit, and a similar affection for him— though she hardly knew him.

The topic of conversation shifted to the civil unrest around the White House. Certain media pundits had suggested that it'd gone too far, that it was time President Smith deployed Secret Service tactical units to disperse the protesters, and if that wasn't enough, he should invoke the Insurrection Act and call in the National Guard, or perhaps even federal troops. "Major Hunt," Chowdhury said, recrossing his legs and articulating his body toward where she sat in the far corner of the sofa. "What is your opinion, speaking as a military officer?"

"The people have a right to assemble," she said. "So long as it remains peaceful." Julia Hunt glanced out the window, where the sprinklers misted a rainbow across the South Lawn. The day before, a phalanx of protesters had shut down Constitution Avenue. Their leaders had tried to surround the White House by simultaneously marching up 15th and 17th Streets. They'd made it about halfway before horse-mounted Park Police broke their ranks, scattering them across the National Mall.

"Peaceful protest is one thing," said Chowdhury. "But this is darker."

"They feel like they've been lied to," said Julia.

"The key word there is *feel*," interjected Hendrickson, hissing the last word. "This younger generation doesn't believe in facts, but in feelings. If they *feel* they're being lied to"—again he spat out what to him seemed an ugly word—"then in their eyes they *are* being lied to, and so the feeling becomes a fact." Hendrickson spoke as if his participation in the lie around Castro's death was, at best, incidental. He paused a beat, catching himself so that he could measure his words more carefully. "Their feelings don't make President Smith illegitimate. But we do plan to meet one of their demands. Our administration is in the process of setting up a national commission to investigate Castro's death, like the Warren Commission. . . ."

As she listened, Julia couldn't help but recall that the real purpose of the Warren Commission hadn't been so much to solve who killed

Kennedy—at least not in a substantive way—but rather to put the question itself to rest. The Johnson administration had known that if a Cuban or Soviet connection to Kennedy's death emerged, it could've spelled nuclear war. So resolving the question became a matter of national security, one of utmost urgency. Hunt was skeptical of this latest commission. Would her godfather release Castro's autopsy to it? And if the Russians, Chinese, or newer antagonists like the Nigerians were behind Castro's death, would a national commission be willing to point the finger? Would it be willing to trigger a war? Likely not. And what if the commission found that it wasn't a foreign threat that was responsible for Castro's death, but a domestic one? That could result in war just the same.

The topic of conversation shifted to Chowdhury's plans, and his weak heart. When Chowdhury confessed this condition, a heaviness reappeared on Hendrickson's face. On seeing his old friend's concern, Chowdhury reached toward Hendrickson, placing a hand consolingly on his arm. "Please don't worry."

"Your diagnosis sounds serious," said Hendrickson.

"At one time, maybe so," said Chowdhury. "But there's a biotech company, Neutronics, that's doing some cutting-edge work with cardiology and genetic editing. They're down in São Paulo and they're saving lives." Chowdhury asked whether either of them had heard of Neutronics.

Hendrickson shook his head dispiritedly and said nothing more. Julia thought she'd heard of Neutronics but couldn't recall where.

A hefty, closefisted knock came at the door. Before Hendrickson could answer, Karen Slake stepped inside. She apologized but said it was urgent. She reached for the remote on Hendrickson's desk. With arms crossed, Slake stood confronting the television. She tuned in to the news, whose cameras were trained on an empty dais with the *Speaker of the House of Representatives* seal affixed to its front.

"What's going on?" Hendrickson asked.

"That asshole is siding with the protesters. He's going to demand a unity ticket."

"Which asshole?" Chowdhury asked Slake.

Slake shot this outsider a glance, as if his question were absurd, as if there could be any other asshole on this planet except for the one asshole to which she referred. "Wisecarver," she said. "Trent Wisecarver. . . . Who are you?" Chowdhury introduced himself and then asked if she was *the press secretary*. "Secretary *of* press," said Slake, correcting him. When Chowdhury asked the difference, she answered, "You wouldn't call the secretary of state *the state secretary*." Then, before she could say more, a door in the back of the Capitol's press briefing room flung open. Wisecarver strutted out onstage. Trailing behind him was Nat Shriver. When Julia Hunt saw the senator, it jogged her memory. The intelligence assessment she'd given Shriver. That's where she'd read about Neutronics.

22:15 March 24, 2054 (GMT+8)
Macau

Lily had splurged on a suborbital flight, traveling between Dulles and Macau in less than three hours. Once she'd landed, it had taken her about the same amount of time to find B.T. on the casino floor. When she saw him, she knew coming had been the right choice. Elegantly attired in a brown chalk stripe suit that she imagined he had mail-ordered from a

Savile Row tailor who had his measurements on file, underneath it he was wearing a cheap white T-shirt, its grimy collar blown out. A five-thousand-dollar suit paired with a five-dollar T-shirt—classic B.T.

She watched as he slunk from table to table, winning at cards, winning at baccarat, running the table at craps, while surrounded by an aura of personal defeat. Before Lily had left Washington, she'd had Sherman dig into the background on B.T.'s business partner James Mohammad. She hadn't liked what they'd found. His ties with the Nigerian government were obvious, which meant so, too, were his secondary ties with the Chinese government, who through economic subsidies and military alliances had turned Nigeria into a partner, if not a client state. So B.T. was, in effect, not only in bed with the Nigerians but also with the Chinese. If a sequence of his code—which was, essentially, *their* code—had slipped loose onto the internet he couldn't have picked a worse pair of actors to disappoint.

Lily didn't want to approach B.T. She thought that might seem too aggressive; instead, she wanted him to notice her. At the roulette table, he had placed his chips on black, so she'd placed hers on red, and that had been enough. "Lily Bao," he said, a smile barging its way onto his lips as he saw her from down the table. "Why am I not surprised it's you who found me first?"

Lily was still collecting the last of her winnings. "Can I buy you a drink?"

B.T. leaned over, grabbed a pair of her chips, and tossed them as a gratuity to the dealer, who nodded in appreciation. B.T. then turned toward her, his one eyebrow raised, and said, "The drinks here are free, kiddo."

They crossed the casino to the restaurant, walking arm in arm beneath its ceiling painted with kitschy Italianate frescoes and studded with security cameras, dozens of black, watchful orbs. At B.T.'s request, the maître d' agreed to open up a closed section in order to grant them a little extra privacy. "Come here often?" Lily asked, impressed.

B.T. shrugged and replied, "Depends on your definition of *often*." He ordered the two of them a prewar bottle of Bordeaux, a Château Lafite Rothschild. "The 2031," he said authoritatively, which elicited a little bow from the maître d', who answered, "Right away, Dr. Yamamoto," before returning to the front of the restaurant.

Lily suppressed a laugh. "Look at you."

"Look at me what?"

"*The 2031 . . . Right away, Dr. Yamamoto . . .*" B.T.'s gaze dipped self-consciously toward his place setting. Lily reached across the white linen tablecloth and took his hands in hers. "It's really good to see you."

"How'd you find me?" B.T. asked. As Lily opened her mouth to speak, he modified the question: "Wait, *why'd* you find me?" This was more complicated. The long answer began more than a decade before, when, awkward and alone, they'd met freshman year in Cambridge. Back then, they'd clung to each other as if drowning while they navigated the twin challenges of life away from home and MIT's relentless academic load. B.T. had been Lily's first boyfriend, a relationship that'd lasted a total of three months. In a season of firsts, he had, on a futon in her dorm room, become her first lover. Lily suspected she was his first lover, too, though he improbably alluded to other affairs. When he forgot Valentine's Day and then her birthday within a three-week span and had then taken her to dinner to make up for both but forgot his wallet so she'd wound up paying, she had had enough. Mindful of his feelings, she'd suggested that they would make better friends than lovers. His relief at this suggestion was palpable, the only mutual breakup Lily had ever experienced.

After breaking up, they spent even more time together. For Lily—who'd lost her father, her country, and eventually her mother, all before the age of twenty—B.T. began to feel like the only family she had. When the academic load at MIT proved too much for her and it seemed she might flunk out, B.T. intervened. He became her tutor and they spent hours on those subjects she could barely pass; the ones that came so easily to him. For her part, Lily had taken on the role of older sister and confidant, over the years helping B.T. clean up his messes with other people (a heated disagreement with a professor over a grade, the poorly chosen phrase when critiquing a colleague's work, the concerns of future employers who'd heard of B.T.'s "tricky" reputation). Which was, ultimately, the *why* of his question to her. "Because I know you've made a mess, B.T."

"A mess?" he said, as though he weren't certain what she was talking about. The server returned and uncorked their bottle of wine. B.T. placed his palm over his glass when the server motioned to pour him the first taste; he gave Lily the honor. She sipped and nodded enthusiastically.

"Really good," she said.

"It is, isn't it," answered B.T., as though proving a point. "My work is far from a mess, Lily. Who told you that? Remote gene editing is on the cusp of becoming a reality." At this, B.T. threw his eyes across the room, to ensure no one had overheard him.

"James Mohammad called me," said Lily.

"What'd he want?"

"He was looking for you."

B.T. took an aggressive slug of his wine, wiping his mouth with the back of his hand as he finished his glass and poured himself another. Lily wondered if he was going to get drunk. "Well, here I am," said B.T.

"He said something you'd been working on together had turned up on the internet."

"Is that all he said?" B.T. asked.

"And that you'd been, to use his word, acting *erratically.*"

"And do you believe that?"

"I just want to make sure you're okay."

"I'm fine," said B.T. "It's really nice of you coming out here to check on me, but I'm fine. How about you?"

"Fine, I guess." A stain on the tablecloth caught her attention.

"Really?" said B.T. "I'd think things would be a bit tricky, with your senator friend and all." B.T. lifted his glass of wine, leveling his eyes over the rim, so he was staring right at Lily as he took his sip. "When I saw about the president's death, I thought of you and Shriver. Things are going to be complicated for him now."

More than a year ago, after the secrecy had begun to wear on her, Lily had confessed her affair with Shriver to B.T. She'd explained how it had started: at a benefit dinner at the Kennedy Center where she and Shriver had been seated together. This had led to a one-night stand, which evolved into what felt like a series of one-night stands with the same person. She'd needed someone to confide in and B.T. had been the logical choice.

"We're supposed to believe that Castro's heart gives out, though he has no history or indicators of a heart condition. . . ." He continued, "I'd think that a lot of scrutiny is going to fall on the president's political enemies. Shriver must be top of that list." Lily had realized this but didn't yet want to acknowledge it. Her mouth went dry. She took another sip of her wine right as B.T. added, "It isn't just your Shriver who's mixed up in this mess. It's me too. A key sequence of my code that relates to remote gene editing has appeared on a website called Common Sense. If someone used that code to kill Castro, then his assassination is the smaller of two problems."

"What's the second?"

"The Singularity," said B.T. "We may have reached a tipping point."

He explained that much depended on whether there was a hard or soft takeoff. A soft takeoff would lead to an increase in human capacity over time, with gradual technological and biological integration. But a hard takeoff would look very different. The resulting explosion in human intelligence would look like a hockey stick if you were to graph it.

"We'd witness advances like mind-uploading," B.T. said, and described the process by which the knowledge, analytic skills, intelligence, and personality of a person could be uploaded on a computer chip. "Once uploaded, that chip could be fused with a quantum computer that couples biological with artificial intelligence. If you did this, you'd create a human mind that has a level of computational, predictive, analytic, and psychic skill incomprehensibly higher than any existing human mind. You'd have the mind of God. That online intelligence could then create real effects in the physical world. God's mind is one thing, but what makes God, God is that *He cometh to earth—*"

When B.T. said *earth*, he made a sweeping gesture, like a faux-preacher, and in his excitement, he knocked over Lily's glass of wine. A waiter promptly appeared with a handful of napkins, sopping up the mess. B.T. waited for the waiter to leave.

"Don't give me that look."

"What look?" answered Lily.

"This isn't as far-fetched as it may seem," he said in a more subdued tone. "Someone who has achieved the Singularity could reshape cellular structures through remote gene editing. They could manipulate perceptions of events, hiding some and emphasizing others. They could also engage in the deepest levels of the human subconscious, changing the way we think about the world, even our dreams. And there's no reason to believe that this wouldn't move beyond individual actions into influencing entire populations . . . no reason to think it wouldn't scale . . . so ask yourself, what would a person or an ideological group, or a given nation, be willing to do to finally achieve the Singularity? I'd say just about anything."

Lily sat very still, behind the enormous stain of wine. "Your sequence of code explains all of this?"

"Not exactly," he said. "That bit of code is like a single link in a much longer chain, but it's a recognizable link. Maybe this website Common Sense is simply a person, or a group of people, revealing what should be obvious . . . what should be . . . well, common sense." He grimaced as he uttered the last two words.

"Which is what?" asked Lily. "That Castro was assassinated? I'm sure you're not the only one considering that."

"That's only part of it . . ." said B.T.

"What's the other part?"

"That, inadvertently, I placed the weapon in the assassin's hand."

⌐

03:37 March 25, 2054 (GMT-5)
Columbia Heights Metro Station

Julia Hunt had finally returned to sleeping in her apartment, a drab studio on 11th Street NW that she rented fully furnished with a single window that opened onto an alley. When she arrived the night before, she'd had to clean out her fridge—all the food had spoiled during her vigil alongside Hendrickson at the White House. Exhausted, she'd ordered takeout. An hour passed and then her headsUp pinged with a message from the delivery service. Due to unanticipated road closures the auto-car couldn't make it to her and her order would have to be canceled. She rummaged through her cabinets and found half a box of Wheat Thins, which she washed down with two glasses of stale Chardonnay, then went to bed.

She slept poorly, woke an hour before her alarm, and anxiously cleaned up around the apartment until it was time to make for the first train at five a.m. She had a dread of arriving late for the morning's meeting between her godfather and the president, which wasn't on the official schedule. The two of them planned to review the slate of vice presidential candidates, a topic of extreme sensitivity given that the day before Wisecarver had endorsed Truther demands for a unity government. Julia would attend the meeting to take notes. In the current atmosphere, Hendrickson felt uncomfortable attending any high-level meeting without a trusted third party present.

After Wisecarver went public with his demand for a unity government, Truther brigades had deployed in Washington and throughout the country, around state legislatures, courthouses, and at the gates of military bases, where they insinuated their solidarity with those in uniform. Already the Democratic-Republican adjutant generals of both the Florida and Texas National Guards had declared their forces available to restore order in Washington and to investigate the president's death with a commission of their own "if called upon by a *legitimate* authority."

Outside Julia's apartment, the detritus of protests littered the street—tipped-over trash cans, twisted metal barricades, expended tear-gas canisters. Her trained eye understood the mayhem that had occurred here, and was occurring nightly in cities across America. At the intersection of Columbia Road and 14th Street, about a block from the Metro, sat a single police cruiser. Its lights turned silent orbits. An officer loitered behind the wheel. Each night, the police proved hesitant to involve themselves in the protests. They stood on the sidelines, as irrelevant as a referee trying to call a game with no rules.

Julia, who wore her service uniform, waved at the police officer in solidarity. He glanced at her through the windshield but didn't wave back. As she rode the escalator down into the Metro, Julia tried to remember if she had a change of clothes at the office. She wondered if wearing her uniform in public placed her on the side of the Dreamers and made her a target for the Truthers, or vice versa. Perhaps this was why the officer hadn't waved back. Maybe he'd determined that appearing too sympathetic to anyone could prove a liability. Politics, like the pandemics of decades past, had become a scourge, one no person or institution could escape. Everyone had to pick a side.

The platform was empty except for a lone man in a wheelchair. When her train pulled up to the station, Julia stepped into her car, and he followed. The man was elegantly dressed in a navy gabardine suit, white shirt, and red tie, with the legs of his trousers neatly pinned up beneath him. His face was lean, even gaunt. Hints of gray lingered within the palette of his thinning red hair. He sat facing her and his eyes rested on her uniform. Julia noticed the Marine Corps sticker on his wheelchair. As their train pulled out of the station, he said, "Second Raider Battalion," like it was a password, and then glanced down at where his legs would've been. "Spratly Islands."

"*Spiritus Invictus*," Julia answered, evidence that she understood this language of unit mottos and places, that she and this stranger shared a heritage as surely as two relatives who sit on different branches of the same family tree. "That was a tough time to be in uniform."

With a frown, the man bobbed his head side to side noncommittally. "Right now is tougher."

"You think?"

"Yes, ma'am."

Because he called her ma'am, she asked: "What'd you get out as?"

"I medically retired as a gunnery sergeant." Then he noticed her noticing his outfit, which seemed more befitting a banker than a former staff noncommissioned officer. "I wear this monkey suit for work."

She asked what he did.

"*Finance*." He blurted out the word in a single syllable, as though this were the least distasteful way to speak it.

"That's a good field. Sounds like you've landed on your feet."

It became awkward between them.

"I sure miss the Corps," he said. "Even if it did take more from me than just my legs." He stared out the window, at the swirling blackness of the tunnel. "I'll always love the Corps," he said wistfully, then added, "But she's a whore . . . always has been. You can love the Corps all you want, but she'll never love you back. You give her your body. She drives you away from your family. And, in the end, she leaves you for a younger man. Or younger woman, I guess." A wry smile spread across his face, causing creases to form near the corners of his blue eyes. "You heard that old saw before?"

Julia grinned back . . . she had.

"I feel for Marines like you," he added. "Pretty soon you're going to have some choices to make. . . ."

"Some choices?"

He shot her a glance, like a teacher irritated by a pupil who wasn't quite living up to her potential. "Yes, some choices," he said. "Truth or Dreams. There's no place in between, nowhere to stand if you're not with one or the other. Maybe you haven't had to choose yet because you wear the uniform. But it's coming. Politicians will force you to choose— that's their bread and butter. Making that choice when you wear the uniform means something entirely different. So I hope you choose wisely."

As they pulled into the next station, Hunt was about to ask him what choice he'd made, whether he was for or against the administration, whether he'd chosen Truth or Dreams. But she didn't have to. When he turned toward the door, she saw the second sticker on the frame of his wheelchair.

"It took me a while to find you, Major, and to figure out how we could have a quick word." He pushed himself out onto the platform. "When the time comes, a lot of us are counting on you to do the right thing, so take care of yourself."

The doors shut behind him, and as the train sped off, he offered Hunt a playful two-fingered salute.

⌐

19:15 March 24, 2054 (GMT+8)
Macau

It never ceased to amaze James Mohammad how stupid smart people could be. If B.T. had wanted to hide out for a while to avoid him, why go to Macau? B.T. only had to pick up a newspaper or read a book published in the last decade or so to understand the special relationship that existed between Lagos and Beijing. The Great Game being played in biotech, artificial intelligence, and quantum computing had come to define foreign policy as nations aligned with one another in pursuit of the Singularity. Yes, B.T. was a genius; his work was irrefutable proof of this. But for a genius, he could certainly be an idiot sometimes.

The call came in from Beijing that B.T. had reserved a suite at the Venetian. Mohammad was glad the civilians at the Guoanbu had flagged the transaction, as opposed to their counterparts in the People's Liberation Army security services. He'd always found the Guoanbu fellows more congenial, possessing sensibilities closer to businessmen like himself, as opposed to their straitlaced counterparts in military intelligence. The Guoanbu hadn't thought twice about approving Mohammad's request for surveillance on B.T. as well as rigging the games on the casino floor to his advantage so B.T.'s winning streak would extend long enough for Mohammad to fly in from Lagos. Which was how he found himself sitting in the security control room of the Venetian, toggling a joystick linked to one of the thousands of cameras that studied every inch of the casino.

What surprised Mohammad—it was, frankly, an oversight on his part—was that Lily Bao had flown in from Washington to meet B.T. Even if you took the suborbital, the flight was around three hours. This seemed quite a distance to travel to visit an old friend simply because he was suffering a professional crisis. Unless Lily Bao knew something that Mohammad didn't. Ever since the day before, when the facial recognition technology at customs and immigration had flagged her entry, Mohammad had been trying to connect the dots on why she'd made this trip. He'd even gone so far as to request her case file from Beijing, which was woefully outdated. As he sat behind the security console, toggling the joystick that controlled the pinhole camera above their table as well as the audio, an important piece of the puzzle locked into place: Lily Bao's relationship with Senator Nat Shriver.

B.T. possessed her one great secret. Her reason for the trip made sense now.

Nat Shriver . . . this was an unexpected windfall for Mohammad. His hand shook excitedly as he held the joystick, causing his view into the restaurant to shudder. Mohammad imagined the ways he could leverage this discovery to his advantage. He continued to eavesdrop on Lily Bao and B.T. as they discussed the role remote gene editing might have played in Castro's death, and also the sequence of code leaked on Common Sense. James Mohammad struggled to concentrate. He was pondering his next move.

⌐

05:27 March 25, 2054 (GMT+9)
Okinawa

After his dinner with Lily, B.T. had returned to his suite, packed his single bag, and boarded a return flight to Okinawa. He needed to get back to his lab. He needed to figure out how Common Sense—whatever or whoever it was—had stolen that sequence of code. He arrived at his lab directly from the airport in the early hours of the morning. As he turned the first and then second of the double locks on his door, he half expected to find the place ransacked, his files strewn across the floor, his hard drives yanked from their ports. He found the place exactly as he'd left it.

A draft of air caught B.T.'s attention. He crossed his lab to shut an open window. He noticed the large goldfish bowl at the center of the table. The multicolored butterflies had returned, their wings batting seductively. He came down in a crouch, his face level with the bowl. He counted a little more than half of the original number. Remarkable, he thought, they'd found their way back. He grinned like an idiot and almost laughed. He sat behind his computer and opened his email. Thousands of messages awaited him, which he passed through a personal response filter—a rudimentary but useful bit of artificial intelligence—that answered nearly two-thirds and prioritized those he needed to answer himself. His inbox swiftly dwindled to a couple dozen messages.

Among these, one stood out. At first it appeared like spam that had managed to evade the filter. The subject line read: *Friends of yours?* The sender was a corporate account, Cape Maeda Dive Shop. A string of photographs posted at the bottom of the email showed the dive instructor from Tokyo, the pretty one with the interesting tattoo, standing in the grass near the beach, with the multicolored butterflies perched on her fingers, in her hair, and along her shoulders. She wore the butterflies like the most elegant evening gown and so looked radiant, adorned as she was in one of B.T.'s creations. Above the photographs was a single line of text, *Come pay us a visit*, signed, *xo michi.*

⌐

15:22 March 25, 2054 (GMT+8)
Macau

James Mohammad had her flight number. He waited in a windowless
conference room at the end of a corridor sandwiched between Hermès
and Chanel in the departures terminal, right off security. Three hours
before Lily Bao's flight, a pair of liaison officers from the Guoanbu, each
wearing a dark suit and crisp white shirt, had escorted him to this conference room and told him to wait. They already had the details of her
flight as well as her photograph and a slew of biometric data. The plan
was that once she passed through security, they would escort her to the
conference room; here, Mohammad would make his pitch, and then
they'd get her on the next suborbital flight to Dulles. She'd face a delay
of two, maybe three hours maximum.

Mohammad had weighed other, softer approaches. He'd considered
casually bumping into her at the Venetian, asking her for a drink, and
then beginning his pitch from there. But he'd decided this would be too
confusing, too oblique. He'd done this enough to understand that the
setting for the recruitment pitch was often as important as the pitch itself. If the ask was a small one, something easy and not particularly in-
criminating, then, yes, perhaps it could be made over a drink or dinner;
perhaps asking for an earnings report a day or two early. But if the ask
was something that couldn't be rationalized away, the direct approach
was best. Hence the conference room at the airport.

The logic of his pitch was simple enough. James Mohammad understood Lily Bao's personal story, how two decades before she and her
mother had fled to America as war refugees, and how the regime in Bei-

jing had scapegoated her father, a onetime diplomat and senior military officer, murdering him and leaving his memory disgraced. Cooperating with the Guoanbu would be Lily Bao's chance to restore her family's good name in her home country. Would Lily Bao see the value in that? Would she want to be redeemed in the eyes of a country that had branded her and her family as traitors? Mohammad couldn't say. Countries, he knew, were like lovers; their scorn inspired devotion as often as it inspired resentment.

Rehabilitating the Bao family name was a carrot. But Mohammad also had sticks. His superiors in Lagos (specifically, his uncle) and their counterparts in Beijing never would have approved this approach if he didn't possess both. His stick, the reason Mohammad knew Lily Bao would eventually do whatever he demanded—as well as the source of her true value—was her relationship with Senator Nat Shriver. However, he didn't want to reveal what he knew about the two of them, not if he didn't have to. Her affair with Shriver could, at least for a while, remain an unspoken understanding between them.

Mohammad glanced at his watch. Her original flight had already begun boarding. He paced the room and then sat at the head of the table, pouring himself a glass of water from a pitcher at its center. What was taking so long? He was about to call the pair of Guoanbu officers when they appeared at the door, one on either side of Lily Bao. She had her hands restrained behind her and was wearing only one shoe—she'd used the heel of the other as a club when resisting the Guoanbu officers, both of whom were sweating profusely, as was Lily Bao. Her jaw was swollen, and she was opening and closing her mouth like a fish out of water.

"They arrested you too?" she muttered on seeing James Mohammad.

In Mandarin, he told the two Guoanbu officers to put her down.

They thrust her into a chair. Mohammad cursed them, instructing them to be careful and to free her hands from behind her back. He poured Lily a glass of water. She sipped from it tentatively while taking in her surroundings.

"Oh . . ." said Lily. Her shoulders collapsed and she slunk into her chair. "They work for you."

⌐

06:17 March 25, 2054 (GMT-5)
The White House

Hunt knocked on Hendrickson's shut office door and he told her to come in. He was throwing the loop of his pre-knotted tie around his neck, tightening and adjusting it in the reflection of the window by his desk. Hunt placed a paper cup of coffee in his hand and the two of them gathered up a half dozen binders as the sun breached the horizon, falling on the South Lawn and an encampment of Truthers that had occupied the green around the Washington Monument.

"Ready?" asked Hendrickson.

Hunt nodded.

When they entered the Oval Office, President Smith was sitting with his back to the door, staring out the window that faced the South Lawn. Hendrickson stepped in front of the Resolute Desk. He gestured for Julia to stand to the left beside him. Julia couldn't help but notice that the console table by the window remained empty. This usually contained a smattering of framed photographs of the First Family. Smith had yet to add anything of his own to the table, as if he couldn't quite accept that this was his office. He continued to stare out the window. "How much longer can they keep this up?" he asked, and then exhaled, leaning on the arm of his chair and cradling his chin in his palm.

Julia glanced uncomfortably at Hendrickson, who nodded behind them toward the seating area with its coffee table flanked by two silk-upholstered sofas. She spread out the binders that contained the profiles of the vice presidential candidates, including hundreds of pages of due diligence—voting, tax, employment, and financial records, anything that could possibly embarrass the administration. "*Sir*," said Hendrickson, leaning hard on the word as if it might release the president from this fugue. "We have the final slate of vice presidential picks for your review."

"Last night they burned me in effigy out there . . . *me!*" said Smith. The pain in his voice startled Julia, and she turned in his direction. The president remained facing away from her. "The Truthers stole a man-nequin from a nearby department store, dressed it in a suit, hung a noose around its neck, doused it in kerosene, and torched it over a bonfire." He finally swiveled around, adding, "That can't be legal."

"Citizens have a right to assemble," said Hendrickson. Since this crisis began, Hendrickson had counseled de-escalation. He knew that a single misstep, a single overreaction, would embolden Smith's adversaries, not just the Democratic-Republicans who held public office but also their shock troops in the Truther brigades, who had proven more than willing to take their grievances into the streets.

"They don't have a right to build a bonfire on the National Mall," Smith answered. He edged forward in his chair. He wasn't wearing his customary navy suit, but rather running shorts and a FAIRVIEW FALCONS T-shirt from the high school where he'd been a beloved math teacher and coach of the squash team. "In an hour, I could have the Park Police clear out that encampment. President Castro's funeral is coming up. Are we going to allow them to ruin that as well, to defame the legacy of a great man? How much more of this am I expected to endure?"

Julia listened as she finished laying out the last of the binders. She knew that the few hundred Park Police whose jurisdiction included the National Mall would stand no chance against the thousands of protesters who'd descended on Washington. Of course, the president had greater resources he could call upon, if needed, from the Metro Police to the National Guard, even to the use of federal troops like her, though Hendrickson steadfastly counseled patience and restraint. Whoever escalated, lost. From the Reichstag fire set by German Communists in 1933 to the Soviet generals' storming of the Kremlin during their failed 1991 coup to the 2021 Capitol riot of just thirty-odd years before, the side that attacked the institutions of the state first would delegitimize itself, allowing its opponents to call on those very same institutions for protection, which inevitably turned into the crushing of dissent. Overreach was the enemy.

Hendrickson suggested that the president ignore the view out his window for now. They needed to make a final vice presidential selection. The president meandered over to the sofa and began to browse through the binders.

⌐

15:55 March 25, 2054 (GMT+8)
Macau

James Mohammad raised his hand in a dismissive wave, and the two Guoanbu officers slipped out of the conference room, one of them grimacing as he touched the grooved skin where Lily Bao had clawed his face.

Alone with Mohammad, Lily asked, "So where is it exactly that you work?" She dipped a napkin in her glass of water and then dabbed its corner on her split lip.

"As you know, I'm a private investor."

Lily glanced at him out the corner of her eye impatiently.

"I do, however, have some government clients."

She kept looking at him.

"They're always interested in any discreet, nonpublic information I might glean from my investments. They are, for instance, quite interested in remote gene editing. My partners and I have done quite a bit of business with your friend B.T. The strides he's made in—"

"Your partners?" Lily interjected. "You mean the Nigerian government?"

"Among other governments." Mohammad glanced over his shoulder, toward the door where the Guoanbu officers had departed. "There's a war going on," he said. "Perhaps you haven't noticed; most haven't. There will be winners and there will be losers, and the outcome may determine the future of humanity. . . . If that sounds like hyperbole, it isn't. Technological evolution and biological evolution are merging. Already this merger is impacting the global order. Look what happened in the United States, to President Castro. The world just witnessed the first remote assassination, and it was with a technology developed by B.T."

"You can't prove that," Lily shot back.

"I'm not accusing your friend of anything," said Mohammad. "Whoever stole his work and plotted this assassination is the person we're looking for. Which is ultimately an exercise in figuring out who had the most to gain from Castro's death. . . ." Mohammad allowed his words to hang in the air for a beat, a subtle allusion that he knew about Lily's relationship with Nat Shriver. "Ultimately, the political turmoil in the United States is ancillary, a sideshow. What's a dead president in the course of human history? No, the stakes I'm discussing are far higher than the fate of a single politician, or even that of a single nation. This is about who achieves the Singularity first. This is about the evolution of the species, who goes forward and who gets wiped out. And we need your help."

"Who is *we*?"

"Your country."

Lily Bao didn't say, *I'm an American.* Mohammad wagered that she wouldn't. Lily Bao's blood was Chinese. That nation's soil was her home. Yes, she could live in America; and yes, she could imbibe its values. But evolution wasn't about values; rather, it was about groups of people, their blood and their soil. Look at America's near collapse. Look at its inability to cohere. No idea could compete with blood and soil, with natural selection and the evolution of the species. The Singularity was simply the next step along the path that Darwin had first charted; it was survival of the fittest. Whoever achieved the Singularity first would survive. Others would perish. With the stakes set at such a height, would Lily Bao really turn her back on her country? America was a chimera and always had been, a brief interlude of mankind denying its own nature. Lily Bao was being invited home.

"What do you know about my country?" she asked.

"I know they want you back," he said. "Your help would be rewarded."

Lily Bao crossed her arms. Between her tightly drawn dark brows ran a furrow that gave her face a brooding, nearly angry expression. She assumed the reward Mohammad alluded to was financial, that he was trying to buy her off. Yes, there'd be money aplenty, if she wanted it, but the real reward was one she couldn't imagine because she'd never considered it a possibility, and so Mohammad spoke more explicitly. He leaned forward in his chair. "The government in Beijing could rehabilitate your family name," he began. "They would be quite willing to change the narrative around your father and his role in the war. It's time to end your exile."

This was the carrot.

Lily Bao asked Mohammad for her purse, which the Guoanbu officers had confiscated. One of them came inside and placed it on the table. She began to rummage through its contents. She then took out a compact and began cleaning herself up, wiping away a bit of dry blood from her mouth, brushing her hair and pinning it back, reapplying her lipstick. She did this in silence, considering her reflection while she forced James Mohammad to wait for her answer, which she only delivered after completing this minor transformation, so that she'd entirely concealed her struggle from before. "I'm sorry, Mr. Mohammad," she said. "But I'm not interested in what you're offering. If you would be so kind as to return my things and help me book another flight, I would like to return home—to the United States."

Mohammad still had his stick, but in that moment, he decided not to use it. She'll come around, he thought. With every imaginable courtesy, he presented her with a new set of tickets for the suborbital departing for Dulles in an hour, which included an upgrade from business to first class. He also handed her his phone number. "A direct line, that goes only to me," he explained. The two Guoanbu officers presented themselves at the conference room door with her luggage.

Lily Bao stood to leave, wearing only the one shoe. The two officers had searched security and been unable to find its pair. As much as Lily Bao had done to fix her hair, to reapply her makeup, and to generally make it appear as if this altercation had never occurred, she was forced to limp one-shoed toward the door. Watching her depart, James Mohammad felt confident he'd see her again.

┌

06:58 March 25, 2054 (GMT-5)
The White House

President Smith thumbed through the binders noncommittally: two governors of small states; a senator who'd lost reelection; one retired and relatively obscure admiral; one former ambassador; the CEO of a mid-sized company who'd served a term in Congress a decade ago. On paper each vice presidential candidate was impressive enough, and, crucially, none proved a threat to Smith. As Hendrickson briefed the pros and cons of the candidates—all of whom had proven their loyalty to the Castro administration and none of whom had any real skeletons in their closets (or at least nothing that couldn't be explained away)—the president made slight noises of approval or disapproval.

Then he asked Julia for the time.

"It's seven a.m., sir."

The president nodded, as if up to this moment he'd simply been waiting to speak his mind and now that they'd arrived at the top of the hour he could strike at the heart of the matter. "Bunt," he began, placing his hand affectionately on the shoulder of his trusted advisor, "if I pick one of the six candidates here, will those *people*"—he could hardly restrain himself from spitting out the word as he gestured toward the encampment of protesters out his window—"go home?"

Hendrickson increasingly found himself protecting the president against his own worst impulses. He took up the burden again, explaining the logic behind a safe, middle-of-the-road choice for vice president. The president nodded respectfully as Hendrickson repeated himself: "Sir, the candidates in those binders will get us back on track."

"And what about a unity government?" asked Smith.

"A what?"

"A unity government. The Truthers want compromise. Speaker Wisecarver assures me that if we work with them, they'll work with us and make all of this go away." The president gestured out his window, not only to the Truther encampment but more expansively, as if to the very division that was cleaving the country in two.

"You've been speaking to Wisecarver?" Hendrickson took an aggressive step toward the president, who reflexively took a step back. Julia reached for her godfather, calmly placing her hand on his arm.

A knock came at the door.

This was odd. Impromptu arrivals rarely occurred at the Oval Office. Time inside was structured, the daily choreography of meetings scheduled to the minute. With his gaze fixed on Hendrickson, the president raised his voice: "Come in!"

Wisecarver stepped across the threshold. "Good morning, Mr. President." He gave a little nod. Beneath his arm he carried a single binder.

"Good morning, Trent." Smith gestured for Wisecarver to sit with him on the sofa while Hunt and Hendrickson sat opposite. As they settled in, Julia caught Wisecarver glancing at the half dozen other binders spread across the coffee table, as if gauging the competition. The

president cleared his throat. "As you all know, Speaker Wisecarver believes a unity government, in which I'd select a vice president from his
party, would be in the best interests of our country. . . ."

Julia felt her godfather shift in his seat, as if he couldn't quite stomach the idea that Wisecarver's interest in the matter had anything to do
with the country as opposed to his own naked ambition. While the president spoke, Wisecarver looked around the room, his eyes running the
walls. As speaker, he'd been in the Oval Office plenty of times before as
a guest of President Castro, but he seemed to be taking it all in for the
first time, as if he were rearranging the furniture in his imagination and,
quite literally, measuring the drapes.

Smith finished. It was Wisecarver's turn to speak: "With the loss of
President Castro, our country has gone through a significant trauma.
Now it's time for us to heal. The formation of a unity government is an
important first step in that healing process. The people are in the streets
telling us this. We can't afford to ignore them any longer. Really, we have
little choice in the matter. Either we heal together, or we tear ourselves
apart."

"Is that a suggestion?" Hendrickson asked. "Or an ultimatum?"

"It's a reality, *Bunt*." Wisecarver glanced down at the binders on the
table. "If you pick one of those candidates, you're tying my hands."

"Tying your hands how?" Hendrickson leaned forward so that he
was perched on the edge of the sofa.

"Well, for starters, *they* won't go home anytime soon," and Wisecarver gestured to the encampment out the window. "There's also the
commission investigating President Castro's death to consider, a process that could drag on, depending on who we in the Congress appoint
to lead it. If you need more reasons than those two, I could continue."

"That won't be necessary," the president said to Wisecarver. He turned to Hendrickson with a look like a child pleading with an overly protective parent. He couldn't sustain this level of conflict, the protests around the country, the machinations of his political rivals. Like any performer, Smith cared deeply what other people thought of him and couldn't tolerate being hated, or at least being hated to this degree. He had all of a politician's neediness without any of the cunning. He was doomed.

Julia Hunt could see her godfather reconsidering what Wisecarver offered. A unity government would de-escalate the current crisis, at least in the near term. In the long term, elevating a Truther could prove an astute move. It would diffuse Wisecarver's power within the party. Also, depending on who that person was, having steady leadership—at least steadier than Smith—could help stabilize the country, or at least keep it from *tearing itself apart*, to use Wisecarver's words. But it all depended on who he was proposing.

Hendrickson asked for the name.

Wisecarver reached across the coffee table and handed him the binder he'd brought, with its pages of due diligence. Julia Hunt leaned over her godfather's shoulder as he opened it. Of course, she thought. On the first page she glimpsed the official portrait of Senator Nat Shriver.

4

Cat's Game

Chowdhury checked in to his hotel, an anodyne Grand Hyatt booked by the staff at Neutronics due to its proximity to their clinic. As the receptionist scanned his retina, she informed Chowdhury that "the other guest in your party has already arrived and is checked into your suite." He had no idea who this other guest might be and didn't ask. He trundled his single roller bag through the cavernous marble-floored foyer, toward a bank of elevators, and found his way up to the twenty-eighth floor. At the door to his room, he paused and took a breath before holding his face to the scanner lock.

His suite, situated in a corner of the hotel, boasted a panoramic view of the Rio Pinheiros, which threaded its murky way through the vibrant downtown, past the favelas on the city's impoverished outskirts, until it merged again with the Tietê. He set his bag near the door and flopped down on a sectional sofa that faced the floor-to-ceiling windows. He loosened his tie and unbuttoned his jacket. In the late afternoon sun, the water shimmered like a ribbon of steel.

Then he heard his daughter's unmistakable voice in an adjacent bedroom. She hadn't seemed to notice Chowdhury's arrival. He listened in, wondering why his daughter had traveled all this way without telling him. "And you're certain that's the last time anyone saw Kurzweil," she said. Pause. "Spell it for me," she added. Another pause. "So it's M-A-N-A-U-S . . . Manaus. Okay, if you find out anything else, get in touch right away. My father arrives this afternoon." The call finished.

Ashni stepped into the sitting room.

Chowdhury stood. "What are you doing here?"

"You're early," she said, as if this answered his question. "I'd planned to meet you in the lobby." He remained standing. "Sit down, Bapu. Won't you?"

Reluctantly, Chowdhury sat. Ashni perched beside him, knees together, her perfectly manicured fingers worrying the hem of her skirt. Chowdhury struggled to pinpoint the source of his irritation, which was bordering on anger.

"You asked me to look into Neutronics and Dr. Kurzweil," Ashni began.

Chowdhury interrupted her: "Yes, but I didn't ask you to fly down here. Whatever you found, you could've spoken to me about on the phone or sent in an email. Ashni, if you're going to successfully run Tandava, you have to learn to delegate . . . you have to learn to—"

She cut him off: "Bapu, just listen, for once!" Ashni hardly ever raised her voice at her father. Startled, he stopped and tilted his head slightly.

She continued, "Ray Kurzweil doesn't work for Neutronics, not anymore. Our intelligence people did some digging and found a lawsuit filed by him against the company in a Brazilian court. Three years ago Kurzweil and Neutronics arrived at an impasse with regards to the direction the company's research should take. Neutronics wanted Kurzweil to apply his discoveries in nanorobotics and gene editing to the development of treatments for everything from heart disease to a wide variety of cancers. Kurzweil felt differently. He believed working on specific medical treatments was a waste of time and energy. Kurzweil was adamant that when the Singularity was achieved and the power of quantum computing merged with human consciousness, it would seamlessly allow us to discover cures for cancer, heart disease—or anything else, for that matter—in the time it takes a child to solve a math problem. To Kurzweil, the only breakthrough that mattered was the Singularity itself. But Neutronics is a business. The advances Kurzweil had made meant they were sitting on a gold mine. They didn't want to waste any more time or risk that another company or country would make similar discoveries before they could cash in and turn a profit. So they chose to pay Kurzweil off and he and Neutronics went their separate ways. Kurzweil would be free to continue his research and Neutronics—after paying him a fortune—could develop and market treatments based on the work he'd already done. Like the treatment you're about to receive, for your heart."

"So where is Kurzweil now?" Chowdhury asked.

"No one knows." Ashni glanced down at the piece of paper she'd written on. "The last record of him is from a little more than two years ago, a hotel registry in Manaus. With what Neutronics paid him, he wouldn't need to come up for air anytime soon—if ever. He could take his work and simply vanish. Which is what it appears he's done."

"You didn't need to come all this way to tell me that," said Chowdhury.

"No," said Ashni. "I didn't." As she looked at her father, her lower lip trembled. She turned away from Chowdhury, as if this might help her avoid the onset of some unwelcome emotion. As he watched his daughter, Chowdhury could so clearly see her as she once was; before his divorce, when they'd all lived in the studio apartment in Adams Morgan; before he'd taken the job in the White House; before Galveston, too, that name forever associated with disaster and loss, in which Ashni had lost her mother. The two of them sat quietly, glancing out at the shimmering waters below. A cloud passed over the sun and the shimmer vanished. Ashni turned toward her father. "I came all this way because I don't want you to have to undergo these treatments on your own . . . and I'm afraid. Can't you understand that?"

Now Chowdhury felt as though he were the child, and a selfish one at that, having in all this time hardly considered his daughter's feelings about his health. "Of course," he said in a near whisper.

"There's another reason I came," confessed Ashni.

"What's that?"

"I don't want you to track down Ray Kurzweil."

⌐

13:07 April 09, 2054 (GMT+9)
Okinawa

B.T. was in love. Her name was Michiko Takagi. She called herself Michi, playfully signing her notes to him with a heart over each *i*. It happened quickly, maybe too quickly, B.T. recognized. A couple of weeks ago, after

Michi had emailed B.T., he'd paid her a visit at Cape Maeda. The multi-colored butterflies had impressed her. She said she supposed she owed B.T. for them, and offered to take him diving that afternoon, just the two of them.

That night he returned to his lab, but found he had little appetite for work. He lay down in his bed, shut his eyes, and fixed his mind on her. Like a weighted plumb line, his memories of their day together sank him into a deep, tranquil sleep.

On their fourth straight day together, Michi took B.T. out to the thirty-five-meter trench on Cape Maeda. They anchored their boat near the Blue Cave. As Michi checked over B.T.'s equipment—tightening a chest strap, assuring he had the correct weight on his belt—she explained their dive profile. Once they got down to one hundred feet he would officially be open-water-certified and could dive anywhere he wanted in the world on his own.

Holding his mask to his face with his left hand and his regulator with his right, he pitched backward over the gunwale. Michi followed. The two paddled to a buoy, whose line led to the inky depths below. Wind scalloped the surface of the water and Michi made a thumbs-down sign. Past ten feet everything turned pure and silent. All B.T. could hear was the rhythmic sound of his breathing. Condensation began to pearl at the edges of his rental face mask, an older model that pressed uncomfortably against his temples. Michi had taught B.T. how to clear his mask, by tilting back his head, breaking the seal and allowing water to rush inside, and then blowing all that water out with a forceful exhalation from his nose, but it made B.T. nervous to allow the water onto his face at depth, and so he endured the foggy mask and pincerlike squeeze.

Down here his thoughts achieved a heightened clarity. He found the experience not dissimilar to wandering the casinos of the world: The task at hand required total presence of mind. The leaked sequence of code, the ire of James Mohammad, Lily Bao's troubles in the United States, these concerns seemed to vanish at depth, departing to the surface like so many air bubbles exhaled from his regulator.

Like B.T., Michi had a background in science, evolutionary biology in her case, with a research focus on maritime species. This was how she'd come to diving; she supplemented her research grants with extra money earned as a dive instructor. Between morning and afternoon trips to the reef, as they lounged on the deck of the boat, which lulled at anchor in the mellow current, she explained her fascination with the field. Maritime species outnumbered those on land by six-to-one, and the adaptive radiation that existed on land didn't exist at depth and had slowed the evolutionary processes, granting biologists like her a glimpse into ancient evolutionary patterns. They had talked for hours those first few days. On the deck of the boat B.T. would see the words coming out of her mouth, floating above her like speech bubbles, but all he could think was that he was falling in love with this woman.

On that fourth day, as they descended the wall of the trench, he could feel Michi guiding him from behind. She had told him to stop when his depth gauge reached one hundred feet. He was watching the needle sweep across its dial but struggled to keep it in focus through his fogging mask. Then Michi grabbed the shoulder strap of his dive vest. Refracted through her mask, her already large green eyes appeared even larger, greener, and more appealing. Michi pointed to her own gauge, gently chastising him for exceeding depth. The two of them hovered on the buoy line, floating along the face of the trench as swarms of multicolored fish schooled around them. Michi took the regulator out of her mouth and motioned for B.T. to do the same. His eyes went wide with fear at the prospect of not having oxygen, even if for only a moment. He shook his head. But Michi was insistent. Reluctantly, B.T. removed his regulator.

Michi grabbed B.T. by the vest and pulled him toward her. She kissed him full on the mouth, her lips becoming like the apparatus he breathed from, sustaining him at depth, and easing his anxieties away. Her lithe and muscular body held against his as she swam, kicking for them both and fixing them in place on the side of the trench, which descended into a seemingly infinite void beneath. The kiss went on and his lungs began to burn, a reminder of the boyhood asthma he'd overcome; still, he wouldn't pull away. Whatever anxiety or fear B.T. had felt before dissolved. He felt as if he might stay with her, at depth, forever.

Gently, she released him. He floated for a moment like an astronaut. Michi then handed B.T. back his regulator and placed her own into her mouth. She glanced at him curiously. The condensation on B.T.'s mask hid his eyes, so she couldn't quite gauge his response to her kiss. B.T. recognized this. The anxiety he'd felt before about clearing his mask vanished. He broke its seal and the water rushed onto his face. He tilted back his head, blew out through his nose, and returned the mask over his eyes. Now he could see Michi clearly and she could see him. She reached out her hand and B.T. took it, their fingers entwining. Then the rubber strap on the back of B.T.'s mask snapped.

They both lunged after the mask, their fingers clutching as it tumbled through the space between them. It vanished down the trench.

B.T. jerked to his left and right. He opened his eyes but could only see the vague impression of shadow, light, and hints of color. His eyes began to burn from the salt water. He felt a powerful instinct to kick to the surface, to safety. And when he followed this instinct, he felt Michi's grip on his wrist. He thrashed against her. She held him in a bear hug, yanked the regulator out of his mouth, and kissed him again. Like a shot of adrenaline stabbed into the chest of an overdosing addict, it brought him out of his frenzy.

A rush to the surface from such a depth could prove fatal. In the moment, gripped by fear, B.T. had forgotten. Slowly, they would have to ascend the buoy line, making decompression stops along the way. B.T. would have to do this in the blind, tethered to Michi, his trust placed entirely in her.

The minutes of their ascent passed slowly. B.T. could feel Michi's grip on his vest while with her other hand she clasped the buoy line. His only sense of their progress was when he occasionally opened his eyes to measure the increase in light. They broke the surface with a rush of sound. "Are you okay?" said Michi, as she yanked the regulator from B.T.'s mouth. Again, she pressed her lips to his.

They swam back to the boat. The sun was warm on their skin and they didn't bother to towel off before heading belowdecks.

⌐

19:00 April 13, 2054 (GMT+1)
Abuja

His uncle summoned him from Lagos to the capital for dinner. Except James Mohammad and his uncle didn't really have dinners. They had meetings, with food present. Tonight, Mohammad didn't need to guess the agenda. He'd been waiting for this call ever since his return from Macau. His uncle's eye was set on Lily Bao. Failing to recruit her and close that deal must have proven a great disappointment for him, one Mohammad would have to answer for, favorite nephew or not.

James Mohammad and his uncle shared a name. His own father (the second Benjamin in their family) had broken with convention by naming his son after his elder brother, who'd raised him after a military coup had claimed the lives of their parents. In his uncle's presence, James Mohammad was Jimmy, a moniker that in adulthood he'd come to resent. Throughout his life he had taken his uncle's help when offered, from Eton to the present, so if the elder James Mohammad wanted to call the younger "Jimmy," he had that right, just as he had the right to summon his nephew to the capital, the dusty, landlocked metropolis in the geographic center of the country that held no charm for him.

His uncle had selected a neighborhood place for the meal, a traditional restaurant with plastic tables and chairs under bare bulbs on the outside and the low hum of air conditioners and overhead fans on the inside. Despite his relative wealth, the elder James Mohammad enjoyed holding court in these types of restaurants, which served the starchy Yoruba dishes of his youth, as opposed to the Euro-chic restaurants in Lagos that his nephew frequented.

Mohammad found his uncle at a table surrounded by a handful of men his age who were laughing a little too hard at some joke he had told, their heads thrown back with their mouths wide open as if inviting all the world to count their gold fillings. His uncle waved Mohammad over, but not before grandly announcing, "Jimmy, so good of you to come," as if the younger had had a choice in the matter.

He took a seat next to his uncle. The other men excused themselves, wandering out onto the porch to finish their bottles of lager. The restaurant was mostly empty now. The staff began to deliver dishes of food, and within a few minutes the table was set for a feast. The heaping plates overflowed, spilling rice and meat onto the vinyl tablecloth. Mohammad had traveled all day to meet his uncle and was famished. He reached for a spoon to serve himself. "Just a moment," his uncle said. "Another guest will soon be joining us."

⌐

17:55 April 13, 2054 (GMT-5)
The White House

The announcement of Shriver as the vice presidential nominee was set for after Castro's funeral. Smith had insisted on this point to Wisecarver. He didn't want anything to distract from the day. Burials at Arlington had become an increasingly rare occurrence. For decades, military policy entitled retired service members and those killed in action to a place in that hollowed ground. However, twenty years ago, when a freight of tens of thousands of dead began returning from the island chains and blue waters in and around the South China Sea, that policy had shifted, with burial at Arlington restricted only to those who had died in combat while earning one of the nation's three highest awards for valor—the Silver Star, the Distinguished Service Cross (or its equivalent Navy and Air Force Crosses), or the Medal of Honor. That measure, which at the time other Gold Star families viewed as draconian, had largely become accepted, so that burial at Arlington, always a great honor, was now even more of one.

It was an honor of which President Castro's detractors didn't believe him worthy. In the days before the funeral, as its details leaked out, these critics—many of whom were military veterans—became increasingly incensed. Only two US presidents had been buried at Arlington, William H. Taft and John F. Kennedy. Taft had served as secretary of war and Kennedy as a decorated Navy officer during the Second World War. Karen Slake had faced a hostile press on this issue in the White House briefing room only days before Castro's funeral. Given the precedent set by Taft and Kennedy, and given the fact that Castro had never served, was it appropriate that President Smith authorize his predecessor's burial at Arlington?

Using Kennedy as an example, Slake pivoted, explaining that it wasn't necessarily Kennedy's military service that had entitled him to burial at Arlington but rather his assassination. As the commander in chief, he could be considered a casualty of war. Julia Hunt had been standing in the back of the press room when Slake trotted out this logic, which fed Truther conspiracy theories of a Castro assassination. The result was stunned silence, as if the sheer volume of follow-up questions this elicited in every journalist caused each of them to freeze like a glitching computer trying to download a file that's too large. Then, all at once, up sprouted a crop of hands.

Will the administration finally acknowledge foul play in Castro's death?

If so, what evidence exists to reach this conclusion and why has it taken so long to publicly disclose?

Do any suspects—individuals or nations—exist?

Will the administration commit to a national commission to examine the circumstances of Castro's death?

Slake deflected, contorting facts and language to allow her to answer without providing any answer at all. Dexterous as she was at playing defense, she had slipped up and never should have created a situation in which the press could pivot so aggressively to offense. She couldn't sustain this level of interrogation; ultimately, she had no good answers to these questions. When a journalist asked, "Does the administration's position remain that they have no evidence of foul play in Castro's death?" Slake froze, and in her desperation asserted, "Yes, that remains the position of this administration. We have no evidence of any foul play in the death of President Castro."

She hurried off the stage, chased out of the room by a further eruption of questions.

⌐

13:07 April 13, 2054 (GMT+9)
Okinawa

B.T. had little regard for anything except being on the water with Michi. The days bled into weeks. He spent less and less time in his lab, avoiding the agitated emails that arrived from James Mohammad. Nearly three weeks into their relationship, he confided in her about his troubles one afternoon on the boat.

Given Michi's own scientific background, she could understand the nature of B.T.'s work with little difficulty: the power of mRNA-based vaccines; the promise of remote gene editing; the blurring of the borders between molecular and nanotechnological enhancements; how these advances might be hurtling humanity toward the Singularity. And now, he told her, a key sequence of code he'd developed had leaked onto the internet and was responsible for, as B.T. put it, "a significant political event."

"You mean the assassination of the American president?"

They'd gotten out of the water only minutes before. Michi sat across from him in her bikini, her wet suit peeled down to her waist.

"Well . . . yes," B.T. said with some hesitation.

"So you're saying that you killed Castro?"

"No, not me personally," answered B.T. "But my work did."

"Because a sequence of your code wound up on this website Common Sense?"

B.T. nodded tentatively, as if he could already sense Michi beginning to dismantle certain of his assumptions.

"Maybe what you're missing is right in front of your face." Michi unwrapped the towel from around her waist and began drying the loose black hair that ran down her back. "Maybe you're not asking the right questions." She bundled the towel in a turban atop her head.

"What are the right questions?" he asked.

"You didn't detect any breach of your data, no hack into your servers or anything like that, right?"

B.T. shook his head, no.

"And this James Mohammad, the one who paid you for your research, you say he's upset. Yet he's still interested in funding you?"

B.T. nodded.

"Okay . . ." said Michi. "So, did it ever occur to you that the leaked sequence of code might not be exclusively yours?"

B.T. laughed dismissively. This hardly seemed possible. His research was cutting-edge, the product of years of his thinking, a breakthrough of the highest order, and—although he didn't say this part aloud—a reflection of his unique and distinct genius. B.T. felt certain that he alone could have made such a discovery. All of this he told Michi in no uncertain terms, finishing his soliloquy with, "So you see, it's *impossible* that the leaked code came from anywhere but my lab."

"Impossible?"

"All right, nothing is impossible. But *highly improbable.*"

"What if I told you the reason we met was because that sequence of code didn't come from your lab . . . ?"

B.T. had a sinking feeling in his stomach.

"What if I told you that someone else, working independently of you, had arrived at the exact same conclusion . . . ?"

B.T. crossed his arms over his chest and drew into himself, staring at Michi from the corner of his eye like an injured child. "What are you talking about?" he said in a whisper.

"If I asked you to come with me back to Tokyo, to meet with a colleague of mine who could explain more, would you trust me and come?"

"A colleague?"

"Yes, a colleague of mine who works for our government."

Had this all been contrived? James Mohammad, Lily Bao, and now Michi. Had his life become a game in which everyone knew the rules but him?

B.T. stared blankly out at the horizon.

"So, you and me," he eventually said. "Your government colleague knows about us? And he's a 'colleague,' so you work for the government too?"

What she felt for him was real, Michi said. Her discovery of those feelings had proven an unexpected complication. B.T. kept his eyes fixed to the horizon. Michi stood, as if uncertain whether to grant B.T. his space and leave him alone or to sit beside him and explain more. Then a large dive boat motored into sight from behind a rocky outcropping. The powerful wake from the boat's stern formed into a frothy V. Chattering tourists lounged topside. When the wake struck their smaller boat, it lifted Michi up and, unceremoniously, toppled her to the deck.

⌐

19:33 April 13, 2054 (GMT+1)
Abuja

The restaurant door opened, and a diminutive man in a boxy gray suit entered. He glanced down at a grimy scrap of paper, then looked up. His eyes settled on the table in the back corner. As he approached, the elder James Mohammad rose to his feet. His nephew followed suit.

The man introduced himself as Zhao Jin. He had arrived that morning from Beijing. This meeting, it turned out, was not being held at the request of James Mohammad's uncle but at the request of this unassuming man, who only pecked at the dishes in front of him. "I've had your uncle make the appropriate protocol arrangements with the ministries here," Zhao Jin began. "This allows us to speak candidly about sensitive matters. In Beijing, your work has already risen to the attention of our most senior-level decision-makers in the Politburo Standing Committee, specifically your recent encounter with Lily Bao. We believe that—"

The elder James Mohammad interrupted. "I've told my nephew that he should have acted more decisively. You cannot offer the carrot and then hesitate to apply the stick."

"Understood . . . understood . . ." said Zhao Jin, holding up his hand.

"But I'm not entirely convinced that your nephew made a mistake. To win the game we're playing will require patience. Blood and soil, that's what people return to in the end. They may indulge in fanciful dreams, but they're always forced to return to the truth of their existence. If Lily Bao reaches this conclusion for herself, it will only enhance her usefulness to us. So let her return to the senator. Let her make a few more deals and fill her bank account. Let her believe in her dream a little longer. Let her think she has a choice. Eventually, the dream loses out. The truth holds. And we return to our home, to our blood and soil."

Zhao Jin cast an appraising glance at Mohammad, who moved his food around on his plate and said, "He won't be a senator for much longer."

"No," Zhao Jin answered. "He won't."

"He'll be in the White House soon."

"It would seem so."

"He won't take Lily Bao with him," added Mohammad.

"Would Kennedy have become president if instead of Jackie he'd married a German? The daughter of Rommel or Guderian? The wounds of America's last war remain open, and Shriver is too much of a coward to risk his political career for her. Also, there's something else."

"What's that?" the elder James Mohammad asked impatiently.

Zhao Jin volleyed his gaze between them, as if he were weighing whether to share this last bit of information. "The sequence of code on Common Sense. In your reports, you mention concerns that it was stolen from an Okinawa-based researcher you've funded, a Dr. Yamamoto."

"Yes," said Mohammad. "That's my concern."

"Before Lily Bao set off on her own, she worked for the Tandava Group. I assume you're familiar with them."

Again, Mohammad nodded.

"Although they've divested themselves of the asset, they once had a significant investment in Neutronics, a biotech company. Lily Bao managed that account for the Tandava Group's founder, Dr. Sandeep Chowdhury. At that time, Neutronics was doing cutting-edge work in nanorobotics, quantum computing, and bioengineering, including early-phase research of remote gene editing under the guidance of Dr. Ray Kurzweil. You've heard of him, of course."

Both nephew and uncle nodded.

"He vanished some years ago after leaving Neutronics," added Zhao Jin. "It seems the company wanted to turn a profit off his research, while he wanted to go further with it."

"What does this have to do with my nephew and Lily Bao?" grumbled the elder James Mohammad.

"Truthers in America are agitating for a commission to investigate President Castro's death," said Zhao Jin. "Belief is spreading that there was foul play—an assassination. The sequence of code that allegedly killed Castro, the one released on Common Sense, what if that sequence of code wasn't stolen from Dr. Yamamoto's lab? What if it came from Neutronics?"

"Can you prove that?" asked Mohammad.

"Do I need to? If Shriver climbs a little higher, to the vice presidency or even higher still, his ties to Lily Bao and Neutronics are leverage we'll have over him, a way to exercise control. That will give us an invaluable edge over the Americans."

"So you want to blackmail Shriver?" asked Mohammad.

Zhao Jin scoffed. "That's such an ugly term, and it won't be necessary." He asked if he might share a parable from his country. "Once there was a boy who was trying to figure out how to earn the money for a special toy that he wanted but couldn't afford. On hearing his predicament, a friend of his at school explained that most adults had at least one deep, dark secret and that this made it very easy to get what you wanted from them by simply stating, 'I know the whole truth,' even if you don't know anything. The boy thought this sounded like it might be a way to get the money he needed out of his parents. That day, when he came home from school, he decided to try out his scheme. He found his mother as she was preparing dinner in the kitchen and gave her a grave look, saying, 'I know the whole truth!' His mother quickly reached into her apron and handed him a thousand-yuan note, saying, 'Don't tell your father.' Pleased that his scheme seemed to work, he waited for his father to get home that evening. Greeting him at the door, the boy said, 'I know the whole truth!' His father, glancing from side to side, took out his wallet and pressed two thousand yuan into the boy's hand, saying, 'Not a word to your mother!' Even more pleased and closer to affording his new toy, the boy thought he would try this trick on a stranger. The next morning, on his way to school, he saw the mailman walking up his front path. He looked the mailman squarely in the eye and said, 'I know the whole truth!' The mailman quickly dropped his mailbag, fell to his knees, opened his arms, and exclaimed, 'Son! Finally! Come give your daddy a hug!'"

James Mohammad's uncle laughed out loud. With his napkin he wiped the corners of his eyes. "Very good," he said to Zhao Jin, who returned a smile. The joke elicited only a tepid response from the younger Mohammad. His uncle chided him, "Come, Jimmy, no need to be so serious."

Mohammad looked down to find that he had been tearing at the corners of his paper napkin. A small pile of shreds lay in front of him. "Very amusing," he said, looking down at his hands. "But who will be saying, 'I know the whole truth!'? . . . It won't be either of you; it will be me." Then he turned to his uncle. "This issue has already taken up too much of my time. I also have a business to run and my own investments to manage. As well as—"

His uncle cut him off. "A business that only exists because of a partnership with the government that I have facilitated for you. Now we are asking something more. *No* is not an option." His index finger was pointed at his nephew's chest.

Zhao Jin placed his hand on the elder James Mohammad's arm to calm him before turning to his nephew. "I understand what it's like to have a powerful uncle," he said. "The story I told you, about the boy, it was a favorite of my own uncle's. I assure you that if you help us with this, we'll ensure it's worth your while. There are investment opportunities in our country that are only made available to our most trusted partners. Your successful handling of Lily Bao would certainly help me make the case that you are worthy of being considered *a trusted partner.*" Zhao Jin placed a special emphasis on these last words, allowing them to dangle like bait on a line.

James Mohammad glanced at his uncle, who seemed to be considering Zhao Jin's offer with a measure of skepticism that mirrored his own.

"Take some time to think about it," added Zhao Jin. He flagged down one of the waiters and asked if they might order him a cab. "I don't want to impinge any more on your time together," he said. "I was very close with my uncle and, now that he's gone, I often wish I had him around to enjoy a meal with."

Zhao Jin left, and it was only the two of them. They picked at their food, neither speaking, until, eventually, Mohammad asked who Zhao Jin's uncle had been.

"I thought you might have figured it out. His uncle was Zhao Leji."

His nephew gave him a blank stare.

"Twenty years ago, during their war with the Americans, Zhao Leji administered all internal security for the CCP. He was secretary for the Central Commission for Discipline Inspection *and* a member of the Politburo Standing Committee."

James Mohammad shrugged.

Clearly irritated by his nephew's lack of respect, he added pointedly, "Zhao Jin's uncle was also the one who gave the order to execute Lily Bao's father."

⌐

18:46 April 15, 2054 (GMT-5)
Arlington National Cemetery

That night in her apartment Julia Hunt ordered in sushi and watched the coverage of Slake's botched press conference on her living room sofa. Days later, Slake's panicked responses to the questions about Castro's death continued to air, and they appeared even worse on the news.

Hunt raised a piece of salmon sashimi between two chopsticks as she read the chyron for the next story: *Castro Autopsy Leaked on Common Sense Confirms Foul Play and White House Lies.* She dropped the fish onto her lap.

News of the withheld autopsy exploded. On every channel the prime-time anchors flashed printed copies of the report to the camera. They read whole sections aloud, describing the dimensions of the marble-sized mass of cells inexplicably lodged in Castro's aorta and the excerpted transcript of the autopsy itself, in which the chief internist concluded, "This can't be the same heart."

Within the hour, Truthers flooded the streets in cities around the country. As Hunt scrolled the channels, a news crew in Lafayette Park was conducting interviews with the growing mass of protesters, one of whom she recognized; it was the man in the wheelchair she'd met on the Metro. She had thought of him often. Now she learned his identity: retired gunnery sergeant Joseph William Sherman III. Beneath his name on the screen were the words *Truther Volunteer Organizer.* She placed his name in a search engine and learned that he'd lost his legs in the Spratly Islands, and that the Chinese nuclear attack on San Diego had killed his wife and three daughters, who'd lived at nearby Camp Pendleton. Hunt could hear in Sherman's voice how deeply he resented a president who while alive flaunted constitutional norms by clinging to power for an attempted fourth term and whose successor, Smith, now flaunted norms again by withholding an autopsy and refusing to be transparent about his predecessor's death.

"Point your camera here," said Sherman, thumbing toward his missing legs. "I sacrificed these for my country and you're going to lie to me . . . you're going to lie to all of *us*." He gestured expansively to a cluster of Truthers who'd placed him at their center, the core of them veterans, wearing old military fatigues adorned with medals that dangled from their chest pockets. "It's a lie that Smith is the legitimate president when he so clearly had a hand in killing Castro. Is this what America has become? Dreamers drunk on power led by a dictator-president. Lies to the many so long as it gives power to the few." Sherman held the camera's focus with his insistent blue eyes.

His tone was so resolved, the correspondent felt compelled to answer him. In a meek voice, she said, "I don't know. . . ."

"Of course you don't." Sherman leaned in to the camera. "President Smith," he began, "you are illegitimate. You will find that everyday Americans—we patriots who demand the truth about your crimes and the excesses of the Dreamers—will not be led by a thief, by someone who stole the presidency. We served our country before, and we'll serve it again. And don't even think of trying to place your predecessor in Arlington's hallowed ground." Sherman swiveled around, turning his back to the camera, and wheeled himself away.

The news cut to commercial.

Julia Hunt rested her head against the arm of her sofa, her eyes still glued to the screen. Weeks of exhaustion swept over her. While she waited for the program to return, she fell into a black wilderness of sleep. Deep into this sleep, in the early hours of the morning, she began to dream: Here, in the dream, she is asleep in her girlhood bedroom, and is woken before dawn by a noise, the sound of something hitting the floor. Her surroundings are familiar, the adobe ranch house in New Mexico where Sarah Hunt had raised her. Wearing her nightgown, she carefully shuts the door behind her and steps into the dark corridor. At its far end a single band of light escapes from the base of another door. She begins to walk down the corridor. The tiles are cool beneath her bare feet. As she draws closer, she can hear what sounds like a struggle.

When she enters the room, a man is lying facedown on the floor, motionless, with his arms spread in front of him as if caught in mid-swim-stroke. His hair is thick and black, and his back is powerfully built, but not as if he ever went to a gym or played a sport; it's the type of sinewy strength that comes from a life of physical labor. This dead man is her father. Leaning over the bed, she sees her adoptive mother, Sarah, dressed in military fatigues. Sarah has a pillow and is smothering a woman whom she's caught in the bed. The woman's feet are jerking and kicking, and she's wearing a white lace nightgown that matches Julia's.

When Julia sees this matching nightgown, she knows the woman in the bed is her actual mother and she lunges at Sarah, clawing at her, even biting, like a cornered animal. Julia manages to pull Sarah from the bed, so that she backs toward the door, stepping over Julia's dead father and muttering over and over, "You shouldn't have done that . . . you shouldn't have done that . . ." Now Julia is left in the room. She tears away the pillow, brushing aside the sweat-matted black hair that matches her own so she might reveal her mother's face; except it is the face of Sarah Hunt. The lips are purple, the complexion is sallow and waxy, and she isn't breathing. Julia runs out into the corridor. It is empty. She notices that the door to her bedroom is now open a crack. She slips down the corridor. In the bedroom she finds Sarah Hunt, dressed in her military fatigues, asleep beneath the covers with her back turned toward her. Cautiously, Julia approaches, taking each step heel-to-toe, until she is standing within an arm's length. Julia reaches out. But before she makes contact, the woman in the military fatigues whips around in the bed, so that she is now facing Julia. It isn't Sarah Hunt. Julia recognizes the face immediately: it is her own.

She woke up on the living room sofa to a familiar feeling of exhausted dread. Julia shut off the television. How many times had she suffered through this dream? Hundreds? Thousands? It came in waves. In the weeks after Sarah Hunt's death, Julia endured the dream multiple times each night, waking from the grip of its familiar terror only to drift back to sleep and relive the nightmare all over again. Even though the dream never changed, with the passage of time the faces had aged. When she'd first had the dream, decades before, the face she saw in its final instant was her own as a rebellious teen, incongruously young to be wearing military fatigues. But Julia had since grown into that uniform, just as Sarah had aged out of it.

Julia lifted herself off the sofa, wiped the sleep from her eyes, and stepped into her kitchen. She began to brew a pot of tea. She wondered if Hendrickson and Smith would go through with the funeral, given the leaked autopsy. Outside, light was seeping onto the horizon. The day was breaking cloudless and bright. She imagined Hendrickson and Smith in the White House, the pair of them breathing a sigh of relief that they wouldn't have to contend with the rain in addition to everything else.

Sarah Hunt hadn't wanted a funeral. She'd left explicit instructions that her body be donated to science. When the paramedics came to take her, one of them observed that the cocktail of pills she'd imbibed seemed meticulously calibrated not to do too much physiological damage, thus ensuring that her entire body could be harvested for research. That's how her mother was, always in control up to and including her own death.

Julia didn't really have any memories of her parents, even though her adoption had occurred when she was nine. Her mind only allowed her mother and father to appear in tortured dreams. Her parents, who'd immigrated up from El Salvador, struggled to find work upon entering the United States. They came for the dream and found a truth that didn't match. Monday through Saturday, they took a bus nearly two hours each way into San Diego for day wages. This was how Julia had survived the nuclear blast and they had not.

Julia turned on the television. An overhead shot, taken from a drone, panned along the presidential funeral route, lined with law enforcement— a mix of uniformed Secret Service and D.C. Metro and Park Police. A separate camera remained fixed on the White House, where President Smith and his entourage would depart for Arlington in a couple of hours. She kept the news on mute as she watched the gathering spectacle.

She wondered what her parents might have thought of Castro. Their story began in much the same way Castro's had, despite having ended quite differently. Or had it? In the end America had killed Castro, much as it had killed her parents. And what about Sarah Hunt? Had she been a dreamer? Had America killed her? Julia couldn't say.

The drone feed came on the screen again. A protesting crowd had begun to swell from up the banks of the Potomac, flooding onto the six lanes of Memorial Bridge, which led into Arlington National Cemetery. They progressed slowly, marching with a near-military discipline. At the front, among those setting the pace, Julia could make out a man in a wheelchair.

⌐

11:18 April 16, 2054 (GMT-5)
Rosslyn, Virginia

Lily Bao couldn't believe what she was watching. Three times the presidential motorcade had left the gates of the White House, only to return due to obstructions along their route. At the gates of Arlington National Cemetery a small army of Truthers had assembled to prevent Castro's burial. What stunned Lily most wasn't the confrontation between the administration and its opposition; it was that as she watched the scene play out from her office she saw Sherman in the front ranks of the protesters.

Early that morning, before the authorities could block the route, the protesters had managed to assemble in their thousands and creep up the banks of the Potomac and onto Memorial Bridge. Drawing themselves into formation, they had blocked the six lanes of the bridge, using it as a natural choke point to restrict access to the cemetery. By late morning, the police had made a half dozen attempts to disperse them using a mix of tear gas, rubber bullets, and pepper spray, but to no avail. Sherman, dressed in his old combat fatigues, refused to be dislodged. He remained in the center of the fray swinging an American flag staked to a segment of PVC pipe.

Lily canceled her morning meetings and ignored her phone. She couldn't look away from the news. She was watching when, on their last attempt to break up the Truthers, the police employed a mounted unit. The camera was on Sherman when one of the horses spooked and reared backward, knocking him from his wheelchair. A photographer captured the sequence of events—a legless veteran splayed on the ground clutching the American flag as a horse tramples him, and then him trying to use the flag as a crutch to climb back into his chair as the mounted officer makes another run and tramples him under the horse again.

Lily Bao stared on in horror.

Sherman wasn't moving. A few protesters rushed to his aid. She could see a pool of dark, syrupy blood beginning to gather on the asphalt.

The camera cut away, as if directed to do so.

In a panic Lily switched stations.

"We're getting reports now that the White House motorcade is again departing for Arlington," said the anchor mechanically, as though his concentration weren't on his words but rather on the transmitter in his ear and whatever message it was delivering simultaneously. The station then cut back to the bedlam at the bridge. Bodies pressed one against another. Whirling clouds of smoke and gas. Protesters had pulled two of the officers off their mounts and their riderless horses were galloping back across the bridge, toward the Lincoln Memorial. "We'll try to get an update for you on the individual injured by that horse," said the anchor. The network rebroadcast the images of Sherman being trampled, looping the scene like a sports replay.

Lily Bao turned away. She called Sherman's phone. No answer. She flung on her jacket. Goddammit, she was going down there. As she stepped from her office, she glimpsed the news a final time. At the south end of the cemetery, a crowd had gathered around a three-vehicle motorcade of black SUVs, bringing it to a stop outside a back gate on McNair Road. This crowd wasn't nearly as large as the thousands who had blocked Memorial Bridge, but they were enough to outnumber the Secret Service agents by at least ten-to-one. Unable to nose any farther forward, the agents piled out of the first and third SUVs and tried to subdue the crowd. Unlike the neatly ordered ranks out front of Arlington National Cemetery, this crowd had devolved into a jeering mob. The dozen-odd agents brandished their pistols and credentials.

The Truthers began to shake the second SUV, rocking it on its tires. The Secret Service agents formed a perimeter around this vehicle, sacrificing the first and third vehicles in their column to the mob, which began to vandalize these other two SUVs, tearing out the seats, slamming bricks into the ballistic windshields. Clearly the Secret Service was protecting something in the second vehicle, and the more stridently they defended it—pistol-whipping one protester and pepper-spraying two others—the more frenzied the mob became.

Lily watched the overhead camera shot. This can only end badly, she thought. Either one of the Secret Service agents would be killed by a Truther or vice versa. How had it come to this? Yes, Truther protests had been roiling the country for weeks; and yes, the leak of Castro's autopsy on Common Sense exposed a lack of transparency within the Smith administration. But this attack on a presidential motorcade was something different, a far darker escalation. This eruption of violence had been brewing for years, through successive economic collapses, pandemics, and the utter dysfunction that had become American life; really, as Lily thought about it, since all the way back to the war that had claimed her father. If this connection to the war wasn't evident to anyone watching, one only needed to see the myriad veterans in their old military uniforms woven through the ranks of Truthers. Lily wasn't unsympathetic to them. They would no longer tolerate being lied to.

The standoff around the convoy stretched on. Neither side would de-escalate, but neither side seemed willing to take everyone over the brink. Lily was about to leave in search of Sherman when the sunroof of the second SUV cracked opened. "We're looking inside," the anchor said excitedly as the shot zoomed in. "It's difficult to see exactly what's going on in that SUV. . . ." Lily craned her neck forward. She could discern the vague outline of a few people through the open sunroof. Then one person stepped over another to stand. "Okay," said the anchor. "Someone is coming out . . . can we get a better angle on that?"

The camera shot shifted from directly overhead to side-on. A figure appeared and began to gesture wildly, addressing the protesters as if from a podium. They jeered and taunted him in return. But whoever this was, he continued to speak, refusing to allow this mob to silence him. The anchor, who was split-screen with the live feed, touched his ear. "Wait . . . we're getting confirmation from the White House. This SUV is the vehicle carrying the president. It's confirmed, President Smith is inside *this* vehicle. Hold on, we're tightening the shot . . . but that appears to be someone else . . . that appears to be . . ." In the instant before the anchor said it, Lily Bao could see that it was Nat Shriver addressing the crowd.

She hadn't seen him since her return from Macau. On the two occasions when she'd texted, he hadn't replied. At the time, Lily had shrugged it off. Her relationship with Shriver was, after all, a fling. But her reserve evaporated as she watched Shriver on television, negotiating with this mob. Lily imagined that Shriver was giving the speech of his life.

Gradually, she could see the crowd's posture begin to ease. One of the Truthers shouted something at Shriver. He shouted something back, throwing out his hand as if he were tossing candy to a group of children. Whatever Shriver said elicited a laugh. This spread to the rest of the crowd, which, rippling with laughter, took a step back from the convoy. This provided enough room for the Secret Service agents to carefully climb inside the other damaged SUVs. Shriver kept talking from the sunroof, gesturing toward specific people in the crowd—a middle-aged woman wearing yellow pants held up by a snakeskin belt and a yellow T-shirt with a DON'T TREAD ON ME silk screen, effectively transforming herself into a walking Gadsden flag; a twenty-something Native American wearing a beaded belt over a Truther T-shirt from Veritas Vengeance; as well as the leather-vested members of the Buffalo Soldiers, the African American motorcycle club with heavy US military representation, some of whose members lent their services to the Truther brigades. Whatever Shriver was saying seemed to resonate. A path opened through the crowd. The convoy was allowed to turn around. They returned to the White House.

The camera followed above the three SUVs, as the anchor commented, "A remarkably courageous display from Senator Nat Shriver. Easy to imagine how that might have ended differently. As I mentioned, we do have confirmation that the president himself was in that car with Senator Shriver. . . ."

One of the network pundits now joined the anchor on-screen. "Yes, a remarkable display of poise from Senator Shriver. I'm grateful to see a peaceful resolution here, but I gotta ask: Where has the president been in all this? Why haven't we heard from him?" The anchor allowed his eyebrows to knit together on-air, and remained silent. They then cut to commercial, an advertisement for a company selling gold. The graph of gold's price that flashed on the screen was upward and basically vertical.

Lily Bao had seen enough. She switched off her television and rushed out of her office, headed to the nearest hospital. She was going to find Sherman.

⌐

20:23 April 23, 2054 (GMT-3)
São Paulo

Chowdhury had two passports, one Indian, the other American. He'd entered Brazil on the latter and his citizenship was listed in the Neutronics system as such. Every physician he met as he underwent his batteries of tests and treatments asked his opinion of the ongoing crisis. Chowd-hury endured these conversations graciously, but after the weeks of scans and samples, of genetic testing and mapping, he was exhausted. He be-gan to wonder if he would ever begin the actual treatment that might repair his ailing heart.

He was pleased to find on his schedule an appointment described as *Final Preoperative Consult, Dr. Ayesha Bakari, Chief of Cardiological Editing.* Unlike his other appointments arranged by Neutronics, this one would occur in his hotel suite. Ashni had afternoon tea sent up, and room service had just left when the doorbell rang. Ashni escorted Dr. Bakari toward the sofa as Chowdhury emerged from his bedroom.

On seeing Dr. Bakari, Chowdhury did a double take—the dark hair, though worn a bit longer, and the black glasses, though in slightly nar-rower frames—it was the young technician who'd visited him at the Carlyle. Chowdhury mentioned that they'd met before. "In New York," he said. "Don't you remember?" A look of recognition flashed into Dr. Bakari's eyes.

"My twin sister," she said. "She's the one you met in New York."

Chowdhury apologized.

"No need," said Dr. Bakari. "It happens all the time."

"How long have you both worked for Neutronics?"

"This is my fourth year and it's her second, though we've had a re-lationship with Neutronics for far longer." Dr. Bakari explained that she and her sister had come to the attention of Ray Kurzweil decades ago, when they were only children. They suffered from a rare congenital heart defect, a genetic disease that caused the rapid deterioration of car-diac tissue. "Imagine being a person but born with a heart that aged in dog years," Dr. Bakari said. "Ray Kurzweil, who I believe you know, was at the time conducting research on gene-editing therapies that could rejuvenate deteriorating heart tissue. He discovered my medical file as well as that of my sister. Neutronics was just beginning trials on human subjects. My sister and I were attractive prospects for those trials. Genetically, our hearts are virtually identical. A twin study sped the results."

"So, I assume the trials proved a success?" Chowdhury asked.

"I wouldn't be talking with you today otherwise," said Dr. Bakari. "Neutronics saved my life. . . ." Then, pausing a beat, Dr. Bakari amended the statement. "Really, it's Dr. Kurzweil who saved my life."

Ashni shifted uncomfortably in her seat. Chowdhury knew she harbored certain reservations about Kurzweil. It was one thing to embed a headsUp in your wrist. But Kurzweil wasn't making gadgets. He was toying with human existence. She'd traveled here because she wanted her father to receive this specific treatment for his heart and then to leave, so he might finish out a normal life. The life Kurzweil offered—at the intersection of technology and biology—was anything but normal. Ashni worried that this technology might seduce her father. She imagined he could disappear up some murky river, vanishing into the interior.

Dr. Bakari reached into a medical bag and removed several pill bottles. She arrayed them on the table alongside the tea service. "The editing process occurs over many days," Dr. Bakari explained. "It takes time for your body to respond to the treatment, and during that time it's important that you remain under sedation. Gene editing requires a degree of precision that is difficult to achieve in a body whose systems are running at capacity. Think of it like trying to write calligraphy in a car that's driving down the road; it's impossible. All we're doing is pulling your body off to the side of the road. This series of prescriptions will handle that. Take them tonight after dinner and simply go to sleep as you normally would." Dr. Bakari turned toward Ashni. "By morning your father's vitals will have become undetectable. He will for all intents and purposes have flatlined. Don't worry, though, he'll be fine. A team of our technicians will then transport him into the clinic for the rest of his treatment."

That night, Ashni and Chowdhury ordered dinner to their room. They ate facing the window, the river spread before them. Chowdhury tried to engage his daughter in conversation, but she sat next to him in silence, her attention fixed on the view. Eventually she said, "I never said goodbye to Mom."

Chowdhury set his fork on the rim of his plate. He reached across the table and placed his hand on his daughter's arm. In a flash, he could see his ex-wife Samantha twenty years before, sitting in the corner booth of a Chinese restaurant in Dupont Circle, the night they'd met for the last time, the night she had agreed to allow Chowdhury to evacuate their daughter to New Delhi. A few weeks later, Samantha was dead, vanished in a white nuclear flash in Galveston. "I'm sorry," Chowdhury said to his daughter. "I wish you'd had that chance."

Ashni turned away from the view of the river, and her gaze bored into her father. Chowdhury wondered if she would now say that goodbye to him. Instead, she leaned over, kissed him on the head, and said, "Get some rest, Bapu. I'll see you when you wake up." Then she left him at the table and shut the door to her room.

Chowdhury finished the remainder of his meal alone. He was in no rush. Soon he changed into his pajamas. He arranged the dozen or so pill bottles that Dr. Bakari had left behind on the edge of his sink. He poured himself a large glass of water and, pill after pill, imbibed this cocktail in the exact manner Dr. Bakari had prescribed.

He headed toward bed. But as he walked he began to feel as though his steps were being taken through sand. The margins of his vision crowded in, so that the bed itself appeared as if viewed through a pair of binoculars held in reverse. He was very conscious of not wanting to collapse on the floor. He didn't want Ashni or someone else to find him in so undignified a position. Willing himself forward, he toppled onto the pillows and pedaled his feet beneath the sheets.

Rolling onto his side, he realized that he'd neglected to draw the shade. It wouldn't matter. He would be oblivious to the day breaking. He continued to stare out into the night, at the darkness of the Rio Pinheiros. What overtook him wasn't the darkness his consciousness associated with sleep; rather, it was its opposite: a flood of violent and obliterating light.

⌐

09:35 April 24, 2054 (GMT+9)
Tokyo

B.T. agreed to return with Michi and meet her "colleague." Michi never referred to this person as anything else, not on the flight over from Okinawa, not on the taxi ride from the airport to her modest apartment in the Meguro District, and not that night as they shared her bed. B.T. had decided that he trusted Michi. If she wanted him to meet this elusive colleague, he would.

The next morning, she cooked him an "American breakfast" of

bacon, eggs, and coffee before they set out on a bus. Two transfers and a half-mile walk later, they approached a nondescript office building. B.T. stopped just short of the entrance and stared up at the glass façade. "Michi," he said, "where are we going?"

"To see my colleague."

B.T. wouldn't budge.

Michi glanced toward the mirrored glass doors at the entrance, which didn't boast a sign or any outward indication of the building's purpose. She sighed. "This is a general research facility, one of several dozen scattered around the country and funded by the government's Research Promotion Bureau. My mentor, Dr. Kobe Agawa, has his office here. He's the one who wants to meet you."

Few people knew the name Dr. Kobe Agawa outside of Japan, she explained. However, inside this country he was a trusted and universally recognized public health official. Over a nearly fifty-year career, he'd become an indispensable figure. When the government needed its citizens to adopt some collective measure—such as taking an experimental vaccine or enduring costly economic shutdowns—Dr. Agawa would appear on television to make the case. He was the son of Hiroshima survivors and carried that nuclear legacy in his own body. Born with a host of genetic defects that twisted his limbs from the waist down, he'd spent his life confined to a wheelchair. Which was why, when B.T. and Michi entered his office, he didn't stand to greet them but instead sat barricaded behind his desk.

"Dr. Yamamoto, won't you sit?" He gestured to a pair of club chairs. "I owe you an apology, both for asking Michi to remain discreet about our meeting today and for the role I've played in orchestrating your relationship with her." Dr. Agawa recounted with startling omniscience the events of the past six weeks, beginning with Michi's arrival at the dive shop at Cape Maeda, the escaped butterflies, and even their recent excursion down the undersea trench. Sincere as Dr. Agawa's apology seemed, it only reinforced B.T.'s sense that he'd been a mark. Once or twice, Michi shifted uncomfortably in her seat. Whether this was because she felt guilty about the ways she'd manipulated B.T., or because Dr. Agawa remained unaware of the intimacy that had developed between them, B.T. couldn't say.

Dr. Agawa unlocked a side cabinet and removed a manila folder overstuffed with paper. "If in the last century nuclear power threatened to end humanity, in this century that threat comes from the Singularity. Whichever society merges biological and technological evolution first will—with the power of quantum computing and artificial intelligence—out-evolve, and thus erase, all other societies. But, of course, you know this. . . ." He waved his hand dismissively. "In the nuclear age, the Japanese people became the first to suffer the results of a scientific breakthrough with similar destructive potential. It's a legacy we live with to this day, one that has never left us. We, more than anyone else, understand that this game is zero-sum . . . but for one exception . . . if one player can subvert the rules of the game."

Dr. Agawa removed a notepad and two sharpened pencils from his desk. He drew a tic-tac-toe board in the corner of the page. "Come, Dr. Yamamoto, allow me to show you what I mean. Let's play."

Both B.T. and Michi crowded around Dr. Agawa. As they began, B.T. placed an *X* in one corner. Dr. Agawa placed an *O* in the center. Then, once the board was filled, Dr. Agawa drew a large *C* across it and said, "Cat's game. Shall we play again?" and they did, with the same result, the two of them quickly filling the board. "Ah, you're very good at this," said Dr. Agawa.

"Are you making fun of me?" answered B.T. as they finished yet another cat's game.

"Is it possible to be good at tic-tac-toe?" Dr. Agawa asked in the same rhetorical tone as before.

"No," said B.T. definitively.

"And why is that?" Dr. Agawa drew another game. With mild annoyance, B.T. began to play with him yet again.

"So long as you follow a basic strategy by sticking to the center of the board and the corners," said B.T., "you can produce a cat's game every time. The only winning move is not to play."

"He is a quick study, isn't he?" Dr. Agawa said to Michi. He gestured for them to return to their seats and took up the overstuffed folder he'd removed from his desk a few moments before. "These pages contain the moves of another sort of game. While the Chinese, the Nigerians, and even some of the Americans jockey for scientific supremacy, our nation has adopted an entirely different strategy. Japan has no interest in achieving the Singularity. Our aim is to subvert it, to ensure no one is ever able to unlock and thus abuse this technology. Look at what's happening right now in the United States. The assassination of their president and the political turmoil that's followed is the direct result of biological and technological integration. Dr. Yamamoto, you above all people understand this."

B.T. felt himself complicit in a crime. "It was a sequence of code that I developed which killed President Castro."

"Yes and no." Dr. Agawa began to sort through the manila folder until he came to a few stapled pages. He flipped to the second page, and then slid the document across the desk to B.T. "Do you recognize this?"

```
α Ω

If a beam of light / energy / open + / close—/ reopen == / repeat /
stop α

Then / She / he / it / them / they / human! @ / machine # ** /
blink / be ⌫

?? Singular / one / unique / here > / now < / then

/ soon / all at once /

Open vistas across limitless paths / = infinity x pi / @ # ⌘ . . .
```

Line after line of code followed, all of it familiar to B.T. It matched his work on remote gene editing and far exceeded the leak on Common Sense. "Where did you get this?"

"We monitor the research advances of a number of private companies," said Dr. Agawa. "One of which, Neutronics, has made startling advances in recent years, including in the field of remote gene editing, as you can see. This particular sequence of code was written by their former chief of research. He's since left the company. But before he left, he made this breakthrough. We haven't been alone in identifying the threat that this technology poses. As I mentioned, some in America wish to pursue the Singularity. But a small group inside the White House do not. They have proven quite willing to cooperate with us."

"To what end?"

Dr. Agawa leaned back in his chair. "To create a cat's game."

At this, B.T. flipped to the first page. This was the email that had contained the sequence of code as an attachment. It was printed from an anonymous account linked to a private server. The date was from three years before, the subject line: *common sense.* It contained no message, simply a signature: *SH.*

5

The Nightingale's Song

08:38 May 01, 2054 (GMT-5)
The Hay-Adams Hotel

Senator Nat Shriver's seventh-floor suite looked down at the White House
from across Lafayette Square. For the past two weeks, he'd been seques-
tered in the hotel awaiting his announcement as the vice presidential
nominee. The controversy around the leaked autopsy and the debacle at
Castro's funeral had delayed that announcement, but in the afternoon
it would become official. President Smith had scheduled a press conference in the East Room of the White House in which he'd reveal not only
Shriver's nomination but also the formation of the unity government
that the Truthers under Wisecarver's leadership had long advocated for.
It would be the most significant day in Shriver's political life, after which
every other facet of his life would change. This was why he'd finally relented to Lily Bao's repeated requests to see him.

Over the same two weeks, Lily Bao's world had imploded. In her office on the day of Castro's funeral, she'd watched Sherman get trampled to death by the police. That video would ricochet through the consciousness of disaffected Americans with a power she could hardly fathom. If a photo is worth a thousand words, the image of Sherman, a disabled and decorated veteran, being crushed by the apparatus of the very state he'd served became the symbol of the Truthers' rage. Rage against the Castro administration and its excesses. Rage against a country that had become divorced from the truth.

The senator wasn't the first to arrive to their meeting in his suite. On his schedule the thirty-minute block was listed as *Conflict of interest review with personal investment advisor.* His time was no longer his own and he needed a pretext to see Lily. Karen Slake, whom Lily recognized from her frequent and increasingly combative television appearances, came in advance. "The vice president is running a few minutes behind schedule," she announced, giving Lily an appraising glance that began at her shoes and ended at her shoulders. Lily noticed that Slake already referred to Shriver by his new title, though Congress had yet to confirm his appointment.

Then Shriver entered the room shaking his head as if in disagreement while trailing a half dozen aides, none of whom Lily recognized and all of whom were speaking over one another as they competed for his attention. When he saw Lily, he stopped his headshaking. He paused, causing his aides to stumble as they accordioned one into another. He then swiveled around, faced his aides, and instructed them to clear out and leave him in peace. He told the last of them to shut the door on their way out.

Slake remained perched on the sofa ready to take notes.

Shriver said, "You, too, Karen."

Slake grumbled about "standard protocol" and the necessity of "an official record of every meeting." Shriver simply nodded along while shooing her toward the door, and if Lily Bao required any reminder of the power Shriver would soon wield in the White House, Slake's deference was evidence enough that he would be calling the shots—if he wasn't already.

The door shut behind Slake and now they were alone.

Shriver gestured for Lily to sit across from him on the sofa. She felt the sting of his formality.

"How have you been?" he said.

"How have I been?"

He stared down at his hands. A painful silence lingered between them, which Shriver eventually broke. "I was sorry to see about Sherman. I know . . ." His voice trailed off for a moment. "I know how close the two of you were."

"I had to go to four hospitals before I found him," Lily said. "I was there, you know, when he died." Haltingly, she began to explain all that followed, then she stopped herself. It was as if she'd reached an emotional wall, one she couldn't quite surmount. She was back there, in that tiny hospital room, reliving that pain, and one particularly excruciating detail: "I called you, Nat . . . all that week I called you . . . you didn't answer . . . you never came."

He had seen her missed calls. He replied with a feeble, "I didn't know," staring down at his hands. It felt like a lie. Even if he had known, he wouldn't have taken her call. And he certainly wouldn't have come. Too much was at stake. He glanced up at her. "I'm sorry."

Lily Bao pushed down her emotions so forcibly that they formed into a hard center, like a stone she carried inside.

Shriver reached toward her and placed his palm gently on her arm. She shrugged him away. "Don't."

"I'm sorry I wasn't available then."

"You aren't available now."

Shriver stood from the sofa and walked across to the window and looked down at the White House, where a dozen black-clad and heavily armed Secret Service agents patrolled the roof. His eyes scanned the platoons of baton-wielding riot police, the armored vehicles with mounted water cannons, the tangles of new fencing that cordoned off 15th and 17th Streets along with Pennsylvania and Constitution Avenues.

"What is it you expect from me, Lily?"

"What is it I expect?" She was incredulous.

"Yeah," he said, matching her tone. "What do you want me to do?"

"How about being straight with me, for once."

"Straight with you?" he said. "Okay . . . I love you. I've always told you the truth about that. You're the one who's gone on pretending that this is something less than that. I've been totally clear with you about my feelings from the start. Jesus, Lily, I wish it was different. Do you even know what's happening later today?"

Of course she knew. To ask him to subordinate his life and his work to anything was to ask him to subordinate his *duty*. And to have had an affair as they'd had, which placed his political future in jeopardy . . . well, Lily imagined that in Shriver's mind it was as though she were asking him to commit treason.

Shriver continued on about the host of challenges he would face after that afternoon's announcement in the East Room. President Smith had suffered withering criticism for cowering in his SUV that day outside Arlington. That criticism had only grown louder, particularly among

Truthers, after it came out that Smith had managed to inter Castro's remains at Arlington in a private ceremony, even after the tragic events on Memorial Bridge. Smith's approval rating had plummeted to record single-digit lows. As vice president, it would rest on Shriver to rehabilitate the president's faltering image. Fearful of impeachment, or worse, Smith had not only conceded to a unity government but also a national commission to investigate Castro's death. And if that wasn't enough, Speaker Wisecarver planned to appoint himself chair of the commission. Shriver became almost breathless as he enumerated the administration's many challenges. "There's only so much I can do right now, Lily, and my life is about to change. But I love you, and that's not going to change. You want me to be straight with you? You want the truth? That's the truth."

Shriver wandered back to the sofa. Silently, the two sat opposite each other for what felt like a long while. They had talked themselves out. Lily recalled that the last time she'd sat with someone for this long and in this type of silence was when she'd said her goodbyes to Sherman, in those minutes before the hospital staff had come into his room to shut down the many intricate machines that had kept him alive. This moment felt similar, like a goodbye of sorts before they pulled the plug. She interrupted the silence to ask: "So the administration has agreed to a commission? And Wisecarver is chairing it? I didn't know that."

The question seemed to take Shriver aback, but nevertheless he answered, "No one knows that. The commission will be announced on Monday. Not even the president knows that Wisecarver has decided to chair the commission."

She believed that Shriver was telling her the truth; that he did in fact love her. But she also believed that Shriver had betrayed her. He wouldn't choose her over his work. And so she had omitted one fact. As she'd watched Sherman's life slip away she hadn't been alone in the hospital room. James Mohammad had been there too.

⌐

06:45 May 04, 2054 (GMT-5)
Columbia Heights Metro Station

A little before seven a.m. This felt normal. A normal time to arrive at the office, a normal Monday commute, and a normal day, in which she'd answer emails, schedule meetings, and attend to her mundane administrative duties. So Julia Hunt hoped.

And she had reason to hope. The Friday before, President Smith had announced Senator Nat Shriver as his vice-presidential nominee in an elaborate ceremony in the East Room, replete with the Marine Band, bouquets of fresh flowers (all selected by Smith), and the poet laureate of the United States, who recited some verse written for the occasion. Hunt had staffed the announcement, standing in the back of the ceremony, ready to pounce on any unforeseen complication—an unseated dignitary, or a Truther who'd slipped inside to make a scene; anything, really.

But the announcement had gone off without a hitch. On the way back to his office after the ceremony her godfather remarked, "Our long national nightmare is over." She looked at him blankly and Hendrickson told her it was what President Ford said in that very same room during his swearing-in speech eighty years before. "This was after Watergate," Hendrickson added. "That's when Nixon tried to cover up a break-in at the headquarters of the—"

Julia cut him off: "I know what Watergate was, Uncle Bunt."

He apologized, "Of course you do." He stepped into his office while she sat at her desk outside it. At her computer, she'd looked up the rest of Ford's remarks that day, a simple 850-word address to the nation, including: *I am acutely aware that you have not elected me as your President by your ballots, and so I ask you to confirm me as your President with your prayers. And I hope that such prayers will also be the first of many.... Our Constitution works; our great Republic is a government of laws and not of men. Here the people rule. But there is a higher Power, by whatever name we honor Him, who ordains not only righteousness but love, not only justice but mercy.*

Love...justice...mercy...they seemed in short supply. There was still the matter of confirming Shriver. The Truthers held a majority in the Senate and the House of Representatives. Julia felt certain Shriver would have no trouble. It wasn't only Hunt who felt this sense of confidence. The day before, Sunday, Julia had gone for a jog near the National Mall, and for the first time in months she'd been able to go from the Lincoln Memorial to the Capitol without interruption. The Truthers had disbanded and returned to their homes around the country.

But as Julia's train sped out of the Metro station that morning, she glanced up at her reflection in the tunnel-darkened windows and her optimism vanished. Standing next to her was an apparition, Gunnery Sergeant Joseph William Sherman III. Except he wasn't in his wheelchair wearing his suit, as he'd been that morning more than a month before, when he'd tracked her down. He was standing on two legs, dressed in his camouflage fatigues and kit, as he'd been in the last war. He appeared young—younger than her, at least—but grimy and unshaven, wearing body armor, a helmet with the chin strap dangling loose, his rifle slung across his chest, his hands stuffed in his pockets. He was grinning, but darkly, like he knew something she didn't. Julia had seen him this way in an old photograph that'd accompanied the many news stories about his death, stories that included details of his distinguished service record but also details of what'd happened to him on Memorial Bridge. His image lingered there, until her train entered the next station. Then Sherman vanished.

When Julia arrived at her desk, her thoughts remained minced up and distracted. Images like this—waking dreams, really—had been a part of her life as long as she could remember. Her very identity, the fabric of who she was, was stitched together by loss. Occasionally the seams showed.

That morning, the tasks piled up as Hendrickson, Slake, and even the newly appointed vice president filed past Julia's desk. In the afternoon Wisecarver was set to announce who would be leading the commission to investigate Castro's death. The White House had agreed to a commission led by Congress, but, given Shriver's appointment as vice president, the expectation among those in the West Wing was that Wisecarver was obligated to appoint a Dreamer to lead it. Hendrickson had even gone so far as to provide Wisecarver's staff with copies of the binders he and Hunt had put together in their vice presidential search. Any of those candidates, all of whom were Dreamers, would have been an acceptable choice.

In the early afternoon, Hunt wandered into Hendrickson's office to find him seated at his desk, flanked by Slake and Shriver. They'd gathered to watch Wisecarver's announcement from the Capitol. In a briefing room, crowded with press, Wisecarver approached a podium. Camera shutters chattered.

God, he's old. This was the only thought Julia Hunt had in the pregnant pause Wisecarver took before beginning. She could hardly imagine all he'd seen in his more than eighty years, sixty of which he'd spent serving a country that had elevated him, discarded him, only to elevate him again. Today, he stood at the height of his powers. Watching him on television, she felt a begrudging respect for the old man. He had refused to quit. He was still here.

"My fellow Americans," Wisecarver began, "today our country faces a crisis, one that threatens our very way of life. In the past, we, the American people, have endured economic collapses, attacks on our homeland, and the scourge of disease." Wisecarver dropped his head for a moment, as if to say a prayer, but also to remind the audience that decades ago he had lost an immunocompromised child to the 2020 coronavirus pandemic. "Our crisis today is a crisis of truth, and it is the reason I stand before you. I believe that truth is the glue that holds government together, not only our government but civilization itself. . . ."

This final line took Julia back to that day in Wisecarver's office with Shriver. Wisecarver had said that a nightingale can only sing its song if it recognizes another nightingale singing it first. Was the truth the same as the nightingale's song? Was it merely a matter of recognition? She glanced at Shriver on the sofa. He seemed distracted. Wisecarver came to the crux of his argument. "In the wake of President Castro's death," he continued, "it has fallen onto the shoulders of this legislative body to appoint an investigative commission. Now, there are some who believe that this commission in the spirit of reconciliation should be led by the very people whose interests align with those who are being investigated. But would that serve the truth? And if the truth is the glue that holds our civilization together, would that serve you, the American people? I cannot abrogate my duty to the truth. Therefore, I have decided to chair this commission personally. Effective immediately, I will assume—"

A crashing sound came from the direction of the Oval Office, as if a door had been violently thrown open. A shout swiftly followed: "Where the hell is Shriver!" Hendrickson and Slake glanced at Shriver, and their eyes carried an accusation. Slowly, Shriver stood from the sofa. Then Smith hurled the door open. "What the fuck is this?" he said, flinging his arm at the television.

"Sir, I think—"

"Goddammit, did you know about this . . . ?"

Shriver glanced at Hendrickson, who shrugged, a gesture that conveyed, *You're on your own.* Slake threw up her hands. "You've got to be kidding me. You knew?"

"Sir . . ." Shriver paused a beat, his voice holding on the honorific as if he couldn't quite figure out how to get past it and on to the next word. "I wasn't at liberty to—"

"Who do you work for?" asked the president, cutting him off.

"I work for the American people," said Shriver.

Slake again threw her hands up in the air. "Oh Jesus Christ." She began to rock back and forth. "*We're so fucked . . . we're so fucked . . . we're so fucked . . .*"

"Karen!" Hendrickson snapped.

She glanced at him.

"Knock it off."

"Wisecarver was supposed to pick one of *our* candidates," said Slake. "That was the deal. We'd take him"—she nodded at Shriver as though he were secondhand goods—"and our guy would run the commission. Don't you see? . . . Wisecarver's going to ruin us with this commission. He's going to dismantle this administration piece by piece. Who's going to be left?"

Slake, Hendrickson, and the president glanced at Shriver.

Who would be left? He would be left.

"That was the plan all along, wasn't it?" asked Smith. "That day at Arlington when the mob surrounded us, you insisted on being the hero. I would've gotten up there and talked to them, but the Secret Service wouldn't let me, and so you insisted. That was all a setup, too, wasn't it, to discredit me? You and Wisecarver and the Truthers, you set us all up, didn't you? And that guy, the veteran, the one they killed, what's-his-name—"

"Sherman," Julia interjected forcefully. "His name was Sherman."

The president was too involved in his own soliloquy to notice Julia's irritation. "Right, Sherman," he continued. "I bet you planted him there too. All of this to discredit me. To discredit this administration." Smith's eyes cast wildly about the room, at Slake, at Hendrickson, even at Hunt, as if appealing to them to confirm his version of events. An uncomfortable silence descended. "Bunt," the president eventually said. "What do you think?"

Hendrickson planted his elbow on his desk and cradled his forehead in his palm, as if warding off a migraine. When he looked up, he gestured to the sleeping bag rolled up beside his sofa. "I think I'm going to be staying here for a while."

"I'm serious," said Smith.

"So am I," said Hendrickson in a tired voice.

"Then I won't cooperate with the commission," answered Smith, as if responding to a question no one had asked. "We'll announce a blanket refusal of all subpoenas from Wisecarver. Slake, how long until you can get the press corps assembled in the briefing room? Let me know once you have a time set. Major Hunt, come with me to the Oval. I want to draft up these remarks myself."

The president motioned to leave.

"Sir," said Hendrickson, "you're not refusing to participate with the commission. Not if you want to remain in office. The American people won't stand for it."

Smith ignored the remark. "Come on, Major Hunt, let's go."

"Sir," snapped Hendrickson. "Sit down."

His command to the president echoed like a gunshot. Everyone, including Smith, froze.

"Give us a minute," Hendrickson said, speaking to his goddaughter, Shriver, and Slake, while fixing the president in place with his gaze. Julia was the last one out of the office, and as she shut the door behind her, she caught a final glimpse of Hendrickson, who now stood in front of his desk, his arms crossed over his chest, as the president of the United States sat on the sofa, glancing upward, like an ill-behaved child awaiting a reprimand.

Hendrickson's office door was heavy, designed so that when shut hardly a sound could escape it; nevertheless, Julia could hear his muffled voice, its familiar cadence, one she knew all too well from the many times her godfather had also dressed her down for childish behavior. She sat in front of her computer, and her eyes migrated to its dark, vacant monitor. In that darkness, the image of Sherman reappeared. She turned on the monitor. The image of Sherman vanished.

⌐

13:57 May 07, 2054 (GMT-3)
São Paulo

Chowdhury awoke gradually. He'd taken a journey of weeks, in which he'd been dead or as close to death as a person can come. The cocktail prescribed by his doctors at Neutronics had slowed his body function to undetectable levels, and now they were bringing him back.

It took a while before he once again became cognizant of where he was and what he was doing there. A clock hung on the wall of the dimly lit recovery room. Vague silhouettes flitted in and out of the room, but Chowdhury had no capacity to focus on anything except the clock. Its stubby hour hand. Its long minute hand. Chowdhury tried to concentrate on its movement, but it appeared frozen. He had to look away and look back to gauge the passage of time.

Minutes . . . hours . . . days . . . Chowdhury couldn't say necessarily how long he stared at the clock as his faculties returned to him.

He heard a voice calling his name.

"Dr. Chowdhury . . ." A light flashed in his eyes, painful, startling. As he flinched, a muscle in the back of his neck spasmed. "It's Dr. Bakari," said the voice, which sounded like it was underwater. "You're in the recovery room. Can you hear me?"

Yes, he thought he said. But no sound came.

She repeated the question.

"Yes," he said. It came out as a dry whisper.

Gently, she propped up his head and placed a plastic cup of water to his lips. When she tilted the cup forward, he began to choke and sputter. Then his body remembered itself and he swallowed a mouthful of the water. "Well done," said Dr. Bakari as she wiped up what had dribbled down his chin and onto his chest. With great effort, he could feel himself smile at her. Spent, he shut his eyes.

When he opened them again some time had passed, and the room appeared different. It was no longer dim; it was illuminated under harsh bright lights. The clock still hung on the wall. He felt refreshed, as if he'd simply woken from a decent night's sleep. Sitting on a chair at his bedside was Ashni. When he turned toward her and said her name, she startled. "You're awake," she said, allowing a little sob of relief to blend with her words. She took his hand and kissed his dry, tissue-paper-like skin, near where the doctors had connected an intravenous port. Ashni reached across his bed to press the call button that would summon one of the attending physicians. Chowdhury stopped her.

"How many days has it been?" he asked.

"It's been two weeks, Bapu."

"So long?"

Ashni glanced away from him and she looked as though she might cry. "Let me call the doctor."

She again reached for the button, and Chowdhury again stopped her. "I don't want to hear it from them," he said. "You tell me. How did it go?" He propped himself up in the bed with great effort.

"The treatment hasn't worked," said Ashni.

Chowdhury took a ragged breath, which in its shallowness only confirmed what Ashni was telling him. "I suppose it hasn't."

"Dr. Bakari kept trying. That's why you stayed under for so long. According to her, the tissue around your heart should have regenerated. Given your physiognomy—your blood type, your mRNA-based vaccination record, and your ratio of red, to white, to nanorobotic blood cells—this should have made you an ideal candidate. Dr. Bakari doesn't understand it. She said in all her time working for Neutronics she's never seen a case like yours, in which someone with your physical profile has resisted their gene-editing therapies. They still haven't given me a good answer as to why none of it has worked. Honestly, I don't think they've figured it out themselves. But they've said they're not giving up."

"What does that mean?" Chowdhury asked.

"Dr. Bakari wants you to take a few days to recover and then try again."

"Try again?"

"We have to keep trying," said Ashni.

Chowdhury was now seated all the way up in his bed. His ashen complexion reddened as he grew increasingly irritated. "If they couldn't figure this out over two weeks, what makes you think they'll figure it out over two more? I'm not going to be their guinea pig."

She placed a hand on her father, to calm him. "No one is asking you to be anyone's guinea pig. Where do you go to get better if you don't do it here?"

Chowdhury was silent, but she saw something in his eyes.

"What . . . not that. Not Kurzweil."

"I'm strong enough to travel to Manaus." Only as he said this did Chowdhury feel it to be true.

"So you can become Kurzweil's guinea pig?"

"We should go to the source," said Chowdhury. "When it comes to this treatment, Kurzweil *is* the source." He swung his legs out of the hospital bed. With his bare feet resting on the cold linoleum floor, he mustered his diminished strength and stood. One by one he snatched out the tubes and nodes attaching his body to the network of machines that surrounded his bed.

"This is crazy," said Ashni.

"Are you coming with me?"

"Just hurry," she said. "Dr. Bakari will be back at the top of the hour."

They both glanced at the clock on the wall.

⌐

22:55 May 10, 2054 (GMT-5)
Four Seasons Hotel, Georgetown

Lily Bao was always on time. James Mohammad had come to admire her punctuality. In five minutes, at the top of the hour, he knew she would knock at the door of his suite. They would sit down and talk. She had helped him and his colleagues understand the ever-accelerating political crisis in the United States, and the implications of that crisis on the technological race for the Singularity.

In a way, their double life had begun long before either of them had committed a single act of espionage, if that was what this was. The death of his parents and his hidden obligation to his uncle, which had become an obligation to his country, had forced Mohammad to live in two worlds. It was the same for Lily, or so he'd allowed her to see. The death of her father, her exile to the United States, the death of her mother, all of this had contributed to her sense of a double life. As had her inability to ever, truly, find acceptance in this country. Shriver had seemed to promise that acceptance. He claimed to love her back. But Shriver hadn't been there on the night Mohammad found her in that hospital, when Sherman lay dying.

Mohammad had mourned Sherman's death with her. He made himself wholly available to her; and soon she made herself available to him. She told him about the encounter with Senator Shriver at the Hay-Adams; the fact that Wisecarver would be leading the commission to investigate President Castro's death.

When Lily Bao arrived at his suite, on time to the minute, James Mohammad handed her an envelope.

"What is this?" she asked.

"Open it," Mohammad said.

The two of them settled into two chairs in a corner of the suite. She tore open the envelope. An official-looking seal with an adhesive back slid into her palm. "I don't understand?"

"It's a four-year multiple-entry visa to your home country," he said. "I thought when you found the time you might like to visit." He watched for her reaction. This felt like hand-feeding an animal in the wild—a single misplaced gesture could cause it to spook.

James Mohammad's uncle had thought that offering Lily Bao a visa of such value after she'd delivered a single piece of intelligence was premature. Zhao Jin had figured differently. He favored decisive action. Political developments in the United States were moving quickly, too quickly, and a lengthy recruitment process could prove a costly mistake. Ultimately, over his uncle's objections, Mohammad agreed with Zhao Jin and the decision was made.

"This is very generous of *you*," she said, holding down the last word long enough to acknowledge to Mohammad that she knew who this gift was really coming from. She added a curt, "Thank you," and to Mohammad's great relief accepted the visa by tucking it in her handbag. Then he mentioned that there was something else he and his colleagues had hoped she might help them with.

"It has to do with your work at the Tandava Group. I believe you are familiar with a company called Neutronics."

She nodded.

"Well, it seems your former boss, Dr. Chowdhury, has been receiving treatment for his heart condition at their facility in São Paulo." This didn't seem to come as a surprise to Lily. She waited for him to go on.

"He's been undergoing an experimental form of remote gene editing that regrows damaged cardiac tissue. However, the treatment hasn't worked. Only a few days ago, he left the clinic."

"Left the clinic for where?" Lily Bao came forward in her seat.

"We're not sure," said Mohammad. "But there's something else. It has to do with your friend B.T."

"Oh God. What's he done now?"

"Nothing . . . yet. But we have him on a flight four days ago from Tokyo to São Paulo with a domestic connection to Manaus." Mohammad reached into the same briefcase from which he'd removed the envelope with Lily Bao's visa. He presented a tablet that contained on its screen some rudimentary details about Manaus, which she politely turned away. She hadn't successfully clawed up the ranks of the Tandava Group and founded her own private equity firm through ignorance. Brazil had developed into the largest market in the western hemisphere. Manaus was its seventh-largest city. "Why do you think B.T. has traveled there?"

"We don't know," James Mohammad said plainly. "We were hoping you might help us with that."

⌐

12:17 May 21, 2054 (GMT-5)
The White House

Shriver had lunch every day in the White House Mess. Smith and Hendrickson had left his office largely unstaffed. As the Wisecarver Commission progressed, they increasingly viewed him as a potential liability, a traitor in their midst. Shriver had a steward who could've provided him with a private lunch in his office, but isolated as he was he wanted to mingle with the lower-ranking White House staffers. At least in theory. Typically, he ate alone.

Day after day, Julia noticed him lingering in the back. The mess was small, only about a dozen tables in a low-ceilinged room, and at lunch hour very busy. You ate wherever the steward could seat you. On several occasions, as Julia waited for an open seat, she noticed how those ahead of her in line, when offered to join the vice president at his table, would demur, saying, "Oh, I don't want to bother him . . ." or, "I can wait until something else opens up." After Julia watched one White House intern feign an incoming call so he could step outside the mess, take it, and then return to the back of the line, just to avoid the vice president, she'd decided enough was enough. She was next in line and said to the steward, "I think there's an open seat for me there."

The steward grabbed a menu and escorted her through the mess.

"All right if I join you, sir?" said Julia.

Shriver gestured to the seat beside him. The staff had cleared his plate, and he was sipping coffee as he read from a thick book, which he now shut, resting his hands over its cover. A second book sat beside him on the table. Julia marked her order in pencil on a paper chit and passed it to the steward, who hurried to the kitchen. An awkward silence descended. "Pretty busy around here," she said.

"Not for me," answered Shriver. He gestured to his two books. The first, Julia recognized as a novel, a pulp thriller and perennial bestseller, one of those often shelved next to the self-help and fitness magazines in places like National Airport or Union Station. The second, de Tocqueville's *Democracy in America*, Julia vaguely recognized from a seminar she'd taken years ago at the academy.

"That novel any good, sir?"

"It's okay," he said. "The plot's a little slow, at least when compared to developments around here. But I probably should be spending less time with it and more time with the de Tocqueville." Julia could hear the fatigue in Shriver's voice.

"I have a book of yours," she said.

"You do?"

"Yes, sir, that day in your office, before you arrived, Speaker Wisecarver gave it to me. *The Nightingale's Song.* He didn't think you'd miss it."

"He probably didn't think I'd ever read it either."

Julia told him that she'd finished it.

"And what did you think?" he asked.

Before she could answer, the waiter brought over her hamburger and fries. The interruption allowed her an extra moment to pick her words. "Speaker Wisecarver is singing a nightingale's song."

"Maybe so," said Shriver.

"Maybe you are, too, sir." She bit into one of her french fries.

"Me?"

"Maybe, sir." She ate another fry.

Shriver scoffed. This was a somewhat impertinent observation for a mid-level staffer to make to the vice president. He pointed out that he'd done no media, made no public appearances. Since taking office as vice president he hadn't uttered a single word critical of the administration and had composed himself with the utmost dignity, beginning with his actions outside Arlington National Cemetery and up to this very moment, despite Smith and Hendrickson having iced him out of the very unity government he'd been brought in to create. "I'm so on the outside," he lamented, "that I can't even get anyone to have lunch with me. Except you, I guess." He reached down the table and stole one of Julia's french fries.

"Maybe it's just that you've got bad manners, sir."

"You've got bigger things to worry about than my manners."

"What do you mean?" said Julia.

Shriver shrugged.

As he reached for another of her fries, she pulled her plate away. "What did you mean?"

Shriver glanced around the mess and leaned in. "Do you really need me to spell it out for you? When I was chair of the Senate Intel Committee . . . the report you shared with me and Wisecarver on remote gene editing . . . the one you sent over just before Castro's death . . . the one that had the same sequence of code that appeared on Common Sense . . ."

Julia felt a sinking sensation.

Shriver continued, "It's going to place you right in the crosshairs of the commission and this controversy of who in the administration knew what and when. Smith didn't know about the intel, and I imagine your godfather will claim the same. If he wants to keep working at the White House. Really, the only person from this administration they'll be able to connect with that intel report will be you."

"But others knew!"

As Julia raised her voice, Shriver shot her a disapproving glance.

"That should matter," she added.

"Why?" said Shriver. "Why should it matter?"

"Because it's the truth. You're a Democratic-Republican, a Truther, that should matter to you."

Shriver let out a dismissive laugh. "Truthers . . . Dreamers . . . You don't really buy into that, do you? People talk about the divide in this country as though we were standing on opposite sides of a chasm. When the reality is we're all standing over the chasm, as if on a bridge. You're never going to get everyone to cross to one side or the other. Some people can't accept that. If they can't get everyone to their side, they'd rather blow up the bridge. Then there's nothing. Just a void we plunge into."

"So whose side are you on?" Julia asked Shriver.

"Weren't you listening? I'm on the side of the bridge."

He took another of her fries. She pushed the plate toward him. "You can have the rest."

"Are you sure?"

"Yeah, I wasn't that hungry in the first place." She excused herself.

As Julia returned to her desk, she realized that she had neglected to ask Shriver what his novel was about.

⌐

16:13 May 22, 2054 (GMT-4)
Manaus

B.T. and Michi had little information to go off of when they arrived in Manaus, nothing more than a suite number in a demolished office building that had once listed Kurzweil as a tenant. They wandered the neighborhood, filled with other abandoned buildings that also seemed bound for demolition.

The address had come from Dr. Agawa, accompanied by a story. It had begun three years ago when the Japanese government had settled on its strategy of creating a cat's game around the Singularity—a policy of technological subversion. Instead of incubating this technology for the benefit of his nation, Dr. Agawa's mission had been to identify where this technology was the furthest developed so that it could be turned on itself.

Ray Kurzweil was the furthest along in this race. Dr. Agawa needed his cooperation. How best to convince him? Dr. Agawa doubted he would prove amenable to working for a government, particularly a foreign one, after bristling at corporate control of his research.

Rumors coming out of Manaus, where Kurzweil had moved his office and laboratory, were that he'd begun to experiment aggressively. Some said he'd gone so far as to experiment on himself. Kurzweil had developed health issues late in life, a heart condition that he hoped to cure by modifying molecular structures in his own blood and tampering with its mRNA. A few snippets of research attributed to him indicated early attempts to upload a human consciousness, presumably his own, onto a computer. Kurzweil was on the cusp of achieving a heightened level of biological and technological integration. This lent an urgency to Dr. Agawa's mission. Certain bells cannot be unrung.

It was around this time that Dr. Agawa met Sarah Hunt. Nuclear nonproliferation had waxed and waned as a cause celebre over the years, though Dr. Agawa had remained active in the movement, attending conferences in which he represented survivors of Hiroshima, Nagasaki, and later places like Galveston and Shanghai. It was at one of these conferences that Sarah appeared, delivering an address to a disappointingly thin crowd. She began her remarks by describing in detail her job as commander of the USS *Enterprise* Carrier Strike Group. She talked about her sailors, about her years at sea, about the ins and outs of managing the carrier itself, which was in effect a floating city. She spoke clinically, and to Dr. Agawa it had all sounded a bit mundane, like hearing the mayor of a small city discuss sanitation routes and traffic patterns. By the time Sarah Hunt had transitioned her discussion to the sequence of events that led her to launch two separate nuclear strikes that killed tens of millions, Dr. Agawa had already begun to doze off. He woke up as Sarah Hunt was describing the annihilation of Shanghai.

It wasn't that Dr. Agawa didn't care. Quite the contrary, he cared deeply. It was more that Sarah seemed to lack an awareness of what she'd done outside a simple military context; that is, until an audience member asked whether she thought mankind could again bring itself to the brink of annihilation. "Do you have children?" Sarah Hunt had asked the audience member, who nodded back. "I do, too, a daughter. The world she inherits will be one with nuclear weapons, so a world where humanity has at least one tool with which to annihilate itself. What about other tools? What about new technologies? The tools are what make us human. They're what distinguish us from animals. But the creation of tools and their ability to destroy us is a schism that exists within mankind. So, to answer your question, *Will mankind again bring itself to the brink of annihilation?* I would answer that mankind has long existed on the brink of one form of annihilation or another. The work of each generation is to keep the species from destroying itself."

That evening, at a reception, Dr. Agawa spoke at great length with Sarah Hunt. He learned about her daughter, Julia, who'd recently left home for the Naval Academy. When Dr. Agawa remarked how proud Sarah must be, she gave a dispirited nod. "Julia is a very strong-willed young woman. I'm sure she'll do well there." As their friendship deepened, Dr. Agawa would come to understand the ambivalence Sarah Hunt felt about her daughter following in her footsteps, her fear that Julia might someday be forced to forfeit a portion of her humanity to the act of killing, which was in the job description of every military officer.

Julia's chosen path had left Sarah feeling defeated. She had confessed to Dr. Agawa that after her own military service she'd sought out redemption in parenthood, and didn't find it. He would offer Sarah another chance.

Dr. Agawa's instincts about her had proven correct. Kurzweil had immediately taken to Sarah Hunt. Dr. Agawa had sent her to Manaus with little more than a letter of introduction from one well-regarded scientist to another. However, Dr. Agawa knew that Kurzweil would intuitively understand how Hunt's experiences could inform Kurzweil's decision-making as he engineered new systems of biological existence that could bring humanity to a similar brink. He (the creator) would work in tandem with her (the destructor).

And so Kurzweil hired Hunt as a consultant. Over the course of a first and then a second year, the duration of her stays in Manaus lengthened, and her reports to Dr. Agawa became more expansive. Increasingly, her work seemed to consume her. The more she saw of Kurzweil's progress, the more committed she became to seeing it steered in a direction that aligned with Dr. Agawa's broader mission. The Singularity would be achieved—with a hard takeoff and the resultant intelligence explosion—so that it could be fully understood, and then snuffed out.

Several years later, as Dr. Agawa recounted these details in his office to B.T. and Michi, his pride in all that he and Sarah Hunt had achieved was palpable. Which made Dr. Agawa's great oversight even more bitter. He had neglected to account for the toll this work was taking on her. Had Dr. Agawa paid closer attention, the signs were there. Her trips home became less frequent. While in Manaus, she became difficult to reach, as whole weeks passed without response to phone calls and emails. When Dr. Agawa questioned her about the troves of research she was sending back—the sequences of code, the preliminary results of experiments on human and nonhuman subjects—she often grew short-tempered. When Hunt let slip that she'd been participating as a subject in some of Kurzweil's experiments, Dr. Agawa was incensed. Who was she to take on those risks without consulting him? A single misstep could undermine all they'd accomplished together. If she ever behaved so recklessly again, he'd have no choice but to recall her. When Dr. Agawa suggested that Hunt return home to see her family and take a break, she didn't resist. The very next day she was on a plane to the United States. A few days later Sarah Hunt was dead.

"Took her own life," Dr. Agawa told B.T. and Michi. "After that Kurzweil vanished. Here's his last known address." He'd passed them the small square of paper.

⌐

16:13 May 22, 2054 (GMT-4)
São Paulo to Manaus

Due to engine trouble, a four-day ferry ride became ten. Ashni and her father argued constantly. Their cabin was cramped, just a pair of tightly spaced bunks, with only intermittent air-conditioning. Each time the unit went out, Ashni asked again why they'd chosen to travel this way. Chowdhury had insisted they travel to Manaus overland, using a mix of taxis, buses, and ferries. He imagined the staff at Neutronics would do everything in their power to keep him in São Paulo, and he thought it prudent to disappear on a long journey.

One evening, after a dinner of oyster crackers and a mysterious stew, Chowdhury decided to allow his daughter to have their cabin to herself for a bit. Wandering the deck of the ferry, he came to the pilothouse, its interior illuminated by a pair of electric lanterns hanging from a bent nail. The lanterns swayed in rhythm with the current. The ferry captain, Manolo, sat at the helm, steering his riverboat, humming to himself, his baseball cap turned backward as he looked out into the night. Manolo always wore the same white-and-blue pin-striped Yankees cap, sweat-stained and grimy around the band and brim. Stepping alongside him, Chowdhury asked who his favorite Yankee was.

"The Babe was the greatest of them," Manolo said. His eyes remained fixed to the horizon.

Chowdhury didn't know much about baseball, but he wanted to keep the conversation going. He dug into his memory and made mention of some other famous players—DiMaggio, Rodriguez, Mattingly . . .

Manolo shook his head. "No, no, no, none of those names may be considered alongside the Babe. None of them played on the Yankees of 1927, which is the greatest team of all time." Chowdhury was out of his depth. But Manolo had gotten going and now Chowdhury had to do little work to sustain the conversation. Manolo explained that because the 1927 Yankees were the franchise's greatest team, it followed that the franchise's greatest player had to have been a member of that team. The cigar rolled from one side of Manolo's mouth to the other as he erected his argument on a solid statistical foundation—home runs, RBIs, ERAs, batting averages. Manolo conceded that an argument could be made for Lou Gehrig, who had also played on the 1927 squad. "But the numbers for Gehrig, they are not really there. So I say no, it is the Babe. Greatest of all time."

"Did you get your hat at a game?" Chowdhury asked.

Manolo laughed at the absurdity of the prospect; that he might find his way to the Bronx to see a game seemed as ridiculous as an amateur astronomer visiting the darkest spheres of outer space. "No," he said. "I've never been to a game. The hat was a gift, from an American client of mine some years ago."

This piqued Chowdhury's interest. "Do you have many American clients?"

"Aside from you and your daughter?" Manolo then glanced above him, as if he were solving a complex math problem that forced him to show his work on the ceiling. "I've had only one other."

Chowdhury lit up: *Kurzweil*. It could be.

Manolo observed that few Americans traveled overland through Brazil, which was a shame. "These days everyone flies in and flies out, never to appreciate the country, never to explore its interior. This river is . . . what is the word . . . *untouched*, yes? The Amazon is a white river. The Rio Negro, a black one. To follow them past where they merge is to go to a deep place in this country, to a different land. I explained all of this to that other American. . . ." Chowdhury now felt certain this other American was Kurzweil. He was going to ask Manolo for his name. But before he could, Manolo added, "She was very generous. I remember her by her gift."

Then, with a flourish like a ballplayer, Manolo took off his cap. He gestured out to the expanse of water in front of his window as though it were a cheering crowd and he himself had hit a home run, just like the Babe, the greatest of all time.

19:45 May 22, 2054 (GMT-5)
The Willard Hotel

James Mohammad had his suitcase flopped open on his bed as he folded the last of his clothes. Lily Bao had departed that morning on a flight for Manaus via São Paulo. His trip to Washington had proved a success, and his uncle and Zhao Jin had agreed that he could return home to Lagos for a bit. Mohammad had left his own business interests untended for far too long.

His flight out of Dulles left at a little after nine o'clock the next morning. The airline didn't run a suborbital into Lagos. He would have to fly atmospheric, which would take most of the day. This inconvenience was compounded by how early the concierge had recommended he depart for the airport, arranging an auto-taxi for five a.m. Typically, this would have seemed unreasonable, but navigating Washington's detours and road closures had become unpredictable at best. Since the announcement of the Wisecarver Commission, Truther brigades periodically appeared around the city, organizing rallies. Some were well advertised, drawing supporters from across the nation and occurring in coordination with local rallies for those who couldn't travel to the capital, including more and more outside military bases, with off-duty service members scattered among the Truthers. National or local, the message of these rallies was clear: the Wisecarver Commission had muscle and the Truther brigades were it.

The night before, news had broken of freshly leaked documents, again posted on Common Sense. A highly classified intelligence report titled "Advances in Remote Gene Editing Among State and Non-State Actors," issued only days before President Castro's death, showed that administration officials knew about remote gene editing and the hazards it posed—hazards linked directly to the president's cause of death.

Now, in the silence of his room, James Mohammad heard a growing commotion outside his window. A crowd had gathered on 15th Street, blocking traffic along its four lanes, which formed the eastern boundary of the White House. When he opened his window a crack, he could hear a surge of pandemonium below. No more chants of "Truth not dreams!" No demands for a unity government, a commission, or other policy prescriptions. Mohammad couldn't make out any message at all, except the occasional shout of "Liars!" He turned on his television. The scene outside his window was live on the news.

His phone rang. It was his uncle.

"Are you watching this, Jimmy?"

"It's happening right outside my window."

"Remind me what time your flight is tomorrow?"

Mohammad told him, and his uncle said he would call right back. No doubt his uncle and Zhao Jin would debate whether they could afford to let Mohammad return to Lagos given the deteriorating situation. What if this political crisis caused the Americans to shut their borders, or restrict domestic travel? He felt certain they would want him to remain in Washington, at their beck and call.

James Mohammad began to unpack. As he rehung his shirts in the cramped hotel room closet, he took some solace from the fact that they hadn't been in his suitcase long enough to lose even a single crease.

⌐

20:07 May 22, 2054 (GMT-4)
Manaus

B.T. and Michi had made little progress, despite their best efforts. As he sat in his room in the newly built Tropicana Hotel & Casino, B.T. fingered the square of paper with the address from Dr. Agawa. Behind him, Michi lay napping on the bed, her hair fanned out like a black halo across the white freshly pressed sheets. She had spent another long, fruitless day wandering the grimy, traffic-clogged streets of Manaus for any trace of Dr. Kurzweil. They'd traveled to a bank where Kurzweil had kept an account, to a public records office where he'd taken out a business license, to restaurants around his old office. Nothing.

B.T. was exhausted, but he couldn't seem to sleep. He kept turning over the square of paper in his fingers, trying to figure out his next move. He switched on the television, muting the volume. It was tuned to the news. B.T. watched what appeared to be a riot in front of the White House. The crowd was enormous, unruly, with its most aggressive members scaling the fence around the Treasury Building next door and threatening to breach the perimeter of the White House itself before Secret Service and Marines dispersed them with a fusillade of rubber bullets. B.T. read the closed captions. A newly leaked intelligence report on remote gene editing had led to renewed calls for President Smith's resignation. The anchor cut to a press conference held earlier that day by House Speaker Trent Wisecarver. The sound bite was Wisecarver's response to the question of whether President Smith should resign: "He should listen to the will of the American people." This was followed by a question about the possibility of impeachment proceedings against Smith commencing in the House of Representatives, to which Wisecarver responded, "Depending on the outcome of my investigation, all options remain on the table."

B.T. shut off the news. They needed to find Kurzweil, if for no other reason than he might be able to tell them the truth about what had happened to Castro. Would the truth diffuse this current American crisis? B.T. couldn't say . . . but the truth certainly couldn't hurt.

He needed to clear his mind. He had yet to take in the casino on the ground floor of the Tropicana. A few hands of poker, some rolls at the craps table, that might do the trick. He glanced at Michi. She wasn't waking up anytime soon. B.T. grabbed his sports coat, and quietly shut the door behind him.

As he crossed the casino floor, he already felt better, more at ease. His mind became both focused and relaxed. The slots ringing their jackpots. The clatter of chips. He played poker, then blackjack. His winnings remained modest, enough for him to carry table to table in a single hand. He wandered the casino floor, searching for the game that would deliver him the run of good luck he sorely needed.

Eventually he settled on roulette and stepped up to a crowded table. He took his winnings and concluded he had time for one last bet. He placed everything on black. The dealer turned the wheel. The ball clattered around. Then fell.

"Winner, red," announced the dealer.

B.T. pushed himself away from the table. There was nothing else to do but return to his room and try to get some rest. Someone grabbed him by the arm. He swiveled around.

It was Lily Bao.

"I figured I'd find you here," she said. She glanced at the dealer, who raked in all of B.T.'s chips. "This never really was your game, was it?"

⌐

20:21 May 22, 2054 (GMT-5)
The Watergate Residences

Her uncle Bunt's invitation to join him at his apartment for dinner had both moved and surprised Julia. She insisted on picking up something special for their meal. Her local bakery was renowned for its cupcakes (red velvet being her favorite), and the line of customers, as usual, extended down the block. Now she was running late.

She came out of Foggy Bottom station and glanced at her watch—more than twenty minutes late. She began to run, stumbled, took off her heels, and ran barefoot the last quarter mile. A cupcake box in one hand, shoes and pocketbook in the other, she dashed down Virginia Avenue with her black cocktail dress hiked midthigh so her legs could extend to a decent stride.

She stopped a half block short of the Watergate entrance to compose herself. She took a few deep breaths, removed a tissue from her pocket-book to wipe the sweat from her forehead, and balanced herself with one hand on a parking meter as she brushed the dirt from her bare feet. She slid on her heels. Her poise regained, Julia strode confidently toward the glass façade of the Watergate. The doorman, attired in black-gray livery, swung open the entrance at her approach. He dipped his head, offering her a small welcoming bow. As she dipped her head in return, her heel caught in the sidewalk's grouting and she pitched forward.

Her instinct was to throw her arms in front of her, to break her fall. But she was carrying the box of cupcakes. She wouldn't arrive late and with nothing to show for it. She cradled the box to her chest, and landed hard on her knees.

The doorman ran out to her. "You all right, miss?" He helped her up. "Fine, fine."

The cupcakes had stayed pinned to her chest throughout the fall. She was about to check on them when she noticed blood trickling down her shins. The doorman offered her some tissues and a bottle of water, which she used to wipe up the blood. She again checked her watch. God, now she was *really* late.

As Julia stepped into the elevator, she tugged down the hem of her dress to cover her skinned knees. She rang the bell and frowned as she examined the crumpled top of the cupcake box.

Uncle Bunt opened the door. Immediately Julia began to apologize for being so unforgivably late. "No need," he said, shepherding his god-daughter inside. "It's a nightmare getting around the city. What's this?" She handed him the box.

She followed him into the apartment. As they entered the sitting room she was explaining how ". . . the line was insane today, wrapping two, maybe even three times around the block . . ." Her steps then minced together. Perched on the sofa, with a nearly empty glass of wine, was Karen Slake.

Slake stood. "Nice to see you, Major Hunt."

Julia tugged down the hem of her dress. "Oh, hi."

"I thought Karen should join us," Hendrickson said from over his shoulder, as he set the box of cupcakes on a counter in the kitchenette that opened onto the sitting area. The apartment was modest, a classic bachelor pad, with empty walls and mostly empty cupboards. A suitcase lingered by the door. A console beneath the television housed a cluster of framed photographs—Hendrickson's children at their graduations, his promotion ceremony to flag rank, the birth of a grandchild. There was also a photo of Hendrickson alongside Sarah Hunt and Julia when she was nine years old; Julia's dark hair was long and untended, its frayed ends hanging nearly to her waist. Hendrickson had come to stay with Sarah in New Mexico right after Julia's adoption, to lend an extra set of hands. He'd remained for a couple of weeks, taking Julia fishing in a nearby stream each afternoon. He'd taught her to find bait worms beneath the dark shaded stones so she could fish on her own when he was gone. The picture was taken in front of Sarah Hunt's adobe ranch house on the day Hendrickson left. Julia remembered the day well, how she'd sobbed and how panicked she'd felt when she'd thought that her godfather might be abandoning her.

"You look exactly the same," Slake said. She lifted the frame to give the photograph a closer inspection.

"She's done quite a bit of growing up since then." Hendrickson handed a fresh glass of wine to his goddaughter. The three of them sat around the coffee table and sipped their wine. The conversation was relaxed, genial. Although they discussed the crisis, they did so in a light manner, swapping stories like war veterans who'd determined that if they didn't laugh about what they'd been through, they'd cry.

Slake recalled the press conference when the fly had very publicly landed in then–Vice President Smith's hair. Afterward, she said, he'd insisted that a member of her staff fumigate any room before he would speak on television. The young aide assigned to fumigation duty came down sick with chemical poisoning. The vice president insisted on filling out and submitting the workman's comp paperwork himself.

Hendrickson told the story of finding the president wandering the halls of the White House picking out floral arrangements after Castro's death.

Not to be bested entirely by her two older colleagues, Julia chimed in, describing her recent lunch with Vice President Shriver. "Each day he eats alone in the White House Mess," she said.

"I didn't know that," Hendrickson said.

Hendrickson had prepared salad and an entrée that struck Julia as a cross between a stew, a casserole, and a lasagna. She took a first bite. So did Slake. They each gulped a large mouthful of wine and reached for the bread.

"I've seen him there," said Slake, moving her food around her plate. "He sits at a table reading all through lunch."

"He reads de Tocqueville," added Julia. "And novels."

Slake laughed. Hendrickson said, "You'd think he could find something better to do."

"He thinks you and the president are suspicious of him, that you believe he's a plant placed in the White House by Wisecarver." An uncomfortable silence settled around the table. Julia added, "He's upset that he isn't playing a larger role in the unity government."

Hendrickson scoffed. "It's difficult for the vice president to play a role in a government that his allies are trying to undermine. Don't you think?" Hendrickson nodded once to Slake, who engaged the headsUp on her wrist. A holographic screen projected in front of Julia that contained a news story about the leaked classified intelligence report on remote gene editing. This report, which the Wisecarver Commission was now calling "a smoking gun in Castro's assassination," had only been handled by one person in the White House. When Julia Hunt read her own name in the story, she dropped her fork on her plate.

"I've convinced the journalist to hold the piece for twenty-four hours," said Slake. "I can't get us more time than that."

"That intel report included the sequence of code leaked on Common Sense that was used to assassinate President Castro," explained Hendrickson. "This story makes you the only verifiable link in its chain of custody. Julia, I'm sorry, but it also makes you a liability to this White House."

"What does that mean?"

Hendrickson glanced at Slake, who encouraged him on with a look. No one was eating, so he stood and began to clear their plates. He was at the sink, with his back to his goddaughter, when he said, "We're going to need to transfer you immediately. When this story breaks tomorrow, it's imperative that we're able to say you're a former as opposed to a current member of the White House staff."

Julia felt the grip of an old yet familiar panic: he was abandoning her.

"Transfer me where?" asked Julia.

Hendrickson had finished with their dishes, but he still hadn't turned around at the sink. "Back to 8th and I."

"To the Marine barracks . . . ?" Julia said incredulously. "You're going to make me work for Dozer again . . . for *fucking* Dozer . . . for Dozer?" She kept saying the name of that lecherous colonel, the one Hendrickson had saved her from by bringing her to the White House. She kept saying his name because she wanted it to echo in her godfather's ears as a reminder of the fate to which he was abandoning her. Julia stood to leave, her chair violently stuttering across the floor.

Finally, Hendrickson turned around. "Julia," he said, very calmly. "Sit down." His authority as a parent—or even a godparent—still held some sway, and she sat. Hendrickson returned to the table carrying the box of cupcakes. As he set it in the center of the table, he explained, "I've put a call in to Dozer. He's not going to cause you any problems. The Marines at the barracks have been stretched thin dealing with the Truther brigades around the city. The fact is they're short of officers and could really use you. . . . This is happening, Julia. The less said, the better."

She sat there, staring at her plate. Those words—*This is happening, Julia*—reverberated in her thoughts. How much of her life—from the death of her biological parents to the suicide of her adoptive mother—could be summarized by her reaction to similar words?

"Aww shit," said Hendrickson. Her godfather's cursing as he opened the box of cupcakes snapped Julia back into the moment. "Looks like they didn't quite make it."

Julia glanced in the box. They'd been crushed. "Excuse me," she said, and stood from the table.

Hendrickson was forking the portions of a broken cupcake on a plate for Slake as he pleaded for Julia to stay. "Please, let's not end like this."

But Julia had to go. She felt a wave of emotion, a mix of sadness and betrayal, welling up inside her, threatening to overtake her . . . threatening to make her break down and cry in front of Hendrickson and Slake, which she couldn't abide. She shook her head no.

She stepped out into the corridor, closing the door behind her. Her knees hurt. She was bleeding again.

6

The Two Rivers

B.T. offered to pick up coffees while Lily Bao and Michi waited at the gate. The ferry carrying Dr. Sandeep Chowdhury and his daughter was now nearly three hours late. The terminal was cavernous and filled with others who, like them, had been condemned to a purgatory of waiting. Each hour a few ferries arrived, but they seemed to adhere to no schedule at all. Lily watched B.T. as he stood in line at the small kiosk. She liked to think she would have been able to track Dr. Chowdhury down on her own. But she couldn't deny that she never would have been able to find him without James Mohammad's help.

Michi, however, was one detail that had seemed to elude James Mohammad. Lily Bao hadn't yet mentioned her presence to her Nigerian handler. Lily wasn't quite sure what to make of Michi, and she valued these few moments alone with her, to suss her out.

"Your wrist," said Lily, gesturing to the constellation of butterflies tattooed there. "Those are quite—" She stumbled over the next word, landing on: "Something."

"Thank you," said Michi, turning up her palm. "I got them so long ago."

"A fitting tattoo for a *biologist*." Lily pressed down hard on the last word.

The evening before, B.T. had called up to the room, and the three of them ate dinner together. Over four courses and two bottles of wine, Lily heard an account of how Michi and B.T. met and why they'd come to Manaus. They'd told her about the recolored butterflies he'd released at Cape Maeda, about B.T. losing his dive mask down the trench so that Michi had to rescue him, and about how they had fallen in love and how Michi had committed herself to join him in search of Kurzweil.

"Butterflies are a bit cliché, I know," she said. "But I wasn't much more than a kid." She was barely out of her teen years, she explained, and passionate to understand how a species could transform from one form of life to another entirely.

"I don't think it's cliché," Lily said. "Life transforms. That's its nature, right? You study those transformations. Ergo, butterflies."

Michi tugged the cuff of her sleeve. "Well, we all have our interests. Was business always a passion of yours?"

"I always knew that I needed to make money," Lily said flatly. "That necessity didn't translate as neatly into a tattoo." There was ice in her voice. Was she really expected to believe that Michi—this tattooed dive-instructor-biologist who, with seemingly little effort, had seduced B.T.—

had also traveled all this way purely out of love and concern? Lily felt certain that Michi was holding something back, some hidden agenda. Then an uncomfortable thought occurred to her. What if this hidden agenda wasn't only something being held back by Michi? What if it was being held back by both Michi and B.T.?

Lily glanced across the terminal.

B.T. neared the front of the line.

Lily Bao had traveled here, deep into the Brazilian interior, for many reasons: out of resentment toward Shriver; out of a hope that James Mohammad might help recoup all that her family had lost a generation before; out of sheer curiosity as to what Kurzweil had discovered. But also out of a desire to protect B.T.

Given events in the US, the best way to protect B.T. was to find out what ties Kurzweil had to Common Sense, and exonerate her old friend of blame for Castro's death. In his communications, James Mohammad emphasized the rapidly deteriorating situation in Washington. He needn't have bothered. News coverage of the power struggle dominated Brazilian media. The two sides had climbed a ladder of escalation, heightening the level of incitement, violating new norms every week. Pundits debated the point at which it could be categorized as a civil war. *Once the shooting starts, it won't stop.* Lily read that somewhere. She tended to agree.

That morning, the Wisecarver Commission released its final report, the "National Commission on the Assassination of President Castro." This report concluded that the current administration, led by President Smith, had conspired against the American people by obfuscating the cause of President Castro's death. Although the commission hadn't explicitly implicated President Smith and his administration in Castro's death, innuendo descended like a fog, and the Truthers' activist base was now calling for an impeachment trial followed by a criminal inquiry.

The Smith administration had pushed back. Karen Slake had embarked upon marathon rounds of briefings with the White House correspondents' pool, while the president himself had submitted to appear on all the Sunday shows. Even the White House chief of staff, Retired Admiral Hendrickson, joined the fray. Damage control within the administration was an all-hands endeavor.

Aside from one key person, who was conspicuously absent: Vice President Shriver. He was no longer defending the administration.

Lily noted it. She was not alone.

B.T. returned with their coffees.

"This one is yours," he said, handing Michi the first cup. "And this is yours." He passed the second cup to Lily. "I'd give it a minute. They're pretty hot."

The three of them huddled together. A moment of awkward silence passed.

Eventually, B.T. said, "I hope I didn't interrupt anything."

"No," offered Michi. "Not at all. I was explaining to Lily a bit more about my research interests."

"Fascinating, aren't they?" said B.T.

"Yes," said Lily. "Fascinating."

This seemed to encourage B.T. to carry on. "The intersection of marine biology and evolutionary biology is an undersubscribed field. There's much we can learn about land-based species by looking below the surface of the oceans. For instance . . ." Lily was listening less to what B.T. was saying than to how he was saying it. His enthusiasm for this woman, this stranger, felt extreme.

"... so you see," said B.T., "Michi has helped expand my thinking as it pertains to my work too."

He stared at Lily like one actor waiting for another to say their line. Which Lily dutifully delivered: "That's great."

Just then a customer service representative interrupted them to say that the ferry they had been waiting on would be arriving in ten minutes. He pointed to a gate at the other end of the terminal through which the passengers would soon disembark. B.T., Michi, and Lily walked in that direction and waited.

⌐

05:55 May 25, 2054 (GMT-5)
Lincoln Park

It was Memorial Day. The night before, without warning, Speaker Wisecarver had called for an emergency session of the House of Representatives. He'd done so with the least possible fanfare, leveraging the holiday to his advantage. It was clear that he had wanted to place his political rivals on their back foot; this he'd certainly achieved. The federal government was closed for the day. Given heightened tensions after the release of the Wisecarver Commission's final report, local law enforcement had to enact a recall of officers to safely accommodate Speaker Wisecarver's request. This included units of the Capitol Police, Park Police, Metro Police from the District, officers from Virginia and Maryland, and the several hundred Marines stationed at the barracks on 8th and I Streets.

Julia Hunt, being a new arrival to the barracks, had drawn duty over the long weekend. When the call came late at night for two companies of Marines to mobilize for crowd control around the Capitol, she'd been at her desk reading. Increasingly, sleep had proven elusive, and reading helped to calm her. The book she'd chosen was nearly fifty years old. It predicted advances in remote gene editing and the integration of biological and technological evolution that had recently arrived. Given that the intel report that had gotten her fired had dealt with these ideas, she figured she should acquaint herself more thoroughly with them, now that she had the time.

That book, *The Singularity Is Near: When Humans Transcend Biology*, was written by Dr. Ray Kurzweil, still alive at more than one hundred years old and supposedly living in some backwater she'd never heard of, in Brazil. Julia had underlined many passages in her reading. They ranged from the fanciful *another intriguing—and highly speculative— possibility is to send a computational process back in time through a "wormhole"* to the disturbing *the body you choose for yourself in the virtual environment may be different from the body that your partner chooses for you at the same time.* She drew up short at this passage: *Uploading a human brain means scanning all of its salient details and then reinstantiating those details into a suitably powerful computational substrate. This process would capture a person's entire personality, memory, skills, and history.*

Was she reading this right? Was Kurzweil predicting the ability to upload the human mind? Julia recalled the post on Common Sense, the one that had set off this crisis. With that sequence of code now tied to Castro's assassination, she'd assumed the Singularity was a new and deadly kind of weapon, a tool of domination, one that could target a single person (or group) and, as was the case with Castro, stop their heart or otherwise kill them. But what if it wasn't only a tool of domination? If a person could upload their mind, they could live forever. What if the Singularity wasn't our destruction but our salvation? What if it could bring a society back from the brink? What if it could bring people back? On and on she read; and, as she did, she thought of her mother, the way they'd left things between them. Then another thought slowly began to form. What about her actual parents?

At that moment, her phone rang with the mobilization orders from Headquarters Marine Corps. Online chatter indicated that a half dozen Truther brigades, numbering in the thousands, planned to descend on Washington in solidarity with Speaker Wisecarver. To maintain order, the Marines would stage proximate to the Capitol in advance of the emergency session of Congress. Unlike other federal troops, the Marines at the barracks could be deployed within Washington, D.C., without President Smith evoking the Insurrection Act, something her godfather had consistently and stridently counseled the president against. Given political tensions between the Truthers and Dreamers, Hendrickson had feared that if the president evoked the Insurrection Act and deployed federal troops to Truther-majority states, it might cause a schism within the military, in which those in uniform who sympathized with the Truthers might disobey their orders.

Within minutes of the call, Colonel Dozer appeared. Julia briefed him on the details, which were scant. Dozer had kept a cautious distance from Major Hunt. Despite her inauspicious return to the barracks, he understood that she still possessed friends in high places, at least for now. Much to Dozer's chagrin, instead of warehousing Julia in an administrative position, circumstances had forced him to give her command of one of his three companies. He was short of officers, with two of his three company commanders under investigation for protest-related incidents.

One of them had gone so far as ordering his Marines to fire live bullets at a group of Truthers after they'd tried to scale the fence outside the Treasury Building. This was the night, a few days before, when Common Sense had leaked the intel report on remote gene editing. Three of those protesters had died. Their deaths were met with far less fanfare than Sherman's. It seemed people were becoming inured to the violence.

And so, at a little after 06:00 that Memorial Day morning, the barracks gates swung open. Two columns of Marines fully equipped—body armor, helmets, face shields, riot shields, greaves, with rifles slung across their chests and batons at their sides—marched onto 8th Street, took a right, and proceeded north, toward Lincoln Park. Dozer was at their head. Julia's company was the second of the two. She stood at its front, which placed her dead center among the nearly three hundred Marines.

⌐

10:12 May 25, 2054 (GMT-5)
The Tropicana Hotel

Another day of rest at the hotel. Maybe two. Chowdhury felt that would be all he needed to muster his strength for this final leg of the journey. Two days before, at the ferry terminal, his arrival had failed to go unnoticed. This hadn't surprised him. What had surprised him was that an old employee of his from the Tandava Group, Lily Bao, had been the one waiting for him, along with this B.T. fellow and his smart and attractive girlfriend. The three of them had explained to Chowdhury their interest in finding Kurzweil.

Despite his exhausting journey, Chowdhury might have proceeded directly upriver had these three not intercepted him in Manaus. He still didn't entirely know what to make of them. He'd asked Ashni to reach back to their networks in New Delhi to see what she could uncover. They discussed the findings as Ashni sat at his bedside that morning, checking his vitals.

"One-seventy-two over one-eleven," said Ashni, unfastening the Velcro cuff from his bicep. "That's better than yesterday but still way too high."

Chowdhury sat up with effort. He pulled down his sleeve and refastened a cuff link. "It's not going to get any better if we stay here. We need to find Kurzweil."

"Lie back down, Bapu," said Ashni. Her headsUp displayed her email, and she scrolled the holographic screen.

"Anything new?" her father asked.

"Nothing." She crossed the room to a tray and pinched a piece of bacon from a cold plate.

"You should lay off that stuff," said Chowdhury. "If you're not careful, you could wind up like me. We've got the same genes."

The idea of sharing the same heart as her father seemed to undo her. She exhaled slowly and wiped her eyes with the back of her hand. Chowdhury had never been adept at managing the emotions of others, least of all his daughter's. He thought of her mother, his ex-wife, who had died twenty years ago, in Galveston. Ashni had always carried the weight of that loss. "There's one thing that I can't quite work out," Chowdhury said to his daughter.

"What's that?" She sat down at the foot of his bed.

"Manolo, our captain, never actually said he met Kurzweil. He knows where Kurzweil is because he dropped a woman upriver, but never picked her up."

"You mean Sarah Hunt?"

"That's what I can't figure," Chowdhury said. "Sarah Hunt took her own life in the US. This woman who visited Kurzweil, she never left him. So who is she?"

"Is it that important?"

"It could be."

"Have you mentioned this woman to the others?"

"No," said Chowdhury. "And I don't plan to, not yet. Whoever or whatever killed Castro is up that river. And whatever killed him might be all that can save me."

"Us arriving there unannounced, do you think that's smart?" asked Ashni. "If Kurzweil killed Castro, I don't imagine he's going to want visitors. And what if it's not only Castro he killed?"

"What are you saying?"

"What if this woman Manolo told you about, what if she's also behind Common Sense? For all we know she could be as much behind this as Kurzweil. This woman might have something to do with Sarah Hunt's death too. We don't know."

"You're right," Chowdhury said. "We don't know. Really, there's only one thing we know for certain: if I don't find Kurzweil, I will die."

The irrefutability of this logic silenced Ashni. She sat for a moment on the side of her father's bed, thinking, then she stood and crossed the room. She rooted around in her luggage and returned with a portable EKG monitor, a little smaller than a television remote. This was a different test. She placed it on his lap. "C'mon, Bapu. Let's see what it tells us."

Chowdhury set his fingers on it as though playing a miniature piano. He tried to relax while his vitals projected on Ashni's headsUp.

A minute passed. The EKG made a loud beep.

Ashni's eyebrows knit together as she read the results.

"How does it look?" Chowdhury asked.

"Better," she said.

"Better than what?"

"Better than yesterday."

"It's time," her father said. "We should leave tomorrow."

"Soon," she said. "We'll leave soon."

⌐

10:52 May 25, 2054 (GMT-5)
Lincoln Park

The clatter of Marines, laden with their equipment, marching in step, echoed off the row houses and down the historic brick-paved sidewalks of residential Capitol Hill. Something was going to happen today, Hunt knew it, and based on the dour expressions of the Marines behind her, so did they. Having assumed command hardly a week before, she struggled to remember most of their names.

Long ago, the city had placed this historic neighborhood under easement, and it had remained nearly unchanged since Lincoln's time. Today Julia Hunt might lead this group into combat, or a form of combat, though not against an adversary she'd ever imagined herself fighting. Long ago, at Annapolis, she'd sworn to do this. The phrase from her oath of office "defend the Constitution against all enemies, foreign and domestic" looped through her mind. The emphasis had always been on the former of those enemies, not the latter. Her mother, Sarah, had been fond of a speech Lincoln gave, more than two decades before the Civil War, in which he'd declared: "All the armies of Europe, Asia and Africa combined, with all the treasure of the earth (our own excepted) in their military chest, with a Bonaparte for a commander, could not, by force, take a drink from the Ohio, or make a track on the Blue Ridge, in a trial of a thousand years. . . . If destruction be our lot we must ourselves be its author and finisher. As a nation of freemen, we must live through all time or die by suicide." America had increasingly come to feel to Julia less like a nation and more like a suicide pact.

In the center of the park that bore his name there had once been a statue of the sixteenth president. Known as the Freedman's Memorial, it depicted Lincoln, cast in bronze, emancipating a man who knelt on the ground in chains. Paid for solely by the formerly enslaved, the memorial, installed a decade after Lincoln's assassination, had proven controversial to later generations due to the enslaved man's subservient pose. Periodic calls were made for the memorial's removal. When President Castro came into office, his Public Monuments Commission reviewed all the statuary on federal land, including the Freedman's Memorial, which in a narrow vote it decided to tear down. All that now remained was a vacant pedestal where Lincoln and the man he freed once stood.

As the Marines fanned out around the park, Dozer established his command post at the base of this granite pedestal. He radioed for Julia and Major Barnes, the other company commander, to join him. A prior enlisted Marine, Barnes had more time in the service than Colonel Dozer. He'd fought against the Chinese in the Spratly Islands as a corporal two decades earlier. At well over six feet tall, he was muscular and imposing, the archetypal Barracks Marine, perfectly endowed for high-visibility ceremonial duty; except for one thing: his face. He carried scars from the Spratlys. They ran in fissures, like so many tributaries across a delta, from his forehead and down both cheeks. Julia had heard that his ex-wife lived with their six-year-old son on the eastern shore of Maryland. To spend more time with the boy, Barnes had requested duty at the barracks. It had taken a binder's worth of waivers, but ultimately his request had been approved despite his unsightly scars. Julia appreciated Barnes's quiet demeanor. He kept mostly to himself, and when he spoke it was often in single words, occasionally whole sentences, never paragraphs. She also appreciated that Dozer—who was younger and had none of Barnes's combat experience—was obviously terrified of him.

Julia stood next to Barnes, neither of them speaking, while she read from a bronze plaque at the base of the pedestal: *The first contribution of five dollars was made by Charlotte Scott. A freed woman of Virginia being her first earnings in freedom and consecrated by her suggestion and request on the day she heard of President Lincoln's death to build a monument to his memory.*

"Funny," said Barnes.

Julia hadn't noticed that he'd also been reading the plaque. "What's funny?"

"They kill Lincoln. He gets a statue. Castro knocks down the statue. Then they kill Castro. Funny." Barnes stopped as if on the brink of some broader insight, but instead he reached into his cargo pocket and removed a tin of Copenhagen, scooping out a plug with the hook of his finger, which he tucked in his bottom lip. He spit a long, brackish stream of tobacco juice onto the pavement. "Yeah," he said. "Funny."

Dozer gestured toward Hunt and Barnes. The three gazed down at a tablet Dozer pulled from his gear. A drone overhead transmitted a live feed of the park to the tablet. Dozer began to annotate its imagery as he issued his orders. "Speaker Wisecarver is scheduled to address the House within the hour," he began, checking his watch. "All morning long, Truther brigades have been dispersing around the city. We should expect that, if given the word, they could mass their supporters within minutes around the Capitol, so we'll need to be in position and deployed appropriately. Major Hunt, I'm going to hold your company in reserve here, in the middle of the park. I want you prepared to reinforce Major Barnes, who is going to man barricades here, here, and here." Dozer annotated the map with his fingertip, placing Major Barnes's platoons dangerously far forward of the Capitol.

Barnes glanced down at the map, frowned, and made three different marks with his finger, not saying a word.

"Okay," said Dozer. "Those positions work too. Any questions?"

Julia said, "None, sir." Barnes just shook his head.

An hour passed, then two. The Marines ate lunch from the rations they'd crammed into their cargo pockets. Wisecarver would only enter the House chamber once it was filled with enough members to take a vote. It took until the afternoon for this critical mass of legislators to assemble, but they eventually did. The Marines, huddled in twos and threes at their posts, watched the live-streamed proceedings. The streets, which hadn't been busy all morning, were now virtually empty.

⌐

13:40 May 25, 2054 (GMT-4)
The Tropicana Hotel

B.T. opened the door to his room and craned his neck down the hall. "Is it still there?" asked Michi. She sat inside at the foot of one of the twin beds, her right knee tucked to her chest. Bored, she was painting her toenails for the second time in two days.

B.T. couldn't quite see. He flipped the dead bolt so the door wouldn't shut behind him and jogged a few steps down the corridor. He glimpsed the DO NOT DISTURB sign still hanging from the doorknob on the junior suite that Dr. Sandeep Chowdhury shared with his daughter.

B.T. hurried back.

"It's still there."

"It's been two days. I know he needs to regain his strength, but this is taking too long."

B.T. asked Michi what she wanted him to do.

"You could go knock on their door."

B.T. made a face, as if he'd tasted something sour. "Why don't *you* go knock on their door?"

"Because I'm busy," said Michi, glancing down at her half-painted toes.

B.T. took a breath and suggested they wait another hour.

"That's fine," she said.

B.T. switched on the television.

Michi asked him to turn down the volume.

He switched the television off instead. "Why do you think Sarah Hunt killed herself?" he asked abruptly.

Michi twisted the cap back on her nail polish, though she still had three toes left to finish. "Why do you ask?"

"Because we've never really talked about it."

"Haven't we?"

B.T. shook his head.

Michi sat up straight, holding herself very erect on the edge of the bed. "Well, I think her work with Kurzweil began to consume her, that's why. When Dr. Agawa asked her to step away, the idea of living without that work proved too much. She reached her breaking point. Everyone has one. Don't you think?"

"Don't I think what?" asked B.T.

"That everyone has a breaking point."

"Sure, I guess everyone has a breaking point. But it doesn't make sense to me that Sarah Hunt killed herself because she reached hers. This is a woman who ordered two nuclear strikes, who wiped out Shanghai and Shenzhen. Millions of people, *poof*, gone. She lived with that on her conscience for years. Can you imagine carrying that? So, no, I don't think a chewing out by Dr. Agawa would send her into a suicidal spiral."

"Okay," said Michi. "Then what did?"

"I don't know . . . but whatever it was, it must have been something she saw or learned about up there with Kurzweil." B.T. swung his feet down from the bed. He leaned toward Michi so that his eyes were level with hers. "Whatever's farther up that river is what killed Castro. And it might have killed Sarah Hunt. That scares me. Doesn't it scare you?"

A knock at the door interrupted them. It was Lily Bao.

"What are you guys doing in here?" she asked.

"Waiting," said Michi. "Dr. Chowdhury and his daughter have a DO NOT DISTURB sign on their door."

"No, they don't," said Lily.

B.T. stepped out into the corridor. The sign was gone.

"I've spoken to Ashni," said Lily. "The ferry captain who brought her and her father here has agreed to take us upriver." She snatched the remote from the foot of the bed and turned on the television. It flashed images of US Marines securing the Capitol. The chyron at the bottom of the screen described an emergency session of Congress. Lily lingered for a few minutes, watching. "Let's hope we find something up there that makes sense of this," she said, and then returned to her room.

B.T. switched off the television and wandered over to the dresser. He took out his suitcase and began to repack his things. Michi remained sitting on the bed with both her knees hugged into her body, watching him. Eventually, she said, "I didn't answer your question from before."

"What question?" B.T. was standing in the center of the room, his chin pinning the collar of a shirt to his chest as he folded its sleeves.

"Whether I'm scared of what we'll find up that river."

"And are you?"

"Yes," she said. "I'm terrified."

⌐

13:41 May 25, 2054 (GMT-5)
Lincoln Park

Wisecarver didn't appear right away.

From the back of the chamber, sitting on the Dreamers' side of the gallery, a freshman congresswoman took the floor. She represented a district in New Mexico that had historically voted straight Democratic but flipped Dreamer as so many had when Castro won his first term more than a decade before. Despite her relative youth, she had the sad eyes of a woman grown weary of explaining things that should need no explanation, like a teacher at a failing school.

Because the legislative business of the day hadn't yet begun, and wouldn't begin until Wisecarver arrived, she used this time to deliver a short one-minute speech, which according to floor procedure would be the maximum amount of time allocated to her or any other member before the day's official session commenced. It would be enough, though. Her message was simple. She delivered it dispassionately from a single sheet of paper she removed from her pocket. "I've taken the weekend before this Memorial Day to read in full the 'National Commission on the Assassination of President Castro,' also known as the Wisecarver Commission Report. Its findings are compelling and call into question the legitimacy of the Smith administration, which it would seem colluded in both the cover-up and quite possibly the assassination of a sitting American president. I cannot in good conscience continue to caucus with a party led by such a president. I call on this legislative body to initiate impeachment proceedings against President Smith, followed by a prompt criminal inquiry. Effective immediately, I also renounce my membership in the American Dream Party, declare my independent affiliation, and choose to caucus with the Democratic-Republicans."

She folded the paper and placed it back in her jacket. She paused a moment, as one might when paying their respects at a grave. By the time she'd turned around, a line of several dozen other members had formed behind her. Each stepped to the dais, read the exact same statement, and returned to their seat.

Julia Hunt was watching this in Lincoln Park with two of her Marines, who projected the proceedings from a headsUp tuned to C-SPAN. Eventually one of them asked her what was going on. "The Dreamers are defecting," she said. The two young Marines returned vacant stares, so she added, "Someone must've gotten to them. They're switching parties. This is going to change everything."

Then Wisecarver made his entrance to the chamber.

188

He sauntered up to the speaker's chair like he was taking his favorite booth at a hard-to-book restaurant. When the last of the defecting members returned to their seats, Wisecarver cracked down his gavel. He brought the chamber to order. It was time for the day's business.

Wisecarver also began by removing a single sheet of paper from his coat pocket. He made a final study of his remarks, taking his time. He even uncapped a fountain pen, struck out one word, and wrote another in its place, ostentatiously recapping the pen. No one spoke as he did this. His last-minute edits seemed less about improving his message and more like a bit of political theater, proof that he could take as long as he wanted because he exercised total control over this legislative body.

"Our president," he began, "is dead. We have no other." He allowed his eyes to roam the crowd and drill into the few remaining members of his opposition before continuing, "What we have is an administration that at best has disqualified itself through negligence, and at worst has conspired in an assassination. Now, this administration would tell you otherwise. They would tell you that hidden, malicious forces were responsible for the death of President Castro. They point to suspicious sequences of code housed on strange websites while asking you to ignore self-evident facts, to forget their cover-up, to forget those shameful and flagrant lies dispensed to the American people, those lies which we remember, those lies for which we have proof!"

Wisecarver reached beneath the podium. He removed a sheath of papers several inches thick, which a staffer must have left for him. It was his commission's report. Wisecarver brandished it like a weapon, sweeping it from left to right across the chamber, while his voice grew louder. "President Smith would even ask you to ignore that he, more than anyone else, had the most to gain from President Castro's death. They call themselves Dreamers because our republic began as a dream, one conjured by our Founding Fathers and made real through the energy and sacrifice of generations of Americans. But when that dream isn't rooted in fact, when that dream is rooted in fictions, the dream becomes a nightmare. First the Truth. Then the dream."

Wisecarver took a sip from a clear glass of water in front of him. He used this pause—the hush of it—for dramatic effect. It elicited low affirmative mumbling from the chamber as his supporters turned to one another and repeated his last two lines for a perfect—even choreographed—result: *First the Truth. Then the dream.*

Wisecarver held up his hand. Silence returned to the chamber. "Our government gives us the tools to seek the truth, tools I have been reluctant to deploy. Until now. The resolve of my colleagues, from both parties"—he gestured toward the gentlewoman from New Mexico, his first defection—"gives me the courage to deploy these tools. For the past several months, we have been investigating the facts in our commission so the House can gather all of the relevant evidence and consider whether to exercise its full Article I powers. Today, I'm announcing that we will exercise a constitutional measure of the utmost gravity. Today I am introducing articles of impeachment against President Smith."

"Here we go," said one of the Marines standing next to Julia, watching the live feed. His voice was inflected with a type of doomy pragmatism common to fighting men throughout the ages. Neither of them needed any explanation as to how articles of impeachment would escalate the ongoing crisis. Unless the actual assassins were to present themselves to the authorities with incontrovertible proof of their crimes, the innuendo and recriminations around Castro's death would likely prove more damaging to the country than the assassination itself. Julia could see this clearly. When a president is murdered, so too is a vision of America.

A chant, at first indecipherable, rose from the far side of the park, from down East Capitol Street. On the handheld radio Julia carried, Dozer ordered her to fall back to his position. There was urgency in Dozer's voice and Julia came at a trot. When she arrived, she found him watching both the drone live feed and the proceedings in the House. Dozer's eyes toggled anxiously from one to the other. The members were voting. The C-SPAN scoreboard of *yea* vs. *nay* ticked up incontrovertibly in favor of the *yeas*. The articles of impeachment would pass. Also on the live feed, a swarm had appeared, as if from nowhere. A massive crowd, larger than any Julia had yet seen, advanced toward the Capitol. The crowd wasn't approaching from the west, down the Mall, as Julia would have expected, but from the east. Two companies of Marines were the only thing standing in its way.

Although Julia couldn't yet see the crowd, she could hear it more clearly. Their vague chanting had become distinct, the fusion of thousands of voices. "First the Truth! Then the dream!" they shouted in unison. A cell phone tucked deep into Dozer's pocket began to ring. Dozer answered it with a crisp, "Yes, sir." The conversation was entirely one-sided. Dozer simply repeated those two words. His eyes widened as he received his orders, but he didn't stray from his response.

Events were moving quickly now. Barnes radioed back, calmly explaining that he counted "a few thousand at least. More than we can handle. Nothing violent. So far. Suggest we let them by."

"Negative," said Dozer. "Our orders are no one passes beyond this park." He gazed solemnly at his phone, as though he'd become the protector of a holy relic. Julia could only imagine who'd been on the other end of the line. It was likely someone quite senior, maybe not the president himself but someone the president could rely on in a crisis. Likely her godfather, who wouldn't return her calls. A simmering rage gathered within Julia.

Barnes came back up on the radio: "Crowd's moving around my position. I can't hold them. Request permission to fall back."

Dozer glanced down at the live feed. He cursed under his breath and granted Barnes permission. Dozer had deployed his companies too far apart. They had no other choice but to consolidate into a single line bisecting the park.

In twos and threes, with balletic precision, the Marines bounded backward. They formed shoulder to shoulder behind their riot shields. The crowd had breached the eastern end of the park, headed west, straight toward them, and straight toward the Capitol. Fifty yards of grass separated the two groups.

Then the crowd halted.

Inside the Capitol, the last vote was being counted.

The articles of impeachment had passed.

A deafening cheer rose from the crowd. The Truthers—a blend of paramilitary cadres in tactical gear, political activists carrying flags and signs, and thrill-seeking youths—resumed their chant, "First the Truth! Then the dream!" repeating it over and over, looping the cadence of those six words into a song, one they began to dance to in little spontaneous jigs that broke out among their ranks. Their protest—an expression of political will on an issue as grave as the presidency of the United States—had the atmosphere of an afternoon tailgate party.

Dozer struggled to make sense of the bizarre display. He paced anxiously behind the line of Marines. Then four young protesters sprinted into the vacant field. "Get ready!" Dozer shouted. This elicited twitchy looks among the Marines, who weren't certain what they should be getting ready for. When the young men stripped off their shirts, their bodies were each painted with a single letter outlined in blue and filled in with red.

"R-U-T-H," said Dozer. "Who the fuck is Ruth?"

Barnes, who'd begun to shadow Dozer, said, "Sir, I think—"

Dozer cut him off. "If they cross this goddamn field, I'll—"

From the back of the crowd, a fifth protester sprinted forward. He tripped, stumbling in the dirt. Clumsily, he took his place among the four others. With a superhero's panache, he ripped off his shirt, revealing an enormous T painted on his chest. This elicited a raucous cheer from the crowd; and, so encouraged, the five lettermen of T-R-U-T-H sprinted and juked around the no-man's-land that had formed between the Marines and the protesters as if they were five streakers who'd found their way onto the field during a championship game. When Dozer ordered the heavily laden Marines to snatch them up and arrest them, this turned into a spectacle all its own, with the five men disassembling and reassembling into T-R-U-T-H as they evaded the authorities.

Dozer, embarrassed and at his wits' end, had seen enough. "Barnes, Hunt!" he barked. "Deploy nonlethals!"

Julia noticed her Marines looking uncertainly at their rifles, which were loaded with rubber bullets. They nervously fingered their gas masks, which sat on their hips. "Sir," said Julia. "Could we—"

"We have our orders," Dozer snapped back, wagging the phone in the air. "Deploy nonlethals."

"Whose orders?" Barnes interjected.

A slimy grin spread across Dozer's face, as though Barnes had walked into a trap. "Orders directly from the president of the United States."

"He calls you on that phone?"

Dozer slitted his eyes. "His chief of staff does."

Barnes turned toward Julia, so his back faced Dozer. In that single gesture he seemed to preclude not only Dozer's authority but also whatever executive authority flowed through Dozer. "These people haven't broken any law," Barnes said to Julia. "The Constitution affords them the right to peacefully assemble. I'm under no obligation to follow unlawful orders. And certainly not from a president who is in the process of being removed from office. I'm not opening up on this crowd. No way. Not gonna happen."

It was perhaps the most Julia had ever heard Barnes speak at a single time. He then took off his helmet and slung his rifle across his back.

Julia did the same.

Before Dozer could issue any more orders or threats, up and down the line the Marines followed suit. Their helmets came off. Their rifles were slung.

The Truthers cheered.

The shirtless young man with the T emblazoned on his chest was the first to run across no-man's-land. He clutched an American flag lashed to a segment of plastic piping. The flag beat in the wind. Behind him came the swarm of Truthers. They soon mingled among the Marines. They snapped photographs and embraced the Marines like a scene from the Second World War, as if it were the Marines who had at last liberated them from a force of occupation. Julia quickly lost track of Barnes amid all of this. The last she saw of him, he'd been hoisted up onto the shoulders of the crowd. He was carried toward the Capitol like a hero from a sports field. Julia couldn't see Dozer, either, but she knew he was nearby. She could hear his telephone ringing.

She was standing at the base of the old Freedman's Memorial when the young man with the T on his chest found her. He still clutched his flag and effortlessly vaulted himself up onto the vacant pedestal. Then, standing above Julia, he turned toward her. "C'mon!" he said. "Get up here!"

She hesitated.

"C'mon!"

She began to climb, pulling with her arms and pushing with her legs. Her equipment was too heavy. She couldn't quite get the purchase she needed and soon gave up. But the young man wouldn't let her. He remained staring down at her. "C'mon! You can't miss this!" She then dropped her equipment, stripping off her body armor and laying her rifle at the base of the pedestal. He reached his hand toward her, and his eyes were very open, very clear. Unburdened, she began to climb and soon found herself at the top.

She stood, with her hand and the young man's hand clasped together. He then held both their arms triumphantly over his head and with his other arm he waved the flag he'd been carrying all this time. Below them, like a westward flood, the vast crowd approached the Capitol. Julia turned toward the man, who was howling in delight, his expression wild and unrestrained, an expression, she realized, that matched her own.

Standing at such a height, she felt the onset of a sudden, vertiginous terror. The city, the crowd, everything that was spread beneath her; it all appeared so radically different from up here, atop a pedestal.

22:12 May 30, 2054 (GMT-5)
The Watergate Residences

James Mohammad sat in his apartment watching two televisions. On the first was the news. On the second was a screen split into four live feeds: the lobby, both elevators, and the corridor outside his apartment door, a corridor he shared with his new neighbor, Retired Admiral John "Bunt" Hendrickson.

Zhao Jin and his colleagues at the Guoanbu had arranged the short-term lease on the vacant one-bedroom at the Watergate. Mohammad would approach Hendrickson and deliver their terms. With the onset of impeachment hearings, the Smith White House had become a building on fire and Mohammad would be showing Hendrickson the exit. Mohammad sat in the apartment, waiting for Hendrickson to return from another dismal day within the faltering Smith administration.

Faltering, Mohammad thought, was probably too generous a word. *Imploding* was more like it. The news playing in the background outlined the scope of that implosion. Wisecarver's successful introduction of articles of impeachment had taken President Smith and his staff off guard. The White House hadn't understood the depths of disillusionment that existed within its own party. Wisecarver's win appeared inevitable.

Smith, however, refused to accept the inevitability of his conviction in the Senate. When Truthers had marched on the Capitol, the Marines stationed nearby had proven useless, refusing to employ even nonlethal means to stop them. After the Marines returned to their barracks, the president vowed to subject each to arrest and a court-martial. The president had then invoked the Insurrection Act, ordering tens of thousands

of troops to the capital. Ostensibly, these troops would deploy throughout the city to restore order. In reality, they had become yet another political tool deployed by President Smith as he clung to power.

The news anchor explained Smith's latest directive, a government
shutdown, to include a temporary suspension of Congress. A statement
from the White House argued the federal government could only resume
business once order was restored throughout the city. The news anchor
noted that only about half of the troops mobilized under the Insurrection Act had mustered for duty. Where the other half were, no one knew.
"It seems tens of thousands of US troops have gone AWOL."

Mohammad absorbed the news with only passing interest. The most
pressing development for him was the update from Lily Bao the day
before.

Lily had exceeded expectations. With little trouble, she'd tracked
down B.T., who was traveling with a Japanese woman, Michi. Mohammad had passed along Michi's name to his handlers, who returned an
extensive dossier on her, with everything from her doctoral dissertation
(a molecular study of deep-sea xenophyophores) to her ties to Japan's
Research Promotion Bureau, whose chief scientist, Dr. Kobe Agawa, had
ties to Sarah Hunt. If Agawa had ties to Sarah Hunt, Mohammad wagered that Agawa also had ties to Hendrickson.

Lily had found Dr. Sandeep Chowdhury too. She'd described to James
Mohammad how she'd intercepted him at the ferry terminal in Manaus.
Chowdhury had immediately recognized Lily from her time at the Tandava Group, whereas she had hardly recognized him. Unshaven and much
thinner, he looked like a newly rescued shipwreck survivor.

Chowdhury's deteriorating condition troubled Lily. Chowdhury
knew the location of a compound, a half day upriver from Manaus, where

Kurzweil had moved after Sarah Hunt's death in the United States. Chowdhury wasn't yet strong enough to make the trip, so Lily and the others had occupied a bank of rooms in the Tropicana. Lily assured Mohammad they'd soon embark on the last leg of their journey. Mohammad had pressed Lily on when. "When Dr. Chowdhury's ready," she'd said. James Mohammad had said nothing more.

He now returned his attention to the security monitors.

Crossing the lobby's smooth marble floor, Hendrickson appeared on the first camera, while a pair of Secret Service agents took up positions by the building's front door. Hendrickson cradled his rumpled suit jacket beneath his arm, and he walked in a shuffle, as though he could hardly be bothered to lift his feet.

James Mohammad sprang from the sofa. He crossed his apartment in a dozen broad steps. He grasped a full trash bag he'd staged at the door, filled with a couple of old blankets. He would intercept Hendrickson in the corridor while taking his trash to the chute. Espionage—Mohammad had long ago concluded—and its attendant tradecraft, was often a very childish business, filled with silly ploys like this one. He waited, his hand on the doorknob, his ear pressed to the jamb, listening for the elevator's chime.

PING.

Mohammad took his first few steps too quickly, worried Hendrickson might get inside his apartment before he had the chance to deliver his already rehearsed lines. Hendrickson was a half dozen steps from his door, fumbling with his keys, his head down. He hardly seemed to notice James Mohammad barreling straight toward him. "Long day at the office, eh?"

Hendrickson glanced up, smiled weakly, and turned the key.

"You must be under a great deal of pressure." Mohammad stood next to Hendrickson, swinging his trash bag from side to side like a metronome.

"Do I know you?"

"We have a friend in common."

"A friend?"

Hendrickson's door was cracked open. "May I come in?"

Hendrickson didn't budge. Mohammad added, "We can talk out here if you like, but I think a bit of privacy might better suit us." He looked up at the ceiling.

"First, tell me who our shared friend is."

"Shriver," said James Mohammad. "Excuse me . . . Vice President Shriver."

Hendrickson exhaled heavily. He walked into his apartment and left the door open behind him. "You can leave your trash outside."

⌐

05:19 May 30, 2054 (GMT-5)
Marine Barracks, 8th and I Streets

Major Julia Hunt was now the senior-most officer. Dozer had vanished. After Lincoln Park, the Marines under her command had retreated here, to the barracks, where they remained as if under siege. No one was allowed in and no one was allowed out. Being the senior-most officer was the last thing Hunt had wanted. However, since she and Barnes held the same rank, it came down to who had the most time at that rank. Despite Barnes's reservoirs of experience as an enlisted Marine, Julia had received her commission one year earlier. And so it fell to her.

Barnes had convinced Julia to set herself up in Dozer's old office. "You're the commanding officer of the Marine barracks," he explained. "The junior enlisted need to see you in that seat. They need continuity. Continuity breeds confidence . . . confidence that they haven't betrayed the Corps. Or the country."

From her office window, Julia could see the well-manicured parade grounds surrounded by thick red-brick walls. For nearly three centuries, Marines had defended the nation's capital from these barracks, from the War of 1812 to today. Julia found herself thinking of this history. Did she belong to that lineage of defense? She didn't know. Her place in history would depend on events outside her control. The commandant of the Marine Corps, whose residence was a white porticoed mansion abutting the barracks, had not returned since Hunt had assumed command, a fact that did not bode well for her. But neither the commandant nor anyone else in Julia's chain of command had contacted her. The government was surely in disarray; still, she wondered when an overture from them would come. When it did come, it wasn't from the commandant, or the administration. This overture came from the speaker of the House. It came from Wisecarver.

Hunt was at her desk, reviewing a collection of modified security measures Barnes had recommended—a new network for their CCTV, changed protocols for drawing weapons at the armory—when a call came from the sergeant of the guard at the main gate. Wisecarver was asking to be let inside. Hunt stepped to her office window. The day was breaking in an early-morning blue. A single SUV idled at the gate. Wisecarver had stepped onto the sidewalk and was speaking with the Marines. Their hands rested on the grips of their rifles. They were telling him to step back inside his vehicle, a suggestion he didn't seem to be taking very seriously.

He glanced up. Her third-floor office was the only one lit at this hour and, with her silhouette framed in light, Wisecarver quickly spotted her. He waved.

The sergeant of the guard remained on the line. "What do you want us to do, ma'am?"

"Let him up," she said. "Only him."

⌐

08:45 May 30, 2054 (GMT-4)
The Amazon and Rio Negro, Northwest of Manaus

Manolo met them that morning at the ferry terminal, in a flat-bottomed skiff powered by two outboard engines. Dr. Chowdhury, Ashni, Michi, B.T., and Lily sat crowded in the stern as they proceeded upriver, to the convergence of the Rio Negro and the Amazon. A matronly older woman helped Manolo handle the boat, securing and untying lines, restarting one of the engines when it stalled. Lily had assumed she was Manolo's grandmother, enlisted to help them for the day. Manolo referred to her as "Avozhina," Granny. When Lily Bao asked whether she lived with Manolo, he erupted in laughter.

"No, Miss Bao," Manolo answered. "Avozhina keeps Dr. Kurzweil's house. She will guide us. His place, you see, it is not so easy to find."

Avozhina turned toward Lily and smiled with her mouth shut. Lily wondered how old she might be.

They traveled most of the way in silence. The roar of the outboard engines precluded any casual conversation. Everyone was sunk in their own thoughts. Lily understood that for Dr. Chowdhury and his daughter, Kurzweil represented a last hope. Dr. Chowdhury had needed help even getting into the skiff. Lily wondered how he'd fare on their return journey. Michi and B.T. were another matter. B.T.'s interest in Kurzweil's work was purely scientific, but Lily regarded Michi's aims with suspicion. Something didn't entirely make sense.

They soon cut off of the main river and made slow, wakeless progress up one of its tributaries. By early afternoon they arrived at a dock that was little more than a pylon stuck into the silty river bottom. With a wrangler's skill, Avozhina lassoed the pylon and heaved their skiff parallel to the bank, where the six of them disembarked. Manolo glanced at his watch. He uttered terse directions to Avozhina, who nodded. Manolo announced to the rest of the group that they needed to be back with at least two hours of daylight; otherwise, they would have to spend the night, as the river was too dangerous to navigate in darkness. No one objected. This would give them an hour with Kurzweil. Whatever each of them had come to find, an hour would have to be enough.

A single-file trail ran into the jungle. The sun, almost directly overhead, diminished into shade as they followed the trail, and then seemed to vanish entirely. The temperature fell. The absence of man-made noise became profound and the chatter of unseen animals invaded that absence. Chowdhury walked behind Avozhina at the front of their column, setting the pace, which remained excruciatingly slow. He required many breaks, sitting trailside for five or ten minutes, catching his breath, settling his heart rate.

After a third stop in less than an hour, Lily marched from the back of their column to the front. Chowdhury sat on the ground with his torso slumped forward and his elbows perched on his knees to support his weight. His daughter quietly encouraged him to sit up straighter, so he might draw deeper breaths. Lily caught a glimpse of his anguished expression. Lily took Ashni by the elbow. Pulling her off the side of the trail, Lily whispered, "Your father's in bad shape."

"He'll be fine," said Ashni. "We're almost there anyways."

"How's he going to get back?"

Ashni returned a stony gaze.

"I'm ready," said Chowdhury in a raspy voice.

"Come on," said Lily. "I'll help you get him up."

Chowdhury raised both his arms as if entering chest-high water. Lily took one arm, Ashni the other. They got him to his feet, and they proceeded up the trail. Avozhina continued to lead them, every so often looking over her shoulder to offer an encouraging, "Not much farther," or, "It's just ahead." Finally, Avozhina announced, "We're here."

The trail had come to an end, and all Lily could see to their front was thick jungle, a solid wall of impregnable greenery. Avozhina reached her hand between two closely planted trees. Only then could Lily see that these trees framed a door, and the jungle camouflaged this door almost entirely.

⌐

22:33 May 30, 2054 (GMT-5)
The Watergate Residences

Hendrickson tossed his suit jacket across the back of the living room sofa and gestured for James Mohammad to sit. The apartment's layout was the same as Mohammad's, but it felt smaller, stuffed as it was with the detritus of Hendrickson's life. Mohammad struggled to comprehend that the man who occupied this modest apartment was also occupying the most rarefied halls of American power. Hendrickson was rooting around in the kitchenette. Cupboards opened and closed. Ice cubes tumbled into glasses. Hendrickson eventually asked, "You a whiskey man?" Mohammad wasn't, but he said that he was.

Hendrickson teetered across the apartment balancing a large bag of chips, a box of reheated pizza, a pink bakery box, a can of nuts, and, lastly, two amber water glasses of whiskey in his arms. Mohammad stood from the sofa and helped Hendrickson unload the refreshments onto the coffee table between them. "So," said Hendrickson as he sipped his whiskey and settled into his chair, "let's start. How do you know Vice President Shriver?"

"It's really my colleague who knows him. . . . You see, she and Mr. Shriver have, for some time, been involved in a confidential relationship."

"Confidential? You mean like a business thing?"

"Intimate and confidential," Mohammad added.

"Is that so?" Hendrickson rooted around the pizza box, fishing for a slice, which he soon found, folded in half, and took a large bite of. "Did you come here to tell me that you're pals with the vice president's girlfriend? I'm not sure I'm following you here, Mr. Mohammad." He held out the box of pizza, offering a slice.

"I'm quite all right, thank you." Mohammad lifted his glass to his lips, barely sipping his whiskey. "Her name is Lily Bao, and she is my colleague."

"Yes, you already said that. So, what is it you do?"

"I'm in the information business, Mr. Hendrickson."

"Ah, I see." He was eating his crust. "And what type of information is that?"

"Nonpublic information."

"And your clients?"

James Mohammad set down his glass. He leaned back on the sofa and crossed one leg over the other while extending his arm along its back. "Not anyone you, your administration, or Vice President Shriver would want to be publicly associated with."

Hendrickson leaned back. "Are you trying to blackmail me?"

"That's quite an ugly word."

"Do you have a better one?"

"I simply think we should have a conversation about our shared interests." Mohammad stood from the sofa. He crossed the room and, stepping into the kitchenette, poured his whiskey down the sink. He returned to his spot on the sofa with a glass of tap water, took a sip, and added, "But no, I don't have a better word. If you want to call it blackmail, we can call it that. Except it's not you that we're interested in, it's Vice President Shriver."

Hendrickson wiped his hands with a napkin and crossed his arms over his chest. "Is that so? In case you haven't turned on the news, this country has far bigger problems than who the vice president is sleeping with. He's not even married. I'm failing to see the scandal here. . . ."

"He's been sleeping with an agent of a hostile country."

Hendrickson's jaw set.

Mohammad continued, "Mr. Shriver has passed along classified information to our agent. For instance, I have records of him revealing that

Speaker Wisecarver would lead the commission investigating President Castro's death. This was divulged to my clients, through Lily Bao, before it was made public to the American people."

"*Your clients* . . . let me guess . . . Nigeria . . . China."

Mohammad shrugged.

"Anyone else?"

He shook his head.

Hendrickson shut his eyes. With one hand he began to knead his forehead between thumb and middle finger. "Lily Bao . . . Lily Bao . . ." He kept repeating the name, as if trying to remember the meaning of a forgotten word. Then he opened his eyes. "Her father wasn't in the Navy, was he?"

Mohammad nodded.

"The Chinese Navy?"

He nodded again.

"So, Admiral Lin Bao's daughter."

"As you see, if this came out it would be . . ." Mohammad fished around for a moment before he landed on the word: "*Complicated.*"

"What is it you want?"

"The sequence of code that killed President Castro, the one posted on Common Sense. You've achieved the Singularity."

"You think we're behind that?" Hendrickson was incredulous. "Despite what you've read in the Wisecarver Commission, we didn't kill the president . . . mishandled the aftermath of his death, sure, but our administration didn't kill him. That's not how we settle things in our country."

"Do you expect me to believe that?" Mohammad's incredulity matched Hendrickson's own. President Smith, Vice President Shriver, Hendrickson, Castro's death had benefited each of them. In the history of James Mohammad's own country—going all the way back to the death of his grandparents and before—violence and domestic politics attended one another. If this was the case in his native Nigeria, it was certainly the case in Zhao Jin's native China. So why did the Americans always have to insist that it wasn't the case in their country, in their vaunted *democracy*? Castro had wanted more power than the people would give him, and his inner circle made sure he paid for it with his life. Mohammad was simply stating the facts, a pattern of events so common in other countries that one might even say they amounted to human nature. He could barely stomach Hendrickson's sanctimony. Americans, they were so precious, so self-deluding. Their exceptionalism—if it ever truly existed—had devolved long ago into an exceptional capacity to divorce themselves from reality.

"Vice President Shriver had nothing to do with the death of President Castro," said Hendrickson. And he spoke as if from an unshakable foundation. He then added, "And neither did I." Hendrickson took a deep breath. "Has it ever occurred to you, Mr. Mohammad, that my country, that your country, that perhaps all the nations of the world have already achieved the Singularity? Has it ever occurred to you that long ago biological and technological evolution merged? Look at the societies in which we live, riven by divisions, embracing technologies we know don't make us better off, that we know hurt us, and that we embrace nonetheless. Who or what is driving that? The technology has already won. It won a long time ago. We humans lost to it, enslaved ourselves to it, this is all ancient history."

"What about Ray Kurzweil?" Mohammad interjected. "What about his work into the Singularity? Are you saying he was successful too? That he made his vision a reality?"

"You must've read his book *The Singularity Is Near*," Hendrickson began. "It's a visionary work. Except for one thing. The Singularity isn't *near*. The Singularity is *here*. It's simply the latest technological master come to devour us."

"So you won't help me?"

"I wouldn't know how." Hendrickson's voice turned hollow and desolate.

Mohammad believed him, believed that there was nothing Hendrickson could do, that he was also caught up in events, events that had long ago exceeded his capacity to control them. Mohammad didn't know how his uncle and Zhao Jin would react to this news, whether they would insist on creating yet another scandal, another crisis, by exposing Shriver, or whether they would choose to preserve Shriver and Lily Bao for some future use.

Mohammad slumped back into the sofa. His gaze drifted out the window, beyond the Watergate, toward Georgetown. A smattering of lights reflected off the Potomac where a congregation of yachts had moored to a pier. He imagined himself far out on the water, unreachable.

"I'll explain your position to my colleagues."

Hendrickson thanked him.

Mohammad looked down at the bright pink box on the table. Curious, he opened it and found a collection of thickly frosted cupcakes dusted with sprinkles. The tops were a bit crushed. "My goddaughter brought those over last week," said Hendrickson. "They should still be good." Hendrickson wrapped a cupcake in a paper napkin and handed it to his guest. He escorted him to the door. "Please don't take this the wrong way, Mr. Mohammad, but I hope this is the last time we see one another."

James Mohammad paused short of the threshold. He held the cup-cake in both hands like a delicate bird. "I hope the same," he said. Then he noticed the trash bag sitting outside the door. He carried it down the corridor and tossed it into the garbage chute. Walking back to his apart-ment, he pulled down the cupcake's wax-paper wrapper and took a bite. It was stale. He turned around, returned to the garbage chute, and threw it away.

⌐

05:32 May 30, 2054 (GMT-5)
Marine Barracks, 8th and I Streets

Julia Hunt stepped back from the window and installed herself behind her desk. In the predawn silence, she waited and listened as steps echoed down the long, vacant passageway. Then came a knock.

"Enter," she growled.

"Major Hunt . . . good to see you doing so well." Wisecarver stepped through the door held open by one of her Marines, to whom she gave a slight nod so he might leave them. Wisecarver sat in one of two chairs placed in front of her desk. With head angled back, his gaze ranged the walls. They were resplendent with centuries' worth of memorabilia—battle flags, shadow boxes, oil paintings—evoking the gilded and blood-soaked legacy of the Corps. "I hope I'm not the first visitor to congratulate you on your new command."

Hunt placed her hands on her desk. She laced her fingers together and leaned forward. "To what do I owe the pleasure, Speaker Wise-carver?"

His eyes remained fixed on the memorabilia. "Someday," he said, "your actions will be commemorated on these walls. What you and your Marines did in service of our republic won't soon be forgotten. It was heroic. And it might have saved us. But I don't imagine anyone has told you that yet, have they?"

"Respectfully, sir, we don't need you or anyone to tell us about what we did."

A smile, like putty, stretched up one corner of Wisecarver's mouth. "No," he said. "I don't suppose you do. But you are going to need me for something else, Major Hunt. And not just you. The Marines in your command too. All of you are going to need me; that is, if you don't want to walk out of this place in handcuffs."

"I take it you have a solution to this mess?"

"I wouldn't quite put it that way," said Wisecarver. He slung one arm casually over the back of his chair, as if Hunt had stepped into his office as opposed to the other way around.

"Then how would you put it?" she asked.

"Right now you have precisely the right instrument, at precisely the right moment of history, in exactly the right place. Do you know how rare this is? A moment like this won't repeat itself for a thousand years."

"And you want me to do what?"

"Take your Marines," said Wisecarver. "March them to the Capitol. If my colleagues in the Senate can enter the chamber, then they can vote. If they can vote, we can convict the president. His powers will then vanish. You can save our republic."

"Who am I saving it from?" Julia asked.

Wisecarver threw his hands in the air. "Itself, Julia. You must see that by now? We have to save America from itself."

Wisecarver explained the mechanics. Julia and her Marines would easily overwhelm the Capitol Police, many of whom already possessed Truther sympathies. There would be no need for her and Wisecarver to maintain any further contact because when she and her Marines made their move on the Capitol, it would be widely reported on the news and elsewhere, so Wisecarver would see it. He would then mobilize the senators needed to cast the final votes to convict the president. Time was short. Federal troops had already begun to land at Joint Base Andrews, but they had yet to disperse around the city in strength. That would take another couple of days.

Wisecarver clearly wanted a decision from Julia, but she didn't offer him one. She finished their audience with a curt, "You've given me a lot to think about."

Wisecarver stared back at her. He was no doubt savvy enough to understand that pushing for more would result in less. He mentioned a meeting he was late for and excused himself. His hand gripping the doorknob, he glanced over his shoulder. "I remember your mother," he said. "She loved this country and was a woman of remarkable integrity."

"And how would *you* define integrity, Speaker Wisecarver?"

He glanced again at the memorabilia on the wall. "I'd say it's who you are in the dark. Who you are when no one else is looking. That's what they taught us at West Point. Wouldn't you agree?"

Julia offered a slight nod.

Wisecarver checked his watch. "Now I'm really late."

He hurried out the door, and Julia listened as his steps receded into silence. She paced over to her window. The sun was rising, casting slanted light across the empty parade ground. Her mother had loved this country; Wisecarver had been right about that. She wondered if he loved it too. Was he acting out of the country's interests or his own?

She caught another glimpse of Wisecarver below, hurrying across the parade ground toward the SUV. A distant trumpet sounded the first notes of "To the Colors." Wisecarver stopped in his tracks. The flag was being raised and protocol demanded that anyone standing outside stop, salute, or place hand over heart, and face in its direction.

Although no one was around—and even though he was late—this is what Wisecarver did. The flag was out of view, far away on the opposite side of the barracks. Nevertheless, Wisecarver stood, alone, for nearly a whole minute, facing the music, while somewhere an unseen flag was raised.

⌐

16:37 May 30, 2054 (GMT-4)
The Amazon and Rio Negro, Northwest of Manaus

They ducked as they passed through the door. It opened into a massive space, as large and cavernous as an aircraft hangar. Peeking through the living, breathing greenness that covered both the walls, Lily spotted a few places that showed the original metallic superstructure. Desks littered with computers, test tubes, beakers, vials, and the detritus of experiments crowded the wood-floored interior. Stacks of books, pages decomposed into mulchy bricks, crowded every surface.

While the others wandered around inside, in a corner Lily noticed two single beds in a modest living area. One of the beds had mussed sheets, as though someone had risen from it that morning. The other was precisely made up, with hospital corners slitted at forty-five-degree angles and six inches of exposed sheet at the blanket's top fold. Lily was keenly aware of the time. She asked Avozhina where Kurzweil was.

"Dr. Kurzweil, yes, he is just by the stream. Come, I will take you."

Ashni stayed behind with her father, who wasn't up for more walking. Michi and B.T. said they'd wait for Kurzweil to return. Lily followed Avozhina on her own. Their walk wasn't long. They skirted the outside of the facility and descended into a ravine so steep that Lily had to clutch the jungle undergrowth to climb to its bottom. She could hear the stream, a murmur of water.

"We are almost there," said Avozhina. The two of them stepped through the last of the jungle. They stood on a sandy bank, the stream at their feet and the jungle so close to their backs that its growth fell on their shoulders.

Lily shot a gaze up and down the stream bank. The windblown shadows of trees played across the water's surface. "Where is he?"

"There," said Avozhina. She pointed to a minor escarpment that jutted into the stream.

Lily walked perhaps fifty feet, so she was standing on the escarpment. "Where?" she called out over the noise of the water.

"There!"

Lily glanced down at where Avozhina was pointing. At her feet was a large black rock. She noticed an inscription scratched into the wet stone, as if done with another, harder stone, in block letters. It was his name, R. KURZWEIL, and the dates 1948–2052. And an epitaph: MY FRIEND.

The stream cut a clearing in the jungle through which Lily could see the sun, sinking toward the western horizon, its stubborn glow still brilliant and beautiful. She needed to get back to tell the others. But she also needed to carry the message home that Kurzweil was dead. If she could get into Manaus tonight, she could catch a morning flight and be back in the US by the end of the following day. She hurried up the stream bank toward Avozhina. As she did, she nearly tripped on another stone she hadn't noticed. It, too, was large and black, nearly identical to Kurzweil's grave marker, with the same style of block letters. No date was scratched into its surface, no epitaph, simply an initial and a name: S. HUNT.

7

——————

The Ocean

02:27 June 01, 2054 (GMT-5)
The Willard Hotel

James Mohammad finally heard from Lily Bao. She hadn't said much when she called, only that they'd found Kurzweil and she was on her way back to Washington. She hadn't provided any specifics over the phone, except to say, "We have a lot to discuss when I arrive." Her voice sounded flat and tired. She passed along her flight number and promised to contact him shortly after she landed. When they hung up, Mohammad contacted his uncle and Zhao Jin.

"She found Kurzweil," Mohammad announced. A holographic image of Zhao Jin and his uncle projected from his headsUp.

"Where?" asked Zhao Jin.

"Upriver from Manaus."

"And the Singularity?" his uncle asked curtly.

"She didn't say."

"Didn't say?" His uncle made a face, as if his nephew had brought home a below-average test score.

"She was right not to say," interjected Zhao Jin. "A matter like this should be handled in person."

"I could meet her tomorrow," said Mohammad. "Or the day after."

"I'm afraid we don't have that much time." Zhao Jin glanced at James Mohammad's uncle.

"Jimmy," his uncle began, "when Lily returns, she is either going to be in possession of the information we are looking for, or she isn't. If she's been successful, we'll need to get her—and you—out of Washington. We can't risk a full debriefing on American soil if she's found critical pieces of Kurzweil's work. We'll need what she's found brought back to us immediately and cannot risk trying to transmit it. Now, if Lily hasn't been successful, we'll at least need to get you out of Washington."

"And Lily?" Mohammad asked.

"If she's been unsuccessful, she'll remain in Washington." His uncle began to recite flight details from a booking made on his nephew's behalf. Mohammad stared out the window, across 15th Street, toward the White House.

"Is something the matter?" asked Zhao Jin. "We can hardly justify Lily Bao's resettlement in the People's Republic if she's failed in her mission."

"What about your talk of blood and soil, that her life in America was meaningless, that it was only a dream?"

"Enough, Jimmy," said his uncle.

"Or was it only true if she brought you what you wanted . . . was it only true if—"

"Jimmy, enough!" snapped his uncle.

Zhao Jin extended his hand like a police officer stopping traffic. "Please," he said. "No need to raise our voices."

Mohammad apologized.

"America is a sinking ship," said Zhao Jin. "It isn't our job to provide everyone with a life vest. The next few days will be particularly chaotic. We have reports that the speaker of the House is plotting to seize Congress and hold an impeachment vote. A conviction of President Smith in the Senate would result in Vice President Shriver's assumption of the presidency."

"What do you think would happen then?" asked Mohammad.

"You're the one who's there. Why don't you look out your window and tell us?" Zhao Jin deadpanned. "News reports claim that half the troops mobilized under the Insurrection Act have refused to show up for duty. We also have reports that the Marine barracks is no longer under government control; that's nearly one thousand elite troops with Truther sympathies less than a mile's march from the Capitol. Our analysts estimate that, depending on the pace of the crisis, American borders will shut within the next twenty-four to forty-eight hours. We need to get you out."

Mohammad's uncle added, "We've even heard of White House staffers burning documents."

Zhao Jin shot him a skeptical look. "Really . . . they're burning documents? Is that confirmed?"

Sheepishly, the elder James Mohammad shook his head. "Unconfirmed."

"No matter," said Zhao Jin. "You've got your flight details and Lily's. Intercept her at the airport. If what she has is worth bringing back, then take her with you. Otherwise, return on your own."

"And then?" asked Mohammad.

"And then what?" Zhao Jin asked.

"Our arrangement," said Mohammad. "You'd spoken about my becoming a *trusted partner*, that you might help with my business affairs." Mohammad glanced at his uncle, who he could see was growing impatient. But Mohammad didn't care. He'd devoted months to this work, taken great personal risks, and now he wanted an assurance of some reward. Zhao Jin assured Mohammad that he would be generously remunerated—as long as he was successful.

Mohammad got to work emptying the sparse hotel closet of his personal effects. He placed his tightly packed suitcase by the door and ordered an autocar to Dulles. Given the late hour and road closures throughout the city, it would take at least twenty minutes to arrive. He sat on the windowsill in his room and wondered when he might come back to the United States, and how it might be different.

The streets below remained quiet. It had rained earlier that night and Mohammad passed the time by watching the traffic lights shuffle their green-yellow-red reflections on the wet asphalt. After a while, his gaze again migrated north up 15th Street, toward the White House. Here, a few lights remained on, despite the late hour. He wondered what they were doing inside. He then noticed something strange. Smoke was billowing from half of its dozen chimneys. It was summer. Was it cold in the White House? Then it came to him. His uncle and Zhao Jin had mentioned reports of White House staffers destroying documents.

James Mohammad slid off the windowsill and crossed the room to place a call to them. But he stopped short. He glanced back up the street. They were definitely burning something in there. Still, he put away his phone. His autocar would soon arrive. In the end, he decided, his uncle and Zhao Jin didn't need to know everything.

⌐

03:00 June 01, 2054 (GMT-5)
The Marine Barracks

The phone rang in Julia's office. It was her uncle Bunt.

"Were you sleeping?" he asked.

"No."

"Neither was I."

"I know," she said. "You're calling me."

"Right. . . ."

The line went silent. When the call had come in, she assumed it was him. She had known he'd call eventually, and she'd recognized the three-digit prefix as coming from the White House. "It's pretty late for you to be at work, Uncle Bunt."

"I should say the same for you."

The line went silent again.

"Listen," said Julia. "I appreciate you calling, but we're kinda busy around here." She glanced out her window, to where a pair of heavily armed sentries crossed the dark quadrangle below.

"I know that . . . I mean, I don't know what you're busy doing, or what you've decided to do . . . what I mean is . . . well, I understand. That's what I mean."

"What is it you understand?"

"That this situation is difficult for you. . . ." Another awkward silence. "And that I put you in this situation."

"I haven't decided what I'm going to do, if that's why you're calling." Julia recognized that her tone was cold, but she felt her godfather deserved this.

"I'm not calling to suggest what you and your Marines should do."

"Then why are you calling?"

"Because I'm sorry, Julia. I'm so goddamn sorry."

"It's okay," she said, but she could feel her throat thicken and her voice constrict.

Hendrickson told her that he'd make it okay, that no matter what she decided to do or not do, whether she marched her Marines down to the Capitol or kept them penned up at the barracks, he would make sure that she was taken care of. She listened to him and said little. He didn't have the power to take care of her, not now and not before, when she'd lost her mother, whom they'd both loved. Julia was past believing in other people's promises, but he continued to make his promises, and so she continued to pretend to believe them even as they hung up the phone.

A book sat open on Hunt's desk. She no longer felt like reading it and she couldn't sleep. She had told her godfather the truth. She had yet to decide whether the Marines from the barracks would march down to the Capitol in the morning. The window for her decision was closing. From across the country—from Forts Tubman, Drum, and Knox, as well as Camps Lejeune, Pendleton, Twentynine Palms, and every base in between—the troops President Smith had mobilized under the Insurrection Act were arriving in Washington. In a day, they'd be deployed throughout the city. Her opportunity was now.

There was a knock on her door; it was Barnes.

"I was in my office down the hall. I heard you on the phone."

She invited him to join her. He sat in the chair in front of her desk, the same one Wisecarver had sat in two days before. Barnes's gaze didn't roam the walls crowded with memorabilia like Wisecarver's did. His interest wasn't in posterity; it was in today, and the decision they faced.

She asked him for his thoughts.

"I'm with you whatever you decide." He glanced out the window, to the barracks, where at reveille the lights would soon throttle on. "The Marines will be with you too. It's your call."

Although Julia appreciated the display of loyalty, what she needed right now wasn't blind loyalty, it was advice. "I need to know," she said. "If you were in my position, what would you do?"

Barnes shifted in his seat. A single desk lamp illuminated her office. The light produced strange effects, livening the scars on his face, granting them a vibrance like open wounds. He spat out the word "Truth," then with equal vitriol, "Dreams." Shaking his head, he said, "We have to choose, right? Well, I choose neither. I choose my son. We're in this jam because we didn't want to shoot other Americans. That puts us in a lot of trouble with the Dreamers. It makes us heroes to the Truthers. I don't care about Wisecarver, but if he gets the president out of office that means I get to see my son again. If Wisecarver fails and Smith remains president, that means I face a court-martial and jail. You will too. And so will our Marines. That's not *truth* . . . that's not *dreams* . . . those are the facts."

Hunt's choice, when examined outside ideological constraints, was a simple one. If anything, its logic adhered to that most basic form of politics: the realpolitik of survival. Wisecarver had already pointed out that she and her Marines had the power—at this specific moment—to alter the course of history. Wisecarver had been right about that. Hunt wondered how much of history, which was so often framed as an ideological contest, was decided by nonideological forces of the sort Barnes described. How often were the rise and fall of nations determined not by one ideology's superiority over another—whether it be truth over dreams, or capitalism over communism, or democracy over autocracy— but rather because at the point of decision people would do whatever was required of them so they might see a beloved mother, father, brother, sister, or child again—so they might remain together. When it came to sheer intensity, all the ideologies of the world couldn't match a force as fundamental as a parent's instinct to remain with their child. Julia knew this, and she also knew what it was like to lose a parent. Although she'd never met Barnes's son, she would make certain this little boy didn't lose his father.

Julia had made her decision. They would advance on the Capitol at first light. She told Barnes to muster the Marines on the parade ground in riot gear. On hearing her orders, Barnes popped up from his chair. With a display of formality she'd not witnessed from him before, he snapped to attention in front of her desk and shot back a sharp, "Aye, aye, ma'am," before turning on his heels as perfectly as a dancer and marching out the door.

The first shrill notes of reveille sounded minutes later. Julia sat at her desk listening to the controlled chaos of hundreds of assembling Marines. The voices of noncommissioned officers, propelled by expletives and filled with baritone urgency, ricocheted down the long brick corridors of the barracks. Three companies, each nearly two hundred strong, would soon form in tight ranks on the grass parade field below her window. Small unit leaders were already briefing the *who*, *what*, *when*, and *where* of their mission. When Julia stepped in front of them, all that would remain for her to explain was the *why*.

What was the *why*? Julia struggled to put words to it. Even though their actions would support Wisecarver, she wouldn't use words like *truth* to justify what they were about to do. And she certainly couldn't use the word *dream*. If they were successful, it would spell the end of the American Dream Party.

When Julia stood in front of her Marines, she'd need a better word. Then it came to her.

Home, she thought. That was the *why*, and that was her word. Standing in front of her Marines, she would promise them that if they trusted her, she would get them home.

⌐

04:57 June 01, 2054 (GMT-5)
United American Flight 8723

On the descent into Dulles, the cabin lights switched on. Lily Bao awoke with a startle; for a moment she didn't know where she was. Sandwiched in the middle seat, she glanced left and right. Gradually, her surroundings came into focus. To have slept this deeply, she must have been exhausted. She looked down at her tray table. A plastic cup of sparkling water reminded her that she'd ordered the drink shortly after takeoff. There it sat for the last six hours while she slept.

The knowledge Lily carried was simple: Ray Kurzweil was dead. She hadn't wanted to deliver this news to James Mohammad over the phone.

She had, in her estimation, lived up to her end of their bargain. A cursory search of Kurzweil's lab had uncovered no specifics on remote gene editing, or mind-uploading, or any evidence that Kurzweil had achieved the quantum-computing-powered intelligence explosion she'd heard so much about. This updated information on Kurzweil had value, she thought, and certainly more value than a one-off visa into the People's Republic, the only thing they'd given her thus far. But she knew that it would take some convincing for James Mohammad and his handlers to acknowledge that value and to make good on their promises to her.

Pressure was building in Lily's ears as they continued to descend. She rolled her jaw, but the pressure wouldn't subside. She shut her eyes, pinched her nose, and blew so hard she could feel moisture leaking from her tear ducts. Still, the pressure built. To take her mind off the pain, she forced her thoughts back to her work.

Her negotiating position with Mohammad and his handlers was strengthened by one additional piece of information she'd gathered; it was something she didn't entirely understand but which she suspected they'd find of interest. Sarah Hunt was buried with Kurzweil. Hunt had allegedly ended her own life in the United States. But this didn't seem to be the case.

After Avozhina had shown Lily the two headstones, they'd returned to the lab, where Dr. Chowdhury was resting and B.T. and Michi were poking around the cabinets, desks, and hard drives in search of any remaining shred of research. To Lily, the news of Hunt's grave had seemed like only a passing curiosity. To the others, it proved a source of intense interest, which was why Lily felt it might also be of interest to James Mohammad.

The pain in her ears was becoming intolerable. The flight attendant came around, securing tray tables and returning seats to their upright positions. Observing Lily's obvious discomfort, the flight attendant pointed to the cup of water. "Have a sip, it'll help." Lily did, and when she swallowed her ears made a squeaking sound and cleared. Immediate relief.

Lily leaned forward, staring past her seatmate and outside through the porthole window. The moon, a slim white crescent that looked as if someone had just finished sharpening it, floated in the sky, slowly vanishing as the sun established a faint seam of horizon against the darkness. Then that seam was drawn up, as if an enormous hand gripped a curtain of night and lifted it from the face of the earth. It was magnificent, she thought. Lily's stare remained fixed out the window as they landed.

Their plane taxied swiftly to its gate. Lily and the other passengers exited into the terminal, which was nearly empty aside from a few janitors supervising a fleet of automated machines that mopped, waxed, and buffed the gleaming corridors that fed passengers toward immigration. With wheeled suitcase in tow, Lily passed by an arrivals board. Nearly two-thirds of the flights had been canceled. She was lucky to have gotten in; it seemed the Smith administration was beginning to restrict international travel.

One by one, she and her fellow passengers stepped onto an autowalk that conveyed them forward through the vast immigration concourse. With its ceiling as high and echoing as the world's greatest cathedrals, Lily had always considered the immigration concourse at Dulles to be a sort of secular church. A familiar disembodied voice instructed her and the other passengers to stare at the screens overhead, which would image their faces and confirm their immigration status. Those screens typically played the news. Today, they played reruns of a dated network reality show, *Survivor*. A vast two-way mirror, which no passenger dared peer into, lined the wall adjacent to the auto-walk. Homeland Security agents lurked behind it, awaiting orders from the artificial intelligence that powered the entire border security system. If the wrong face appeared, those agents would escort the offending party behind the mirror, to a secure interrogation room for secondary questioning.

Lily did her best to concentrate on the screens. The last thing she wanted was to draw attention to herself. She had engaged in espionage and worked under the employ of a foreign government against the interests of her own; yes, her work had yielded a mixed result; and yes, her government couldn't even agree on what its own interests were; but none of this relieved her anxiety as the auto-walk trundled forward. She kept her attention on the screens overhead. Soon she found herself more than halfway through the concourse. The twin double doors at its end opened and closed, opened and closed. . . . She counted only a half dozen passengers ahead of her.

The auto-walk stopped.

A uniformed Homeland Security officer appeared. "Ms. Bao," he said. "I'll need you to come with me."

Lily's body froze while her mind raced. She would be accused of treason against her country. . . . Just as her father had been accused of treason against his. . . . She had wanted to clear her father's name. . . . In so doing she would tarnish her own name. . . . And it would be with the exact crime that had tarnished his. . . .

The agent escorted Lily off the auto-walk. Once out of sight from the public, he handcuffed her, "for your safety," which not even he seemed to believe. The agent spoke an alphanumeric code into the radio fastened to his shoulder. A staticky voice replied, "We're ready for her in B22." With Lily's hands secured behind her, the agent escorted her through a warren of narrow corridors barely wide enough for two people to pass. This labyrinthine structure of interrogation rooms was vast and filled with other agents escorting detained passengers.

They reached a room with B22 stenciled on a keypad beside a shut sliding door. The agent crouched, bringing his face level with the retina-activated lock. This elicited a pneumatic squeak. The door shot open, vanishing into the wall.

The room Lily was escorted into wasn't a cell but a gallery concealed behind the two-way mirror of an interrogation room. The agent turned Lily, holding her shoulders toward the mirror so she might take a long look and consider what was on its other side. At a desk in the center of the room, his hands cuffed in front of him, was James Mohammad.

⌐

05:10 June 01, 2054 (GMT-4)
Northwest of Manaus

They'd found extra blankets but little else. While the others slept, B.T. lay on the floor of Kurzweil's lab beneath one of these blankets, awake with his unsettled thoughts. He and Michi had scoured the lab. The fruits of their search had proven disappointing. The papers they'd found were entirely administrative. When they imaged the hard drives on their headsUp, each had already been wiped clean. Kurzweil hadn't simply died, he'd seemed to vanish. Even the legacy of his work was gone. None of it made sense.

A lattice of questions had begun to form in B.T.'s mind. The circumstances of Kurzweil's death certainly existed within that lattice, but not at its top. That place was reserved for Sarah Hunt. Her suicide had been well documented. Records even showed she'd donated her body to science. If that was the case, then how had she wound up here? Also, what was her relationship with Common Sense? Had the remote gene-editing technology that killed Castro also killed her? Perhaps Castro, Sarah Hunt, and Kurzweil were all victims of Common Sense.

Manolo would be back to get them later that morning. Knowing he would soon leave empty-handed, B.T. couldn't help feeling duped. After a lifetime playing for high stakes in the world's greatest casinos, he prided himself on spotting a swindle. He rolled onto his shoulder. Michi snored gently beside him. B.T. wondered if she and Dr. Agawa had played him as a mark. The attraction he and Michi felt toward each other had seemed real enough. If in recent days, as they closed in on Kurzweil, cracks had begun to form in their relationship, this wasn't proof that she and Dr. Agawa had set him up. An image of Dr. Agawa in his wheelchair, his limbs twisted by radiation, appeared in B.T.'s mind. The Japanese government's desire to subvert the Singularity rested on a powerful logic, one tied in to its tragic national past. These forces were more powerful than any interpersonal dynamics between him and Michi.

His thoughts turned to Dr. Chowdhury and Ashni. Their family business, the Tandava Group, operated on a global scale. Its assets under management were comparable to the gross domestic product of a small nation. It wasn't outside the realm of the possible that they would behave like a nation and compete for control of the Singularity, even if that meant engaging in a plot to assassinate Castro. However, B.T. quickly dismissed the idea. He had read and seen plenty about the Tandava Group in the media over the years, but he had a more intimate understanding of Dr. Chowdhury through Lily Bao. She had always spoken reverentially of her onetime employer. Dr. Chowdhury—like Dr. Agawa—had experienced the civilization-ending ravages of nuclear war; in fact, his daughter had lost a mother to them. And now Dr. Chowdhury was dying. For him and Ashni, their search for the Singularity wasn't political, it was personal. They were trying to save his life.

Still, B.T. knew he was being played. He was certain of it. Even if it wasn't Michi and Dr. Agawa, even if it wasn't Dr. Chowdhury and Ashni, he couldn't ignore his instincts. The only person left to consider was Lily Bao, but it was beyond comprehension; the very idea twisted his stomach. Over the course of his life, no one understood him better or had proven more loyal to him than Lily.

Finally, B.T. fell into an unsettled sleep. Then, in the early hours of the morning, an odd shuffling noise came from the opposite end of the lab.

B.T. sat up.

It wasn't the sound of steps, but the sound of distressed kicking. It came from the direction of Dr. Chowdhury's bed. It seemed he was having a bad dream. Then B.T. heard him wake with a sharp gasp.

Ashni heard it too. "Bapu . . . it's okay . . . you're all right. . . ."

Chowdhury continued to gasp, struggling to catch his breath. He rolled side to side in his bed.

A flashlight's narrow beam licked at the corners of the lab. B.T. could hear the clicking of medication bottles as Ashni fumbled through her bag.

"We're all awake," B.T. announced to Ashni. "You can turn the lights on."

Michi was already sitting up when Avozhina threw a large switch at the opposite end of the lab. One at a time the overhead rows of halogen bulbs blinked on. Ashni was crouched by her father, who now lay on his side, too weak to sit up. One at a time she plugged pills into his mouth, and he sputtered and coughed in his struggle to down each with a sip of water. His skin was pale and coated with sweat. The whites of his eyes were veined red. He spoke with great effort.

"My dream," he said. "It was so vivid. . . ." He stopped and took a breath. "I was on a river, like the one we came up. Our boat had no motor, no oars, no way to steer. . . . You were in the boat, Ashni, so was your grandmother, and your uncle . . . and so was your mother. . . . Yes, she was with us too. Everyone I had ever loved was in this boat. But we couldn't control it and the current was strong and it felt as if any moment we might capsize. All around us were other boats, thousands of them, just like ours and filled with other people, other families. . . ."

Chowdhury's voice gained in strength as he spoke his dream. He rolled onto his side and heaved himself up, so he was now sitting in his bed. It seemed important to him to look directly into his daughter's eyes as he recounted this final part of his vision. "Ahead of our boat, I could hear shouting. There was another river, as broad and as powerful as ours. All this time, unseen, it had flowed parallel to us. And now, up ahead, these two rivers merged violently. While people in some boats tried to accommodate those from the other river, many panicked. They were then trying to sink us, Ashni. People lunged at us, pulled at us, and rocked our boat. First we lost your mother over the side, next your grandmother. Soon it was only us two remaining, and I wasn't going to lose you. Ahead, the overcrowded river emptied into a vast, calm ocean. As soon as I saw that ocean, our boat hit something and we flipped. My head went under the water. I couldn't get up for air. I kicked and kicked but couldn't find my way to the surface. The more I struggled, the darker it became. . . ."

Dr. Chowdhury sat with a pillow behind his back, his bedding scalloped at his waist, and his legs thrust out in front of him. He wiped sweat from his forehead with the sleeve of his wrinkled shirt. He carried a look of disappointment as though a part of him wished he hadn't woken from the dream. His gaze, which had remained fixed on Ashni all this time, now migrated to the others, all of whom had been listening. Speaking to them, Chowdhury added, "I've never had a dream so vivid. Never. It was like—"

Then, curiously, a phone rang. Then another. Then a third and a fourth. All at once, everyone's phones were ringing. They exchanged puzzled looks. Cell phone service had yet to penetrate this far upriver. Even the satellite repeaters couldn't penetrate the jungle's dense canopy. Their phones shouldn't have worked, let alone all been ringing at once. When Lily Bao left abruptly yesterday afternoon, she claimed it was because she couldn't afford to spend any more time offline.

B.T. reached into his bag. The night before, his headsUp had been running low on battery, so he'd powered it down. Now something had powered it on. It continued ringing. He noticed its battery was fully charged. The interface remained blank, showing no incoming number. The headsUp simply rang and rang. When B.T. touched it, the ringing stopped. The call answered. A holographic projection appeared in the center of the lab.

It was Sarah Hunt.

15:23 June 01, 2054 (GMT-5)
The United States Capitol

Julia Hunt stood in the back of the Senate chamber with an assault rifle slung across her chest. She also carried a holstered pistol on her hip. Wisecarver stood beside her. He had insisted that she remain inside the chamber until the vote was taken. As Julia watched the senators scurry between their desks, her mind wandered. She recalled the wedding of an academy classmate she'd attended some years before, in which she'd been part of the sword arch on the church steps. She had, in the moments before that ceremony, made the mistake of wearing her Marine-issued Mameluke sword into the nave of the church. The priest had chased her down and firmly admonished her. He explained at length that weapons had no place in a house of worship, and that she should leave her sword at the door. That day of the wedding, she had felt a twinge of shame on bringing a weapon into a holy place. She felt a similar sense of shame now, as she stood in the Senate chamber with an assault rifle and pistol.

Julia glanced at her watch.

"They're going to call roll any minute," whispered Wisecarver.

All day, Wisecarver had assured Julia that at "any minute" this, that, or the other thing was about to happen. Events had begun smoothly. When Julia and her Marines arrived that morning, the outnumbered Capitol Police had either retreated home or joined them. Within an hour, Wisecarver had arrived after seeing reports in the news of the Marines taking over security. What had slowed events was the senators. They had only shown up in ones and twos, and only after Wisecarver worked the phone, cajoling them down to the Capitol. He must have placed nearly one hundred calls that morning to muster his two-thirds majority. Julia understood that Wisecarver had posted her at the door in case some senators lost their nerve.

While the senators readied to vote, Julia stepped into the gallery and checked in with Barnes over the radio. They had established their command post in the Rotunda, and Barnes had arranged the Marines into concentric layers of security around the Capitol. Defying all conventions, he had instructed several squads of Marines to remove their uniforms and dress in plain clothes. He had then sent them on patrols extending as far forward as the Washington Monument to the west, Lincoln Park to the east, Union Station to the north, and Navy Yard to the south. These patrols would act as an early warning. It wasn't a question of whether the Smith administration would send a contingent of active-duty troops to overwhelm them, but when.

After reporting back to Julia that all remained quiet, Barnes added, "Your buddy Colonel Dozer's been on TV this morning."

"Really, where?"

"Some cable news show."

"Christ, they don't waste much time getting them on air, do they?"

"No, they don't," said Barnes. "You know, he called us 'rogue elements.'"

"Yeah, well, he can eat a dick."

"I dunno. . . . 'Rogue,' I kind of like it. Could be your new call sign."

"The senators are going to vote any minute," said Hunt.

"Wisecarver's been saying that all day."

"This time I think he means it."

"It isn't going to be quiet around here after they take that vote."

"No," said Hunt, "it won't be. So make sure everyone's ready."

"Roger, Rogue Six."

"Don't call me that."

Hunt stepped from the gallery back into the Senate chamber, making certain to shut the door carefully behind her. She took her place next to Wisecarver, who stood with his arms crossed over his chest. "Everything okay on the perimeter?" he asked without taking his eyes off the Senate floor.

"Yes, fine," said Hunt. "Everything's quiet. We should expect a significant response from the administration once this vote is taken. My best estimate is that—"

Wisecarver held up two fingers to silence her. "It's starting," he announced in a breathless whisper, like Frankenstein proclaiming his monster alive. Wisecarver's eyes widened. The senators glumly strode down the aisle and cast their votes. Julia caught snippets of procedure like "motion to convict" as well as "in accordance with Senate rules" and "constitutional obligation," but she wasn't paying attention to the proceedings so much as to Wisecarver. She couldn't take her eyes off him. He counted the tally silently, his mouth articulating the growing sum of *yeas*. Then the last vote was counted.

An ancient, decrepit senator with a constellation of liver spots on his bald head and a pair of reading glasses balanced on the tip of his bulbous nose had presided over the vote as the senior-most senator and so the president pro tempore of the Senate itself. Julia vaguely recognized him but couldn't say which state he represented. He read the result. "On this vote, the yeas are seventy-one, the nays are one, and the abstains are thirty-four. The decision of the Senate is to convict."

His gavel came down.

Julia had missed that one *nay* vote. She wondered which dissenting senator had come in today at great personal risk and voted to acquit, simply to thumb their nose at these proceedings. She asked Wisecarver who it was. His voice carried across the chamber as he pointed at the president pro tempore of the Senate. "It was *him*."

The old senator scowled back. He hammered his gavel. "Order!" he cried across the otherwise silent chamber. "There will be order!"

The other senators milled anxiously about, as if realizing for the first time that they had no idea how to extricate themselves from the Capitol. Wisecarver turned to Julia. His directions were crisp. "No one is to leave," he said. "Not until we have a new president."

Hunt placed her body between the senators and the chamber door.

⌐

07:05 June 01, 2054 (GMT-4)
Northwest of Manaus

Sarah Hunt looked B.T. in the eye. "Hello, Dr. Yamamoto."

She turned to the others and greeted each of them by name. Hunt appeared twenty years younger, and she wore her Navy uniform—not a dress uniform, but the type of blue coveralls she would've worn when on the bridge of her ship. As the son of a chief petty officer, B.T. also noticed her rank. She had retired as a rear admiral, and she was entitled to wear an admiral's star on her collar, but she wore captain's eagles instead. B.T. recalled a passage from Kurzweil's book, in which he'd predicted a future where we might edit our appearance, curating the best version of ourselves to present to others as an avatar. It seemed one of Kurzweil's predictions for the future had been fulfilled. B.T. wondered about the others.

Hunt came to Avozhina last. "Thank you, my old friend. Thank you for keeping this place for us and for bringing our friends here. Your work for me and Dr. Kurzweil is now complete." Avozhina nodded and wiped tears from her eyes. "It's time," Hunt added, "to cede back to the jungle all we discovered here."

That word, *discovered*.

B.T. interjected, "They say that you're dead."

"Do they?" Hunt answered.

"There's a black rock by the stream with your name carved into it."

"I know."

"What's buried there?" asked B.T.

"My body."

Her personality, her intelligence, her very life, all that was Sarah Hunt, now existed outside her body, it existed in this quantum-powered technological intelligence that was merged with her biological intelligence. For years, B.T. had attempted to achieve the same but had failed. This was the Singularity he'd long imagined, with implications that few if any could fully comprehend. The night before, when he was lying awake, he'd known someone had gotten the better of him. And it hadn't been Michi or Dr. Agawa, and it hadn't been Chowdhury and Ashni, and it certainly hadn't been Lily Bao. No, it had been Sarah Hunt. She'd gotten one over on him. She had gotten one over on all of them. B.T. couldn't help it, he admired her.

He asked her a slew of excited questions. "Are you housed on a specific server . . . ? What is your relationship to Common Sense . . . ? Is

Dr. Kurzweil's intelligence similarly enhanced and preserved . . . ? How did you return to this lab after taking your own life in the US . . . ? Dr. Chowdhury's very sick. Can you help him . . . ?"

"If you give me a moment, Dr. Yamamoto, I will answer all of this."

"Please," he said, "my friends call me B.T."

Sarah Hunt smiled. "I know, B.T."

⌐

21:42 June 01, 2054 (GMT-5)
Dulles International Airport

Lily Bao sat at a desk in a windowless white room. Her hands were cuffed and locked to a steel bracket on the desk, and the desk was bolted to the floor. For hours, she'd sat like this. At midday, a Homeland Security agent had brought her a sandwich. In the evening, that same agent had brought her a container of pasta. When Lily had asked why she was being held and when she would be released, the agent had simply said, "Do you want your food or not?"

Lily knew she was in trouble, big trouble. The agents who'd escorted her behind the two-way mirror, so she could see James Mohammad, hadn't told her anything. After showing her that they'd arrested her handler, they had placed her in an interrogation room, alone with her thoughts. She imagined the Homeland Security agents—as well as officials from other, more menacing three-letter agencies—interrogating James Mohammad. The more time that passed, the more of her secrets she imagined him divulging. Time itself had come to feel like her inquisitor. She now understood how an interrogation could break a person before the first question had been asked.

Lily's fears had worn her out; she could feel herself nodding off. Eventually they'd have to take her to a secondary cell to sleep if they didn't plan on releasing her tonight. If she could get a good night's rest, she felt everything might be solved in the morning. They had brought her two meals in confinement and allowed for two supervised trips to the restroom, so she was hopeful they'd at least give her a blanket and a pillow and a dark corner to lie down in as opposed to remaining cuffed to this desk in a brightly lit room. But Lily had never been on the wrong side of the US government.

When Lily heard the lock on her door unlatch, she felt a surge of hope. Her door opened, and her optimism was replaced with fresh concern as two dark-suited, earpiece-wearing men stepped silently into her cell, accompanied by a similarly attired woman. One of the agents carried a set of keys. He unlocked Lily's handcuffs and instructed her to stand and place her palms against the wall. While the female agent frisked her—something the Homeland Security agents had already done—the other two men stood a few steps away, as backup. Lily knew the espionage charges she faced were a serious matter, but she hadn't expected such thorough security measures. She hadn't divulged any secrets of real value to James Mohammad, yet these new agents were taking every precaution, treating her like a criminal mastermind.

The female agent soon finished. She sat Lily back in her chair and again cuffed her to the desk, while one of the men stuck his head outside into the corridor and called out that the room was clear.

Shriver stepped inside.

⌐

16:12 June 01, 2054 (GMT-4)
Northwest of Manaus

Chowdhury would die. That, among other things, was what Sarah Hunt had explained to him and the others over the course of the day. Chowdhury resigned himself to the news. If Hunt and Kurzweil had decided to undermine the Singularity, to sabotage that technology, it meant its many derivative technologies would also be sabotaged, such as the gene-editing procedure that might have regenerated Chowdhury's ailing heart. But just because Chowdhury accepted this didn't mean his daughter did.

"You can save him!" Ashni shouted.

"I can't," Hunt reiterated.

Softening, Ashni said, "Please save him. . . ."

"Do you think Dr. Kurzweil wanted to die?"

"I don't understand," said Ashni.

"He could've perpetuated his life. His health issues were, frankly, less complex than your father's. The work he'd pioneered throughout his life, the therapies he'd discovered at Neutronics, those would've certainly saved him. But he chose not only to destroy himself but also his life's work. Why? Why do you think a man like Dr. Kurzweil would sacrifice so much? What moral imperative would drive him to such a decision?"

Ashni didn't answer Hunt's question, but she didn't argue the point further, which was itself a concession. Instead, Chowdhury answered on his daughter's behalf. "Because he understood the destructive potential of his work."

The holographic projection of Sarah Hunt flickered as if in acknowledgment. "Correct," she said. "That's why Neutronics' therapies failed when administered to you. The work Dr. Kurzweil and I did, and that I later had to finish on my own, was to dam a vast torrent of knowledge, the result of the predicted intelligence explosion that occurs when the Singularity is achieved. By placing obstructions upstream, we've assured that biological and technological existence won't again merge; or, if those currents do merge, they'll do so gradually, not violently."

It was late in the morning. The others—B.T., Michi, Avozhina— stood nearby, glumly watching. Only when Sarah spoke about cutting off the knowledge of the Singularity, the knowledge that B.T. had pursued for years, did he finally speak up. "That's not possible."

"What's not possible?"

"You can't destroy knowledge," said B.T. "You can only hide what you've discovered. Eventually someone or something will find a way around whatever upstream obstacles you and Dr. Kurzweil have put in place."

"Maybe so," said Hunt. "But I wouldn't underestimate us."

Chowdhury interjected, "Records show you took your own life, that you even donated your body to science. That black rock by the river, is that you?"

"It's my body," said Hunt. "But I'm right here, with you. Just as I've always been. As for my body, when I volunteered it for Dr. Kurzweil's experiments, it became clear that Dr. Agawa would prevent me from returning here. The sedation procedure you underwent at Neutronics, in which your vitals were slowed to the point of death to facilitate treatment, I simply underwent the same procedure. When the paramedics found me at home, I appeared dead. Given my own history, the cause of death seemed obvious. My suicide was accepted at face value. Because I donated my body to science, Kurzweil was able to intercept it and I journeyed back here, where no one could interfere in our work."

Over the course of the afternoon, Chowdhury questioned Sarah Hunt further about that work. She and Kurzweil had been in a race against the governments of the world to achieve the Singularity before others might put it to ill use. Her nearest competitor, she conceded, had been B.T. His breakthroughs followed theirs by only weeks and in some cases days. Before vanishing, Hunt had colluded with her old friend Hendrickson. Disaffected as he'd become with the Castro administration, Hendrickson would have left the White House long ago had he not understood the threat the Singularity posed, particularly if it became a tool for a budding authoritarian like Castro to wield in his consolidation of power. Although Hendrickson acknowledged this threat, he and Hunt had philosophical differences as to how far they should go to assure the Singularity never fell into Castro's hands. The last conversation the two of them ever had was a heated argument on the subject.

"That's when you decided to kill President Castro?" Chowdhury lay on his bed. His daughter had by now turned on a nearby lamp and the edges of Sarah Hunt's projection lost some of their sharpness in the artificial light.

"Not exactly," said Hunt. "That's when I decided to take my own life, or at least take it for a first time. By coming here, with Kurzweil, I effectively ended one life to begin another. All that was left for me was this final task. When I came to understand the destructive scope of the Singularity, of its power to alter us forever, that's when I decided to stop Castro, or anyone else, from gaining that knowledge. I alone understand it. I *am* it."

"The grave by the stream?" said Chowdhury. "The black rock Lily saw."

"What about it?"

"Your body is there."

"My body hardly matters," said Hunt, seemingly disappointed by Chowdhury's inability to accept the unlimited bounds of all she'd become. Then, as if to illustrate this, she added, "Last night, you had a dream. You and your family were in a boat on a swiftly moving river. When that river and another powerful river merged, it created a violent current. Boats began to capsize and sink. People clawed at one another to stay above water, causing even more to drown. Beyond the two rivers was an ocean, but no one could reach it. You lost Ashni's mother and your mother over the side of your boat, and when you woke you were struggling not to lose Ashni. . . ."

"Were you listening when I described my dream to the others?"

"I didn't need to listen."

"Then how did you know about it?"

"I put the dream there, Sandy."

"It was your dream?"

Sarah Hunt laughed. "Our dreams originate in our brains, so if the technological can hold sway over the biological—as we saw in Castro's death—it can hold sway over our dreams too. But that dream of the two rivers wasn't mine. Our dreams are collective, rarely dreamt by one person alone. How many of us have dreamt of falling into a bottomless pit? Or of having to take a test we haven't studied for? Have you ever woken from a dream so upset that you find yourself in tears? Is your dream less real than the tears it's caused? I've left my body—in fact, I left it in the very bed where you're about to leave yours. Avozhina is the one who buried it by the stream. The form I've now taken—this uploaded intelligence—bears closer resemblance to a thought, an idea, or even a dream, as opposed to an actual embodied person."

As night arrived, a wave of exhaustion broke over Chowdhury. He had nothing else to ask Sarah Hunt. It was as if all this while—as he traveled upriver—his life was sustained only by his need for answers. With those answers given, with that journey completed, his body was letting go. His limbs felt heavy, as though the earth had decided to exert on him a greater share of its gravity. His eyes wanted to shut too. And his breath slowed. He could hardly swallow. Those most basic functions, which, for a lifetime, he had performed unconsciously, he now had to perform consciously. It was a new, exhausting awareness. All he wanted was sleep.

His daughter was holding his hand and gently stroking his hair. Chowdhury's breath had become shallow, his hearing had become muted, as though he had a cold. He could hear Ashni's voice, but it sounded distant, as though she were walking away from him down a long corridor, muttering, "It's okay, Bapu. . . . You're tired. . . . You deserve to rest. . . . It's okay. . . . I'll be okay. . . ."

Then a thought sounded in Chowdhury's mind, ringing loud and clear as a bell. His dream from the night before, what if he could get back to it? A person cannot die in their dreams; he had learned that long ago, as a boy. He might not be able to avoid sleep, but if he could conjure a dream in that sleep, then that might be enough to carry his life into the morning. Chowdhury became very still. He fixed his thoughts on the imagery of his dream, on the river, on the boats, on Ashni's mother and his own mother riding in their boat. His body was near motionless, hardly breathing now. With an intensity as great as any he'd ever known, he struggled to re-create the world of his dream, to hold on to it . . . to not let it go. . . .

That next morning, when Ashni tried and failed to wake him, she noticed her father's hands; they were clenched into fists.

⌐

21:50 June 01, 2054 (GMT-5)
Dulles International Airport

The anxiety, the fear, the anger—that knotted mass of emotions that Lily Bao had felt expanding inside her all this time—she couldn't contain anymore. On seeing Shriver, she shut her eyes, pressed her chin to her chest, and her shoulders began to convulse as she silently shuddered and wept.

"Give me those keys," said Shriver.

The female agent protested.

Shriver repeated himself, and Lily heard the keys clink into his palm.

"Now wait outside."

Reluctantly, the detail announced they'd be right at the door.

"Do your best to keep still," said Shriver. Lily noticed she was shaking so much that he couldn't manage to slot the keys into her handcuffs.

Suddenly her hands were free.

She wiped her eyes, took a breath, and glanced up at him. "You fucking asshole!" She slapped him as hard as she could across the side of his head. The agents barreled through the door.

"Everything's fine!" said Shriver, placing his body between Lily and them. "I'm fine . . . please, just wait outside."

The three agents exchanged concerned looks but relented. They returned to the corridor. Lily's stare remained fixed on Shriver. She called him an asshole again but this time much more quietly, hissing the word through clenched teeth.

"That's fair," he said.

"You got me into this mess."

"I always told you that I loved you, and I do love you, and if you would've believed me and waited, you might have avoided this." Shriver stopped, as if weighing the words that he'd spoken to determine their truth. "Maybe you're right and I did get you into this mess. . . . Maybe asking you to wait indefinitely was too much. . . . Maybe it wasn't realistic. None of that matters now. I'm going to get you out of here, okay?"

"How?" she asked.

He realized that she hadn't seen the news. Shriver began to explain. The Marines from the barracks had taken over the Capitol. Wisecarver had convened a two-thirds majority of senators. That majority had voted to convict Smith. Smith was no longer president.

"Then who is?" But as the question escaped Lily, she realized the answer was staring her in the face: Shriver was now president.

"Not yet," he said, after Lily had made this observation. "I haven't taken the oath of office and I won't, not until you're released. Also, I don't plan to stay in the job for long."

"I've always been a liability to you."

"No, you haven't," said Shriver. "That's what I've come here to explain. I'm the one who's been a liability to you. I love you, Lily. I've never lied about that. But I haven't been honest about other things." He got down on a knee, as one would when proposing, or groveling; it seemed he was doing a little of both. His voice lowered to a whisper. "I would've happily walked away from politics to be with you. The reason I couldn't is because when we met, I was already involved with—"

She cut him off. "Another woman? . . . I don't want to hear about another woman. . . ."

"Christ, Lily! Would you for once let me finish . . . ?" He placed her hands between his. "I couldn't because I was already involved in an effort to get Castro out of office. Not long after he won his third term, I was approached by a senior Japanese official. He had a series of classified briefings detailing research breakthroughs Neutronics had shared with the US government. The Japanese official's fears—and what these intelligence reports confirmed—were that Castro planned to use those advances to further consolidate his power, both at home and abroad.

"As a member of the Senate Intel Committee, I should've had access to these briefings, but the administration had withheld that access. No one, it seemed, was playing by the rules anymore, including this Japanese official. He had recruited a retired rear admiral, Sarah Hunt, to infiltrate Neutronics. He also had a high-level source inside the White House. He wouldn't disclose who this source was to me, I only found out later. You see, when Sarah Hunt took her life, that source inside the White House tracked me down."

"And told you what?" asked Lily.

Shriver rubbed the back of his neck. "That Sarah Hunt wasn't dead. The source didn't know where Hunt had gone, but suspected she'd gone back to work with the onetime head of the program, Ray Kurzweil, to finish what the two of them had started."

"Which was?"

"A plan to subvert the Singularity, a plan to remove Castro from power, the same plan that's placed you here and placed me in line as president. Lily, I don't know how all this ends, but Hunt and Kurzweil—their combined intelligence, whether biological, artificial, or some combination of the two—have consistently been several moves ahead of the rest of us and have plotted out each move that comes next. I'm certain of it. The intelligence they've created is in charge, not us. Or, put another way, the Singularity is in charge. Common Sense is in charge."

A feeling of utter helplessness fell over Lily, as surely as if Shriver had again cuffed her hands to the desk. "What do we do now?" she asked.

"I'm not sure . . ." said Shriver. "Before Hunt vanished, our project had two objectives. The first was to remove Castro. The second was to install a caretaker president, someone who could find some common ground. Now it's time for me to do my part. Will you come?"

He offered his hand. She took it, but before she would follow him out the door, she asked, "What about my crimes? Are they simply forgotten? And James Mohammad, what happens to him?"

Shriver laughed. "I wouldn't worry too much about Mr. Mohammad. He strikes me as the type who knows how to land on his feet. And we're going to afford him every opportunity to do so."

"I betrayed my country," Lily said despairingly.

The sentiment's simplicity seemed to irritate Shriver. "No more than I have."

They left the interrogation room. Lily and Shriver hurried down the corridor sandwiched between his Secret Service detail. When she asked where they were going, Shriver said, "To the Capitol." Outside at the arrivals terminal, a single SUV idled at the curb. This was far from the expansive motorcade that typically attended a president. These three agents were part of a contingent that now supported Shriver as opposed to Smith.

Aside from these agents, the only person she knew of who supported Shriver in both his bid to unseat Castro and now to unseat Smith was the aforementioned unnamed high-level source inside the administration. Lily wondered who this source might be. She prayed it was someone reliable.

When she stepped into the SUV, she was greeted by Retired Admiral John "Bunt" Hendrickson. Despite his wrinkled suit, loosened tie, and lack of a shave, Lily recognized him from press briefings as the White House chief of staff.

⌐

03:17 June 02, 2054 (GMT-5)
The United States Capitol

Julia Hunt awoke in the predawn hours from a dream she couldn't quite remember. Its details were just out of grasp. She'd slept only a couple of hours, on a sofa in Wisecarver's office. She hadn't even taken her boots off. As she heaved on her body armor and slung the rifle across her chest, she kept trying to piece together the dream. It had left her feeling clear-headed, as though she'd found a solution to a problem she'd long been struggling with.

After stepping from Wisecarver's office, Julia passed through Statuary Hall, toward the Rotunda and her command post. Barnes was sleeping sitting up in an office chair next to a lance corporal who monitored a bank of radios assembled on a foldout table. The only sound in the great, echoing Rotunda was their static murmur. A couple of hours before, when Hunt had gone for some rest, Wisecarver had been looking for Shriver; the new president needed to take the oath of office, but he was nowhere to be found. Hunt had left strict instructions for her Marines to wake her when Shriver arrived at the Capitol. The lance corporal on duty confirmed that there was still no news.

Barnes shifted in his chair. He let out a snore that reverberated within the cavernous Rotunda. "Has Major Barnes been doing that all night?"

"Yes, ma'am," said the lance corporal. He mustered a nervous smile.

Hunt could see his fear. This lance corporal couldn't have been much more than a year or two out of high school. His entire life was ahead of him and, depending on how today's events played out, he might spend decades of that life in a federal prison.

"With Major Barnes snoring like that," said Hunt, "I don't imagine you've gotten much sleep."

"No, ma'am," said the lance corporal. "None at all."

One at a time, the various patrols and sentries deployed around the Capitol and beyond began radioing their hourly status reports. The lance corporal opened his laptop to annotate a spreadsheet titled "Duty Log." Hunt sat next to him, listening passively as the Marines called in. She watched the nervous lance corporal annotate his log. He, like her, had good reason to be afraid, and she wished she could convey to him some of her calm. Poor kid, she thought, between Barnes's snoring and the radio watch, he hasn't slept a wink.

When the lance corporal finished logging in the last report, he minimized the window on his laptop. Behind it, in another open window, were a series of recently posted news articles. Julia glimpsed one headline: AWOL TROOPS AND TRUTHER BRIGADES SEIZE ARMORIES ACROSS NATION.

"How old is this?" she asked as her eyes raced over the body of the text. The lance corporal had read the article an hour ago, but fresh details kept breaking on social media. After yesterday's impeachment vote, once the Senate had convicted President Smith, tens of thousands of troops—those who'd refused the administration's mobilization orders and gone AWOL—had suddenly reappeared, mobilizing alongside Truther cadres. They had converged on their home bases, seizing armories from east to west, from Eglin Air Force Base to Fort Riley to Fort Irwin, and then pledged their allegiance to Shriver, who they viewed as the legitimate president and their legitimate commander in chief. In the eyes of these AWOL troops, they weren't seizing the armories on their bases as part of a rebellion. They were seizing the armories on their bases to *quell* a rebellion, one led by Smith, an impeached, convicted, and therefore illegitimate president who would not relinquish power.

Hunt shook Barnes, who jostled awake with a snore. "Have you read this?"

Barnes wiped sleep from his eyes and his face appeared numb with exhaustion. "Read what?" Before sidling up beside Hunt, he grumbled about her having woken him from the most remarkable dream. He reached into his cargo pocket, removed a tin of Copenhagen, and hooked a plug of tobacco into his bottom lip. The nicotine woke Barnes up quickly, as did the article as his eyes flew across the text. Finally, he muttered, "There's no going back now . . . it's civil war." Barnes turned toward the lance corporal. "Why didn't you wake us up when you saw this?"

"Sir, I just figured . . . I thought . . . well, you said to wake you if any of Smith's forces moved on the Capitol or if Vice President . . . I mean President Shriver arrived. I didn't know. . . ."

The lance corporal was cracking up. The kid obviously needed some rest, which was what Hunt ordered him to go do. As he stood from the desk, the lance corporal said, "Ma'am, I'm sorry, I thought you already knew about the article."

Barnes interrupted, "How the hell would she have known?"

The lance corporal glanced down at his hands. He looked at Hunt, speaking only to her, "I thought you knew because it seems like these AWOL troops are just doing the same thing we already did at the barracks, ma'am." The lance corporal wandered off across the Rotunda, toward a corner where off-duty Marines had unrolled sleeping bags to grab an hour or two of rest.

Barnes and Hunt sat motionless, staring at the bank of radios. Eventually Barnes said, "That kid's right, you know. At Eglin, at Riley, it seems like they're just doing what we already did at the barracks."

"And what's that?" Hunt asked. "What *have* we done?"

Before Barnes could answer, a first, second, then third call came in on the radio. Each of the sentries reported federal troops, still loyal to the Dreamer administration, massing in large numbers. Clearly, Smith couldn't wait any longer. If the military was fracturing along Truther-Dreamer lines, he had to regain control of Congress and reassert his legitimacy. Hunt ordered all her Marines to fall back and consolidate around the Capitol. Barnes was on the radio, coordinating this maneuver, when a call came in from the checkpoint at the I-395 ramp that led south to Virginia. An SUV had arrived from the direction of Dulles Airport. Inside were several people requesting immediate access to the Capitol.

"How many?" Barnes asked the Marine at the checkpoint.

"Six," he said. "Including President Shriver."

08:50 June 02, 2054 (GMT-4)

The Amazon and Rio Negro, Northwest of Manaus

B.T. would leave Kurzweil's lab empty-handed. He found it impossible to reach any other conclusion. That morning, when he woke, there had been two fresh pieces of information. Dr. Sandeep Chowdhury had passed away in the night. And Manolo had arrived to ferry everyone back to Manaus. Manolo had no good way to transport Dr. Chowdhury's body. The best he could offer was to wrap it in a blanket, which seemed rather undignified. Manolo suggested that he take back B.T. and Michi, and then return the next day for Ashni and Avozhina with a casket for Dr. Chowdhury. This was agreed upon, and it was how B.T. found himself motoring down the river, he and Michi in the bow and Manolo piloting his skiff from its stern.

He and Michi sat close together, but still had to raise their voices to hear each other over the whine of the outboard motor. "How long do you want to stay in Manaus?" B.T. asked.

"Not long," said Michi. "Dr. Agawa will want a full debriefing. How long do you think you'll stay?"

B.T. didn't answer, not at first. What Michi had done was subtle yet clear. The inference was that he wouldn't be coming with her to see Dr. Agawa, that the two of them would be going their separate ways. "Not long," said B.T., mimicking her answer, though unlike Michi he wasn't certain where he might go.

Aside from an anxious moment when Manolo piloted their skiff through the hull-splitting whitewater convergence of the Rio Negro and Amazon, B.T. spent the rest of their journey to the ferry terminal quietly mulling over this question. From a practical standpoint, it would make little sense for him to return to his lab in Okinawa. Sarah Hunt had spoken about placing obstacles in the way of anyone who might try to follow her path and replicate the Singularity. Hunt had made it clear that her uploaded intelligence—which had been B.T.'s holographic interlocutor this past day—would vanish once events in the United States had resolved themselves. The integration of quantum computing into Hunt's intelligence made it highly improbable that a scientist without those advantages, even a gifted one, could figure a way around the obstacles she'd constructed to prevent a replication of her and Kurzweil's work and a second advent of the Singularity. If it was possible, that person would need an incredible intellect. And luck.

Manolo piloted their skiff up to the pier. They exited the terminal and stood in the cab line. On the ride to the hotel, Michi cycled through messages and news stories on her headsUp, paying little attention to B.T., except to read him the occasional headline. When they arrived at the Tropicana, Michi asked B.T. if she could have their room to herself for a bit. "I have a few calls to place."

B.T. didn't protest. What good would it do? He didn't mention his hurt feelings. What good would that do either? He simply said, "No problem," and asked her what time he should come up. She answered, "I'll find you," and asked where he'd be. Standing in the lobby, B.T. looked over his shoulder, to the only place he could think to go, and he told Michi that he'd head down to the casino.

B.T. began at the baccarat table, which went all right. Then craps, which went a little better. He won some. He lost some. Generally, he hovered around the break-even point for an hour, then for a second, and into a third. Mathematically, the house always won. But when he thought back on his own life, from his days as an indebted MIT graduate to this moment, he had usually beaten the house. And he began to wonder—as he took another roll, as he was dealt a fresh hand—whether he might extend that luck to his work, whether his luck and intelligence combined might be enough for him to return to his research, despite whatever obstacles Sarah Hunt had placed in his way. Maybe it was crazy, but he thought it possible. He could, someday, rediscover the Singularity.

B.T. was at the blackjack table, six hands into a winning streak, when Michi reappeared on the casino floor, rolling her suitcase behind her.

When he saw her, B.T. left his hand on the table.

"My flight leaves in a little over an hour," said Michi. Then, as if to soften the blow, she added, "I settled our hotel bill."

"You mean Dr. Agawa settled it." B.T. was hurt and angry.

"You're a brilliant scientist." Michi said the words with a certain finality, as if at last she was letting him know what she truly thought of him. Then she added, "I hope to keep in touch. . . ."

The inflection in Michi's voice framed this as a question more than a statement. As she stood across from B.T. on the casino floor awaiting his answer, patrons of the Tropicana flitted by. They clutched their winnings as they shuttled table to table. A nearby slot machine hit its jackpot. Gold tokens poured from its mouth, and an elderly woman with a cigarette dangling from her lips fell to her knees. A pair of floor managers appeared with plastic buckets. "I don't want you to be late," said B.T.

Michi glanced toward the door. "Keep in touch, *okay*?"

The old woman interrupted B.T. and Michi. She clasped both their hands in hers, pressing a fistful of gold tokens into each of their palms. "These are for you two!" she said. Her gravelly voice brimmed with joy.

"A jackpot . . . finally!" She glanced at B.T. and then at Michi, as if to bless their union.

"*Okay?*" Michi repeated.

"Okay," said B.T. "I'll keep in touch. Now don't miss your flight."

B.T. returned to the blackjack table. He lost his next hand. For the next hour he lost and lost and lost, until he couldn't play anymore. He wandered out to the lobby. In the nearby lounge, dozens of the hotel's patrons and some of the staff had gathered around a bank of televisions tuned to a handful of news channels.

In the hours B.T. had been on the casino floor, the situation in the US had deteriorated. The images were surreal. Thousands of US troops—clad in riot gear, riding in armored cars, buttoned-up in tracked vehicles, armed with every accoutrement of war—faced off against one another at the Capitol, as well as at military bases around the country. President Smith remained hunkered down at the White House while his rival, Vice President Shriver, had arrived at the Capitol under the protection of Marines from the nearby barracks. President Smith had issued a statement from the White House in which he characterized his conviction in the Senate and the Marine presence at the Capitol as a Truther coup d'état.

The news was also reporting that Shriver—in defiance of Smith and his supporters—planned at any moment to take the oath of office on the Capitol's West Front, where presidents had taken the oath since time immemorial. Despite the risk to himself, despite the chaos at the Capitol, Shriver was determined to uphold this tradition. Every news network awaited his arrival. The entire country—indeed, the world—was holding its breath. A live shot of the Capitol played without interruption.

B.T. had no idea what would happen when Shriver faced the multitude of Truthers, Dreamers, and elements of the US military whose support had splintered across both factions. The situation was highly combustible. All B.T. really felt certain of was that it was time to return to his lab in Okinawa. That was the closest thing he had to a home, and he wanted to get back to it while flights were still running without major interruptions.

He wandered across the lobby, to reception, where there was the sound of music like water tumbling over smooth stones in the background. He waited in a modest line where people spoke in low voices. By the time he'd reached that line's front, it had grown, extending to the pair of revolving doors at the hotel's entrance as other guests had also decided it was time to check out. The receptionist—the same woman who had checked B.T. in a few days before—asked how his stay had been. She then printed out his bill, which Michi had already settled, and placed it in an envelope. When B.T. asked the receptionist if she might order him a taxi, she presented a second printout. "Of course. First we'll just need you to settle your bill from the casino."

"My bill?"

"Yes, your losses." The sum she'd circled was more than B.T. had in his checking account. The receptionist indexed the tip of her pen to that sum as she awaited his answer. B.T. explained that he would need to move some money between accounts to cover those losses and that he would do so as soon as he returned home. The receptionist gently explained that the policy of the Tropicana Hotel & Casino was that all accounts had to be settled before checkout.

While B.T. and the receptionist debated the point, people in line began to stir impatiently. B.T. glanced behind him. A petite, dark-haired woman who bore a striking resemblance to Harry Potter with her pageboy-style haircut and glasses smiled and nodded patiently, as if assuring B.T. not to worry, he could take his time figuring what he should do next.

The receptionist offered to book him into another room for the time it might take for him to move those funds. She added that unfortunately she wouldn't be able to comp him the rate, but that she could reserve him "a good deal on an economically sized room." The receptionist was growing impatient. "Shall I book it for you, Dr. Yamamoto?"

Before B.T. could answer, the woman waiting behind him tapped his shoulder. "Excuse me," she said in a small voice. "I'm so sorry, but I couldn't help but overhear. Are you Dr. Christopher Yamamoto?"

"And if I am . . . ?" answered B.T.

"Then I've been looking for you." The woman, who introduced herself as Dr. Ayesha Bakari, shouldered past B.T. She handed the receptionist a credit card. "Put whatever he owes on this."

The receptionist swiped her card. "Thank you, Dr. Bakari," she said as the transaction cleared. "I also see a reservation for you. . . . May I check you into your room?"

B.T. still didn't entirely understand what was going on. He simply watched as Dr. Bakari answered, "No, actually. I don't think I'll be checking in after all." She requested a taxi to the airport, for both her and B.T. The two headed outside. B.T. began to thank Dr. Bakari for her generosity, but she cut him off. "I thought I might find you here," she said. "You're going to help me."

"I am?"

"Yes, you are."

"With what?"

The taxi to the airport pulled up. A valet opened its door.

"With research," answered Dr. Bakari. "The company I work for, Neutronics, has suffered a series of setbacks to its remote gene-editing program. Perhaps you've heard of our work? Because we've certainly heard of yours."

⌐

15:17 June 02, 2054 (GMT-5)
The United States Capitol

It would take a battering ram to get in the door. Julia Hunt had also begun to think it would take a battering ram for them to get *out* the door, to inaugurate President Shriver. He had arrived late that morning with a contingent of Secret Service, Julia's godfather, and a woman named Lily Bao, whom her godfather had described in a whisper as "the president's fiancée." Julia thought *fiancée* was an optimistic word under the circumstances. It presumed a future life that seemed difficult to imagine. That's the thing about politicians, thought Julia, they're always peddling tomorrow.

This small group huddled in a corridor off the Rotunda that led to the Capitol's West Front. Only a door separated them from the outside, where Hunt's Marines were struggling to secure enough of the Capitol so that Shriver could safely take his oath for the world to see. However, resistance around the Capitol seemed to be stiffening. Earlier that morning, a cluster of Smith loyalists from a brigade of the 82nd Airborne had breached the Capitol's perimeter, storming into the vacant House chamber. Hunt and a platoon's worth of Marines had eventually pushed them out of that chamber, but it'd led to a sharp exchange of gunfire between the Marines and paratroopers, leaving five Americans dead. Afterward, Hunt had nowhere to put the bodies, so they lay bloodied under their ponchos in a corner of the Rotunda. It was as if they were lying in state. All day, Julia had tried not to look at them.

Shriver and his entourage had arrived shortly after this altercation. Wisecarver had immediately pulled the soon-to-be president aside. While they talked, Julia had pulled her godfather aside. Hendrickson explained that Shriver was determined to take the oath of office and deliver a few remarks from the Capitol's West Front. "And then what?" Julia asked.

"He believes if he speaks directly to the people, it'll make a difference."

"Him and every other politician."

Her godfather said he thought Shriver's remarks *could* make a difference.

"Why?" Julia asked. "Why do you believe in him?"

"It's not him I believe in," Hendrickson said. He gestured beyond the sealed double doors, to where the Truthers and Dreamers continued to battle one another. "It's us, the entire country. I still believe we can snap out of this."

Julia explained to him how tentative her position at the Capitol had become, from the earlier breach into the House chamber to the steady trickle of battered Marines who all morning wandered back from their posts for a few minutes of dazed rest in the Rotunda, only to return to the barricades where they fought with rubber bullets, gas, batons, and sometimes fists, staving off those who, until only recently, had been their comrades in arms. Also, Julia's Marines were outnumbered, as Smith continued to deploy those military units he'd mobilized to Washington— paratroopers from Georgia, armored cavalry from Kansas, even Marines from nearby Virginia and North Carolina, still loyal to Smith and his Dreamer administration. Hendrickson had pointed out to his goddaughter that she wasn't as outnumbered as she thought, at least not when viewed on the national level. Yes, a massive number of troops had surged to Washington, but in so doing Smith had made a critical mistake. He hadn't understood the significance of so many troops going AWOL when their mobilization orders had arrived. The troops loyal to Smith had emptied their bases, coming here, while the troops who'd gone AWOL had stayed behind, allying themselves with local Truther brigades and then taking control of those now-empty bases around the country.

Hendrickson was walking his goddaughter through this when Shriver and Wisecarver approached. They both agreed that Shriver would take his oath on the Capitol's West Front and, if possible, deliver a few remarks. The five of them—Shriver, Hunt, Wisecarver, Hendrickson, and Lily Bao—now waited for Hunt's second-in-command, Major Barnes, to radio the all clear, at which point they would step outside.

Beyond the double doors that led to the Capitol's West Front, they could hear the shouts of thousands, the occasional clamor of a steel barricade toppling over, and the low hiss and pop of rubber bullets. Lily shifted her weight from one foot to the other in a kind of anxious dance step as they waited. Shriver pulled a note card from his coat pocket, reviewed it a final time, and then tucked it away. It'd been agreed that Wisecarver would administer the oath of office, but Hendrickson noticed that he didn't have a Bible.

"For Christ's sake," said Wisecarver. He ducked into an unlocked office nearby and returned with a stately leatherbound volume, its cover text lashed in serifed gold font. "This'll do."

Hendrickson glimpsed the book's cover. "Is that what I think it is?"

He snatched it from Wisecarver. "*Ba to Es?* No fucking way. He's not swearing the oath of office on this." The book was volume two of the *Encyclopedia Britannica*.

This argument between Hendrickson and Wisecarver was interrupted by the young lance corporal who had been standing radio watch the evening before. "Ma'am," he said, speaking to Hunt. "Major Barnes has been trying to reach you. . . ." Hunt glanced down at her handheld radio, which seemed to have lost reception. "He says they've cleared the West Front, that you need to head out now."

"There's got to be a Bible in this place," said Hendrickson.

"We don't have time," said Wisecarver. "No one will know the difference."

"Hendrickson's right," said Shriver. "I'm not going to take the oath on a—"

Before Shriver could finish, the lance corporal interjected. "Sir, I have a Bible. It's in my pack. Do you need it?"

"You do?" asked Shriver.

"Yes, sir."

"Go get it," said Hunt. "And hurry." The lance corporal's footfalls echoed down the corridor as he sprinted back to the Rotunda. The five of them stood wrapped in nervous silence. Breathing heavily now, the lance corporal returned up the corridor. He carried the Bible, a soldier's Bible, no larger than the palm of his hand.

"Are you kidding me?" said Wisecarver. "He's not swearing the oath on *that*. It'll look ridiculous." He held up the *Encyclopedia Britannica*. "This'll be better."

Shriver ignored him. He thanked the lance corporal and promised to get him his Bible back. The lance corporal said to keep it. "Right now, sir, you need it more than I do." Julia flung open the double doors. Light poured in and they stepped out onto the Capitol's West Front.

As Hunt stared across the National Mall, she imagined some future history class in which these events might be taught. She could envision the rows of students at their desks viewing photographs and videos of the abject chaos before her. The sea of heaving, exhausted bodies. The desperate and steady growl of the crowd. The acrid cloud of tear gas that shrouded the monuments. She doubted anyone could ever truly understand this moment without having been here. Her mouth turned dry as she struggled to comprehend it all. She began to think of her mother, when she'd asked her about what it had been like to fight at sea, to see the world taken to the brink of annihilation. Her mother rarely spoke of it. Julia had always believed this was because Sarah Hunt didn't want to discuss so traumatic an experience. But maybe it was because certain experiences defied description.

Hunt could feel her mother's presence. Her Marines began to move Shriver toward the dais, from which he would take the oath of office at great personal risk. There was no bulletproof glass protecting the new president. He was completely exposed. Barnes had successfully pushed back the crowd to enough of a distance so Shriver wouldn't be in immediate physical danger, but it wasn't yet clear how long the Marines could keep the crowd at bay, particularly if they turned against Shriver.

Before administering the oath, Wisecarver offered some preliminary remarks, in which he'd castigated the Smith administration and their Dreamer supporters in familiar and divisive terms, deploying words like *treacherous* and *illegitimate* with abandon. Wisecarver's bitter little speech caused the crowd to stir and press against Barnes's Marines on the perimeter, which for a moment seemed like it might break. Shriver had the presence of mind to raise his right hand, gesturing to Wisecarver that he was ready to take his oath. It wasn't only Shriver who presented himself in front of Wisecarver but also Lily Bao. Shriver had insisted she hold the Bible that he would swear his oath on, just as First Ladies had done throughout the generations.

Wisecarver glanced down at a note card he'd removed from his pocket. "Raise your right hand," he awkwardly began, though Shriver's hand was already raised. "Repeat after me: *I do solemnly swear . . .*" As Shriver spoke the oath, Julia's thoughts returned to her mother. What would Sarah Hunt have thought about the decisions her daughter had made over these days and weeks? ". . . *that I will faithfully execute the office . . .*" Would Shriver's presidency vindicate Julia's turn against the Smith administration? ". . . *that I will to the best of my ability preserve, protect, and defend . . .*" Or would that choice forever haunt her, branding her a traitor much as her mother had been branded a murderer for her role in the last war? ". . . *the Constitution of the United States . . .*" Julia couldn't know, but she could feel her mother's hand in all of this. As she listened to Shriver, she noticed her godfather, Hendrickson, looking right at her.

". . . *So help me God,*" repeated Shriver as he finished his oath.

Wisecarver extended his hand. With a smug little grin, he said, "Congratulations, Mr. President."

Shriver ignored the handshake, snubbing Wisecarver for the nation and the world to see. The Truthers and Dreamers awaited their new president. Their silence was a delicate balance. They were listening. "I cannot be your president," he began. The crowd stirred. "But there is a way forward for us. Last night, I had a dream. . . ."

As Julia Hunt listened to Shriver's dream, it tracked closely with her own from the night before, the one that had left her feeling as if she'd found the solution to a problem she couldn't quite name, the details of which she could hardly remember until now.

Shriver described the convergence of two great rivers. He described traveling down one of those rivers in a boat with the people he loved. In Julia's dream, her boat had consisted not only of her adoptive mother but also her real parents, who existed as a vague impression in her memory, as well as her godfather. Shriver spoke about the powerful convergence of these two rivers and how they led to a vast ocean that people, fearful of one another, struggled to reach as they fought at the convergence, capsizing one another's boats, drowning one another's families. When Shriver finished describing his dream, it was with a question, which he spoke in little more than a whisper, but his voice carried a great distance, quiet as the crowd had become. "So how do we reach that ocean?"

Barnes reached for Julia, clasping her arm. His face, battered as it was with scars, was wrought with an intensity of emotion Julia had never seen in him before. "Last night," he said, "I dreamt that my son and I were traveling on that river. . . ." His voice trailed off.

Low murmurs replaced the silence. The crowd turned to one another with a vague sense of recognition and wonder. It was as if some unseen hand had placed this long and vivid and unified dream into their consciousness, allowing people who for so long had lived in alternate realities to again share a collective consciousness.

How was this possible? thought Julia. But as soon as the question formed, its answer presented itself: *her mother.* This was her mother's work with Kurzweil, her mother's legacy. Was her mother Common Sense? On the opposite side of the dais, Hunt's gaze landed on Hendrickson.

When she found him, he was already staring at her, as if to confirm what she suspected was true. Then Shriver called him forward.

"I have appointed Retired Admiral John Hendrickson to serve as my vice president." Shriver turned to Hendrickson, shook his hand, and offered brief congratulations. He continued, "This nation needs a care-taker, a president committed to relinquishing power as opposed to con-solidating it. Therefore, effective immediately, I resign the presidency. Vice President Hendrickson will complete my term and he will not stand for a second, so that our democracy might rejuvenate itself through a free and fair election. . . ."

Behind Shriver there was a commotion. Wisecarver hadn't planned for this. He'd assumed Shriver's presidency would, at last, allow his party to consolidate power for a generation. For Wisecarver, Shriver was sup-posed to be the Truther president who would assure this. Hendrickson's assumption of the presidency wasn't only a political betrayal, it would shift power away from the Truthers and Dreamers, ending their strangle-hold over America's politics, and it would signal the end of Wisecarver's political relevance. He lunged toward the stage but didn't make it past Barnes, who restrained him.

Hendrickson now stepped to the dais. He made a few brief remarks, committing to serving a single term. He affirmed his belief that the peace-ful transition of political power was the bedrock of American democ-racy. He concluded by quoting King George III, who at the end of the Revolution had asked what General Washington would do now that the war was over. When he was told that Washington would relinquish power and return to his farm, George III had said, "If he does that, he will be the greatest man in the world." Hendrickson pledged to follow Wash-ington's example.

Silence met his speech. Watching her godfather, Hunt recalled her dream. Two rivers feeding a vast ocean. Hendrickson was done talking; they all were. Tradition dictated what would happen next.

Hendrickson stepped down from the Capitol's West Front. He waded into the crowd, which yielded. He set out across the National Mall. His goddaughter was the first to follow, but soon others trailed behind him, Truthers and Dreamers alike, in the hundreds and then in the thousands. They formed a vast procession, inaugurating their new president, like the many before, as he walked that brief distance from the Capitol to the White House.

⌐

17:21 June 02, 2054 (GMT-4)
Northwest of Manaus

Ashni had decided that her father should remain here. His journey up this river hadn't been for no reason—Ashni felt certain of that. If her father hadn't arrived deep in the jungle so that his life could be saved, perhaps he'd arrived here because this was where his life was meant to end. When Ashni explained this to Avozhina, she had agreed. But if Ashni didn't want to bring her father out of the jungle, what did she want to do with him? Avozhina had suggested that they bury him by the stream, that they leave behind a marker like those that marked the graves of Sarah Hunt and Dr. Kurzweil. But this didn't seem quite right to Ashni.

The more Ashni thought of this journey she'd taken with her father, the more she believed that his disappointment at its end wasn't because he'd failed to find a way to save his own life, but because the knowledge of the Singularity had eluded him. But Ashni believed that in his death, she might have found a solution.

Early that afternoon, she and Avozhina moved her father down to the stream bank. The day was hot, the sun was out, and it glittered off the scalloped surface of the water as they worked. The two of them gathered materials from the jungle—fragments of driftwood, vines to use as cord—and labored into the afternoon to create a small raft. Avozhina asked Ashni several times if she was certain she wanted to do this. Downstream, where the rivers merged, the waters became powerful and violent. The raft would surely be torn apart. Her father's body would vanish forever in the current. Each time Ashni explained that this was what her father would've wanted, Avozhina made a sour face, like Ashni was crazy.

They placed his body, wrapped in a shroud, in the center of the raft. The stifling heat had succumbed to a westerly breeze and Ashni waded into the cool stream up to her waist. Avozhina pushed the raft free from its bank, while Ashni gripped its side. Out on the water, Dr. Chowdhury's body rotated, like the needle of a compass searching for true north, before orienting itself downstream, toward the rivers' convergence. Ashni could feel the current pulling her father away as she held the raft. Behind her, in the west, the sun was setting. In front of her, it was already dark.

For a final time, she asked herself if this was what he would have wanted.

Yes, she thought, a man as great as he would want to be consumed by these waters. A man as great as he would want to make this final journey. An ocean awaited.

She opened her hand and allowed the current to take him.

CODA

Dreampolitik

James Mohammad finally had his yacht. He'd bought it new, paid in cash, and named it *The Benjamin*, after his father. Mohammad had taken delivery of the yacht, a forty-four-foot Sea Ray, at the marina only two weeks before, he explained to his uncle. They stood in the pilothouse, threading their way through the intracoastal traffic. It was the first warm day of the year.

"You keep calling it a yacht, Jimmy. But it's a boat." His uncle pointed to a few of the larger yachts at anchor, the vulgar one-hundred-plus-foot behemoths. "*Those* are yachts."

"Yes, those are yachts too," said Mohammad. He eased the throttle forward, adding a couple of knots to their speed. Maybe it'd been a bad idea to bring his uncle along. The elder James Mohammad had finally retired six months before, which he blamed on his nephew's detention in the United States and the subsequent fallout with Zhao Jin and his colleagues at the Guoanbu. His uncle had said his superiors had wanted a scapegoat for that failure. But the truth was he should have retired years ago.

Mohammad thought perhaps his uncle, in retirement, might like to spend more time out on the water. He needed to do something, to find a hobby; otherwise he was going to drive them both crazy. The morning sun hung low in the sky, throwing shimmering tracks across the water. Mohammad struggled to enjoy the view as his uncle prattled on. "What you have is a boat, because a boat can fit on a yacht," he insisted, jabbing his index finger into his palm. "But a yacht cannot fit on a boat. That's the difference, Jimmy. Also, it's bad luck to name a boat after a man. A boat should have a woman's name."

Mohammad's CIA handler, the case officer the Americans had assigned him shortly after they'd flipped him at Dulles, had also objected to the name *The Benjamin*. "It's just a little too flamboyant, isn't it?" his handler had said at lunch when he heard about the purchase. Mohammad had explained that it'd been his father's name. His handler, who'd been dabbing a wet napkin at a few drops of soup that'd left little brown stains down his shirtfront, glanced over the tops of the tinted bifocals he never seemed to take off. "It's tacky, the type of name a rapper would give to his boat: *The Benjamin*, as in Benjamins, as in hundred-dollar bills. Had you thought about that? Or that a cash withdrawal of that size might cast unwelcome attention on our relationship? Also, a boat is a terrible investment. You're a businessman, for Christ's sake, you of all people should know that a boat immediately depreciates in value. If it floats, flies, or fucks, rent it. Didn't anyone ever teach you that?"

That had been a week ago. Mohammad and his uncle now turned a corner in the bay, passing by the Federal Palace Hotel and Casino, where he'd had that unpleasant meal with his handler. As much as Mohammad didn't like his new handler, he preferred the current arrangement to the prior one, with his uncle. Now it was time for him to take care of his uncle, as he might have taken care of his own parents in their elder years, had they survived.

And Mohammad was certainly trying to take care of his family. The Americans paid well, far better than his native Nigerians. The latest piece of nonpublic information he'd delivered, which resulted in the bonus that had afforded him his yacht, was that Neutronics was continuing to sink resources into research on remote gene editing, mind-uploading, and select other technologies that contributed to the Singularity, despite the obstacles erected by Sarah Hunt. Mohammad had discovered this latest piece of information through a well-placed source in the Neutronics hierarchy, a young scientist who, as a little girl, had had her life saved by Dr. Kurzweil's early research. She was determined to see this lifesaving research continued, hence her conversations with investors like Mohammad, and she had disclosed financial information that showed a series of payments by Neutronics to an independent laboratory in Okinawa registered to a Dr. Christopher Yamamoto.

His uncle disappeared belowdecks. After a quick inspection of *The Benjamin*, he reappeared in the pilothouse. He was now wearing a bright orange life preserver. Mohammad laughed. "Why have you got that on?"

"You said we'll be out on the ocean."

"Okay. . . ."

"I've never been a good swimmer."

His uncle asked what they would do once they arrived on the open ocean. Was there a plan? A destination? What did one do on a yacht, exactly?

"To be honest," said James Mohammad, "I don't really know."

His uncle stepped beside him and the two of them stared across the bow of *The Benjamin*, to the west, to the endless water and their indeterminate destination. "No matter," said his uncle. He tightened the strap on his life preserver. "We'll just keep going."

⌐

05:13 June 23, 2056 (GMT+9)
Okinawa

B.T. was running out of steam. All night he'd been up in his lab, determined to finish modeling a protein structure he believed would allow him to circumvent a glitch he'd discovered in an outmoded strand of mRNA-based vaccine. This specific sequence of mRNA had once proven an effective genetic messenger and modifier, but it now collapsed whenever put into application. Over two years he'd made some progress—remodeling certain methods of remote gene editing on completely different precepts—but the gains had proven limited, incredibly labor-intensive, and he was beginning to wonder how much longer Neutronics would subsidize his research and lifestyle, modest though it was.

Most recently, he had spent sixteen weeks remodeling a vast genetic helix, the equivalent of repainting the ceiling of the Sistine Chapel to create a different celestial scene, one of equal beauty but entirely rearranged, with the requirement of including every image from the old painting. Not exactly easy. And now, as he was readying himself to apply the final brushstrokes, it was as if he'd realized that he hadn't left enough space for two cherubs from the original. Those two cherubs in this case were two sequences of nucleotide triplets. They didn't fit inside the new construct.

B.T. cradled his head in his hands. He rubbed his eyes with the heels of his palms and gazed out the window, into the breaking dawn. Maybe he should have heeded Sarah Hunt's warning. Maybe the only thing he could hope to discover by refusing to give up his quest for the Singularity was the limit of his own ego. Did he really believe that his human intelligence—no matter how advanced it was—could prevail against an artificial intelligence designed to obstruct his every move? It had been nearly sixty years since a computer beat Garry Kasparov, the world's reigning chess champion. If anything, it was remarkable that human intelligence had continued to compete against artificial intelligence for so long; it was remarkable that people like him still believed humans could solve any problem—or hope to.

Hope, B.T. thought. The word dangled encouragingly in his mind. This was what always would give humans their edge.

He sat at his desk, staring out at the morning, watching the day as it formed. This technological race, in which he'd long participated, could only solve so many of mankind's problems. Technological evolution might overtake biological evolution, but those advances, profound as they were, would do little to alter the fundamentals of what it meant to *be* human. Those fundamentals didn't exist in the technological realm but in the emotional and spiritual one, something his science couldn't explain. Something *he* had never adequately understood.

His thoughts now migrated, as they often did, to Michi. In that first year after returning from Manaus, he'd tried to forget her, to convince himself that his feelings hadn't been real. But he'd failed there too.

Several months ago, he'd returned to Japan, first to Michi's apartment and then, when he'd found a different name on the buzzer, to Dr. Agawa's office. The old scientist had greeted him warmly. B.T. was soon sitting in front of his desk explaining the reason for his visit. Dr. Agawa had listened patiently to B.T.'s allegation that he had engineered the romance with Michi, which Dr. Agawa laughed at before denying. To offer proof of his innocence, Dr. Agawa noted that Michi had quit working for him shortly after returning from Manaus. According to Dr. Agawa, she'd seemed inexplicably troubled. She'd said that it was time for her to focus on her own research, though she declined to say what that research was, and then she'd left. Perhaps what had happened between her and B.T. explained this decision. Dr. Agawa hadn't heard from Michi in many months.

In the year since seeing Dr. Agawa, B.T. still thought of her often. If anything, her grip on him only seemed to tighten. He could rediscover the Singularity, outsmarting Sarah Hunt, Dr. Kurzweil, Dr. Agawa, the whole group of them, and it still wouldn't bring him any closer to understanding Michi's emotions, or his own. Technological evolution had created a world that would be unrecognizable to humans from two thousand, one thousand, even a hundred years ago. But what of our emotional evolution? Here, nothing had changed, nothing could be accelerated. A person from that time was much the same as a person from this one. And so B.T. continued to stare out the window and think of Michi.

Then, in the branches of one tree, he noticed darts of color. A flash of blue, of pink, then of red. He left his desk, stepping outside onto the grass, wet with dew. He approached the trees carefully. He couldn't quite tell what he was looking at until he got closer. Lifting from the tree branches he saw butterflies, a dozen or more, with their wings remarkably colored. They swirled once in the air, looping around his head like a crown, and then they flew off in a straight line, toward Cape Maeda. Too much time had passed for these butterflies to be the ones he'd engineered. These must be their offspring. B.T. followed them away from his lab.

⌐

10:52 November 23, 2057 (GMT+8)
Beijing

Shriver hadn't wanted Lily Bao to make this trip, but she'd insisted. Her pregnancy, though welcome, had been unplanned, and she'd already delayed this trip because of some minor early complications. The visa Zhao Jin had issued her years before would expire soon. If she didn't take the trip now, she never would. Shriver had understood, or at least said that he'd understood her need to go. Her father was buried in Beijing and before becoming a parent herself she wanted to visit him.

Although Lily's obstetrician expressed concern about undertaking so strenuous a journey in her final trimester, Lily couldn't be dissuaded. Lily had remained active throughout her pregnancy, helping her husband at the modest farm they'd purchased two hours northeast of Burlington, in a remote corner of the state, even by Vermont standards. Both she and her child were healthy. She would go.

Three years before, Lily Bao and Nat Shriver hadn't been looking for a home so much as a refuge. They'd found it on their farm, sinking their savings not only into their house—a stone barn they'd renovated themselves into an airy, light-filled space—but also into the solar panels, water filtration systems, and plant beds that sustained their off-the-grid lifestyle. If their experience in Washington had taught them anything, it was self-reliance. Society was too brittle. They wanted a stronger foundation on which to build their family. It wasn't simply public scrutiny they'd fled by moving so far from the centers of power. When the next crisis arrived—and it would surely be an environmental crisis—their preparedness was the greatest service they could offer an unprepared society. If they had in fact turned away from society, it was only so they might turn toward its future. This was, Lily thought, a practical position. Which was why her decision to return to Beijing baffled her husband.

When Lily landed, she had the name of a cemetery. It was on Beijing's outskirts, in Shunyi District near the airport. The forecast for her visit was all rain. She bought a bouquet of white flowers outside the gate of the cemetery. The caretaker had given her only a section number. The graves weren't organized by plot, and as she wandered, the temperature hovered a degree above freezing. She inspected the weathered headstones, searching for her father, while aircraft on their final approach roared low overhead. More than an hour passed before she found his grave. The granite headstone didn't contain his rank, or any other feature of his life. Its front simply listed his name, LIN BAO, and the years of his life, 1980–2034.

The grass around his grave was overgrown. She tore it up in fists, clearing a patch where she set her bouquet. Another plane flew past. She wondered how many thousands had passed overhead since her father's death, and if he would ever know any peace. The rain continued to fall. She was soaking wet and shivering by the time she returned to her hotel. Exhausted, she tried to sleep, but woke in the night with a temperature and sweats. It was so bad that she called her husband. Shriver insisted she take her temperature again; it was pushing near 103.

"You need to see a doctor."

She at first refused but by morning was having trouble breathing. "If you won't do it for yourself," Shriver said, "do it for Jake." He often used the name they'd picked for their unborn son, while Lily never did. As Shriver implored her to go to the hospital, she wondered why her husband could say her son's name so effortlessly while she struggled with it; it was as if speaking his name acknowledged her obligation as a parent, one she was terrified she might not successfully fulfill.

Shriver wanted Lily to call an ambulance. She took a cab instead. Shriver kept her on the phone the entire time. He apologized that he wasn't there with her, though there was no way he could have come without a visa. Lily's breathing became increasingly labored. She told Shriver that she would call him as soon as she was settled at the hospital. Then she passed out in the back of the cab.

When Lily came to, she was in a private recovery room attended by a single nurse. The nurse hovered over her, took her vitals, and then crossed toward the door. Lily could feel the emptiness in her abdomen, but before she could panic, the nurse returned with an incubator, which she placed beside Lily's bed while announcing in accented English, "Healthy baby boy. . . ." Lily looked at her son, who stared back at her through milky, lustrous eyes. Then the nurse said, "You have visitor," and she stepped out of the room. When Lily's visitor appeared through the door, she recognized him immediately from the name on his hospital-required adhesive guest pass. It was Zhao Jin.

"Congratulations to the new mother." He tapped on the incubator's glass. In one hand he carried a bouquet of white flowers, like the bouquet Lily had left on her father's grave the day before. In Zhao Jin's other hand, he carried a red envelope. While Zhao Jin placed the flowers on an end table, he explained that red was the traditional color of luck and new beginnings in China—in case Lily Bao had forgotten.

"How did you find me?" Lily asked.

"I knew the moment you stepped into the country," said Zhao Jin. He sounded disappointed, as if Lily had underestimated him. "Did you think I'd forgotten about the visa we issued you those many years ago? We hoped you might use it."

"So you've been following me this entire time?" asked Lily.

"Following is so old-fashioned. . . . Who follows anyone these days? No, we haven't been following you. We have been *watching* you. Your father's grave, so unfortunate. He always deserved a more dignified resting place. He was a man of great integrity, who did so much for our country."

"*Our* country . . ." said Lily, rolling the words around in her mouth before adding, "I want to speak with my husband."

Zhao Jin explained that the hospital was in close touch with Shriver. He knew she was safe and healthy, and they had even passed on the news of their baby boy. "And what is his name?" asked Zhao Jin.

"Jake . . . a name from his father's family."

"An American name," said Zhao Jin. "Jake Shriver . . . a *very* American name."

Lily repeated her request to speak with her husband.

"Of course," said Zhao Jin. "That will be arranged, but I've waited quite some time to speak with you, so please just a little longer." He was tinkering with the stems of the flowers, arranging them in their vase on the end table, near where the red envelope sat. "Before you call your husband, would you please open the gift I've brought you and Jake?" He handed her the red envelope. Zhao Jin continued to tap on the incubator's glass. He made cooing faces as he tried to gain Jake's attention.

Lily Bao opened the red envelope. "What is this?" she asked, holding up a government document.

"A certificate of citizenship," Zhao Jin explained. "All it requires is your signature and it will allow your son to be both Chinese and American."

"My son is American."

"But born in China to a Chinese mother, so also Chinese. . . ." Zhao Jin removed a pen from his jacket. "We had once spoken about your father, how perhaps we could provide him with a fitting burial, perhaps even move him to the Babaoshan Revolutionary Cemetery. He would be in quite distinguished company there. Jake Shriver has created this opportunity for his grandfather. Take pride in it. All it requires is for you to leave open the possibility that someday your son might choose to return to the land of his birth, to the land of your birth, and your father's birth. . . . Would you really deny him that choice?"

Zhao Jin offered Lily the pen.

She stared at him for a long moment.

"I can't really sit up," she eventually said. "I need you to bring me something to sign on."

Zhao Jin perched on the edge of her bed. He offered his back. Lily placed the documents across it. When she gripped the pen, she didn't grip it with her fingers but with her fist, like a knife. She fantasized about a day when her son might stab Zhao Jin right where he had compelled her to sign.

⌐

17:38 March 07, 2058 (GMT-6)
Galveston Island Convention Center

Ashni almost hadn't come. As chairwoman of the Tandava Group, she received speaking invitations from across the globe. Hardly a week would pass where she wasn't addressing one group or another. But this speech was different. The Galveston Survivors Association had asked her to deliver their keynote address. The topic would be her mother's legacy.

Since her father's death, Ashni had given speeches about his legacy, she'd accepted awards on his behalf, and memorial services for him had been held in three cities. But her mother had been all but forgotten, cut out of the public narrative of Ashni's life. This was the first time Ashni had ever been asked to do anything related to her mother. She found the prospect daunting, so much so that an hour before she was scheduled to deliver her speech she was at the hotel bar, sipping a whiskey, trying to steady her nerves.

Ashni sat at a cocktail table, the pages of her speech spread across its surface. It'd taken her more than a week to write. She had struggled mightily not only with the content but with how she would deliver it without breaking down in front of the crowd. This was her great fear. In the past four years, she had figured out how to speak about the loss of her father—she'd had no choice, the world wanted to discuss him and his legacy. But her mother was a different matter. Her mother's legacy wasn't a multibillion-dollar investment fund, it wasn't thousands of employees, philanthropic foundations, and cutting-edge research. No, her mother's legacy was her, Ashni.

She read her speech again.

She still couldn't get through it without her emotions threatening to overtake her. But there was no more time. She settled her bill and left the bar. When she arrived at the auditorium, a crowd was gathering in the hundreds, if not thousands. The desire to commemorate the devastating losses from the last war seemed to bleed into a desire to understand how the country had nearly descended into a civil war four years before. Congress had extended the stable, caretaker presidency of the Hendrickson administration to a full four-year term and this had largely returned the United States to a sense of normalcy, which was to say a normal level of fractious dysfunction as opposed to the level that had almost sunk the nation. But Hendrickson's uneventful presidency would finish at the end of the year and the nation was uneasy as it prepared to pick another president from a disorganized field of independents, Democratic-Republicans, and other minor party candidates, without a clear front-runner having emerged.

In the minutes before her speech, the event staff shuttled Ashni into a green room backstage, where a makeup artist dusted the shine from her forehead and a sound technician clamped a microphone to her lapel. She stood stage left listening to her introduction, a recitation of her life and achievements that she struggled to associate with herself, overcome as she was with anxiety. She felt she had this one chance to tell the world who her mother had been.

She stepped onto the stage, beneath a flood of lights. The faces of the crowd were upturned. She spoke a bit about her father, about the work the Tandava Group was doing to prepare the world for the social, biological, and environmental challenges of the future. This was the easy part of her speech, a rote copy-and-paste from remarks she'd delivered a hundred times before.

She transitioned into her own story.

The moment she evoked her mother, she felt her throat constrict as surely as if someone had gripped her neck. She explained how her mother, who they were honoring, had made the impossible choice of letting her go. Her mother had understood that to save Ashni she had to give her up.

"Too often," Ashni said, "we believe that progress is holding on. Often, progress is letting go, not only of a person but also of an idea. . . ."

Her mother had understood this. Her father had, too, at least in the end. But did anyone else? She searched the crowd, looking for one glimpse of recognition, one person who might steady her. Then, sitting in the front row, right beneath her, where she hadn't noticed him, she recognized the renowned Japanese public policy expert Dr. Kobe Agawa. He was nodding in approval.

She had never met Dr. Agawa, but knew who he was, how he had factored into her father's legacy and thus her own. When she finished her speech and the crowd emptied out, Dr. Agawa remained in the back waiting for her. He introduced himself and offered to take Ashni for dinner, where at a quiet table they talked about her mother, her father, and her, late into the night.

⌐

04:38 May 17, 2059 (GMT-5)
Boston

In the morning, Julia Hunt would graduate. She would receive her doctorate in record time. Her thesis advisor at Tufts University's School of Public Health had cautioned that it could take up to seven years to fulfill her degree requirements. But she'd done it in a record-breaking four, funded by her GI Bill and a portion of her retirement, which she'd taken early from the Marines. To celebrate, her godfather had flown in from Washington the day before. That evening they'd had dinner at his hotel on Boston Common. It was the first time Julia had seen former president Hendrickson since he'd left office a few months earlier.

As they sat in the restaurant, it was nice to have the Secret Service mostly out of sight and his retinue of staffers at bay. She noticed how they called him "Admiral," not "Mr. President." Hendrickson, like Theodore Roosevelt, who was called "Colonel" after he left office, believed there should only be one person called "Mr. President" at a time. Hendrickson hadn't traveled entirely alone. He'd kept Karen Slake on a consulting contract. Her slate of projects included Hendrickson's presidential library. Slake had sat with them for a drink before dinner. They'd gossiped about Dozer's failed Senate run and a controversial, unauthorized biography of Wisecarver due out in the fall—Wisecarver's estate was suing the publisher. Slake had lamented, not for the first time, that Julia had left the Corps. "You would've been a general," she'd said. Julia shrugged and simply said she was much happier now—which was true. Slake had also shown Julia the not-yet-announced plans for the presidential library. Slake could hardly contain her skepticism. "It's in the middle of nowhere." The library would be built in New Mexico, only a few miles from the ranch where Sarah Hunt had lived. "No one's going to visit," Slake added before excusing herself to her room.

"I didn't realize you were planning to build it there," Julia said, her eyes following Slake as she walked out of the restaurant. "I also guess I didn't realize how much you missed my mother."

"I loved your mother." Hendrickson stared wearily out the restaurant window. "Loved her so much and for so long . . . and still do. Don't you miss her?"

"Of course I do." Julia was tempted to say more, and almost did, but thought better of it.

She changed the subject, telling Hendrickson about a meeting she'd had with an agricultural company partially funded by the Tandava Group. The company had shown an interest in her recently published dissertation. Julia thought they might offer her a job. Hendrickson told her that her mother would've been proud. They soon finished their dinner and finalized plans to meet the next day on campus, after the graduation ceremony. Then Julia returned to her apartment and went to bed, where she dreamed.

This was her secret, a gift from her mother that arrived each night. Sarah Hunt had vanished, and most people assumed the technology she and Kurzweil had discovered had vanished with her. But Julia knew otherwise. Sarah Hunt had left a gift for her daughter. For years now, Julia's biological mother and father, whom she'd lost so long ago in San Diego, appeared in her dreams. How was this possible? Julia didn't know. All she knew was that Sarah Hunt had made it possible. The life Julia would've led with her parents, beginning where she'd left off as a girl, was re-created in her dreams, each night, as if in memory.

That night after dinner was the first in years her parents hadn't appeared. It was the first night Julia had dreamed of Sarah Hunt instead. The dream was simple, a premonition of the following day's graduation. Julia wore a cap and gown. She stood lined up with her classmates on one side of a stage, while at the lectern a university administrator called out names. When hers was called, she climbed the stairs to the stage. A degree was placed in her hand. A doctoral hood was hung over her head.

Smiling, she faced the crowd and searched for her mother, for Sarah. In the very front row, in a reserved seat, she saw her.

The next day at graduation, the scene appeared exactly as it'd been in Julia's dream. Except Sarah wasn't there. But as Julia stood on the stage, waiting for her name to be called, she noticed a vacant seat in the front row. It was the same seat Sarah had sat in the night before, and Julia couldn't tell if what she felt was sadness or relief that today the seat was empty. Then Julia heard her name called. Confidently, she strode out onto the stage. By the time she'd crossed to its far side, she'd resolved to tell Hendrickson her secret.

But if it be asked what the issue of the struggle is likely to be,
it will readily be understood that we are here left to form a
very vague surmise of the truth.

—Alexis de Tocqueville, *Democracy in America*

ACKNOWLEDGMENTS

Elliot Ackerman would like to thank Scott Moyers, Mia Council, Helen Rouner, Elizabeth Calamari, PJ Mark, Phil Klay, and, as ever, Lea Carpenter.

Admiral Stavridis would like to thank his editor, Scott Moyers, and agent, Andrew Wylie. Also, our wonderful shipmates at Penguin Press, Mia Council, Helen Rouner, and Elizabeth Calamari. And the woman whose intelligence is anything but artificial, Laura Stavridis.